"LIFE WENT ON"

EVENTS IN RAUNDS AND BEYOND DURING & AFTER THE GREAT WAR

VOLUME 2 – 1917 TO 1918

+

1919 TO 1921

COMPILED BY
STEVE BENCE & ANDREW DACE

A
RAUNDS WAR MEMORIALS RESEARCH GROUP
PUBLICATION

The Raunds War Memorials Research Group is indebted to the

Heritage Lottery Fund

whose generous grant continues to make our publications possible.

First published in 2011 by the
Raunds War Memorials Research Group
35 Lime Road
Southam
Warwickshire
CV47 1EQ
UK

www.raundswarmemorials.org

ISBN: 978-0-9556541-2-1

Front Cover: A suitably-themed fancy dress float
from a war-time Hospital Week Demonstration.
(Vorley/SJB)

Back Cover: A piece of commemorative china from the Great War
with the Raunds crest, made by Arcadian China and
backstamped with a retailer's mark of F W March. Stationers, Raunds.

Prepared for publication by Steve & Megan Bence

Printed by Warwick Printing Company Limited,
Caswell Road, Leamington Spa, Warwickshire CV31 1QD

CONTENTS

ACKNOWLEDGEMENTS

Many people and organisations have once again supported us in the production of this publication, and to all of you we offer our grateful thanks.

However, special thanks have to be extended to the following for their invaluable contributions:

The **County Archivist and staff** at the **Northamptonshire Record Office,** for once more unearthing some fascinating Rance archive material for us.

Andrea, Dennis and the team at **Kettering Library,** as patient and as helpful as ever.

Sally and the girls at **Rushden Library,** always welcoming and supportive.

Michelle at **Raunds Library,** for hosting the launch of this book.

Brook Street News, Raunds, (opposite the Post Office) our principle retail outlet since 2007.

Chantelle, Max & Maddie Dace, for always keeping Daddy on his toes.

Angela Vernals, grammatically correct and dictionarily supreme.

Maggie Bence, of the multi-stringed bow.

And finally .....

Everyone who has bought **"A Wall Unto Us"** &/or **"Life Went On, Volume 1".**

Steve Bence & Andrew Dace

INTRODUCTION

Welcome to Volume 2 of our Raunds Great War Diary; more than two years have passed since the publication of Volume 1, so we thank you for your patience.

As before, with a few exceptions, all of the narrative is taken from articles appearing in the Kettering Leader, Northamptonshire Evening Telegraph or Rushden Echo, which are stored on microfilm in the local libraries, or from the Church of England School records, St Mary's* Church Parish Magazines and Wesleyan Methodist Church records held at the Northamptonshire Record Office.

And in order to maintain the atmosphere of the period, the words and phrases utilised are as they were written by those journalists and scribes nearly one hundred years ago.

Again we have tried to only use photographs that have not appeared, to the best of our knowledge, in any previous publication, and we hope that the subject matter of the newspaper reproductions more than makes up for their inferior quality. The source of each photograph is individually acknowledged.

Wherever the name of one of the town's Great War victims is mentioned, his name appears in **bold type**, followed by his corresponding page number from **"A Wall Unto Us"** (copies still available!) in brackets **(x)**; references with a suffix "a" are for additional men found since the publication of "A Wall" whose details can only be found on the "Addenda/Corrigenda" page of the "Publications" section of our website. Significant events of the Great War appear in ***bold italics***.

The currency quoted throughout is good old pounds, shillings and pence (£sd). For the uninitiated, there were twelve pence (d) in a shilling (s) and twenty shillings in a pound (£) and a guinea comprised of twenty-one shillings.

And where court cases are reported, the identities of all parties involved have generally been kept anonymous in respect for the feelings of any surviving relatives.

* *

* *As explained in the superb 1988 book "Raunds, Picturing the Past", by David Hall, Ruth Harding and Cyril Putt, the church at Raunds is actually dedicated to St. Peter. However, during the late Victorian period through to the time of the Great War, the commonly used name was that of St. Mary's, the early 16th-century patronal saint.*

In this volume, the years 1917 and 1918 are covered in the same detail as in Volume 1; however, for the period from January 1919 to October 1921 (bringing us up to the unveiling of the town's War Memorial), some of the more everyday, repetitive events have been omitted to keep the book to a sensible size.

We join the town again in January 1917, thirty-six men had been lost in the war to date and life at home was becoming more and more directly affected by the conflict.

Escalating demands by the military for men were causing increasing problems for the owners of the boot factories as they tried to fulfil their War Office contracts with a workforce that was diminishing in both numbers and skill levels. The critical circumstances, however, provided a unique opportunity for the ladies to prove their worth and arguably did more to advance the cause of women's suffrage than any hunger strike, fence chaining or suicide-by-horse ever did!

Meanwhile in the High Street, the range, quantity and quality of goods available in the shops also grew less as the country strained to produce more of its own food against a backdrop of attacks on merchant shipping and the need to maintain effective supply lines for the men at the front.

So having set the scene, we hope that you enjoy reading the continuing story of Rance's "Great War", and its sometimes uncomfortable return to peacetime life.

Steve Bence & Andrew Dace

February 2011

Chapter 1 – January to March 1917

The Great Fire and the Tsar's abdication.

JANUARY – The Bishop of Peterborough, writing in the first Parish Magazine of the New Year, said "As we bring to an end another year of war and suffering and look into the unknown twelve months we have much to thank God for: a country still untrodden by the foot of the invader; a nation that is drawing ever closer into a family fellowship; men by the thousand who have 'loved not their lives unto the death'; and women who have been doing that which they have been given to do, and enduring that which they have been given to bear."

The vicar, the Rev Cyril Clowes Aldred, acknowledged the gifts of £1-0s-0d from G W Darlow, for the Churchyard Fund; and £1-5s-0d from the Rev W S Bethway, for the School Building Fund. Sadly, the magazine, in the "Died in the Service of Their Country" column, also confirmed the deaths of **Charles Archibald Vorley (117)** in September, and **Stanley Frederick Nunley (84)**, in December.

Raunds Temperance Band arranged a dance in the Temperance Hall on Thursday evening, **4 January**, the proceeds being for New Year gifts to the bandsmen serving in HM Forces and local War Charities. Miss Ivy Adams acted as MC over the 120 or so present and dancing was indulged in from 7pm until midnight.

The death of **Edgar Jarvis (64a)** was confirmed on Friday, **5 January**. The Raunds-born Northamptonshire Regiment private had actually been killed in action on Friday, 24 November 1916, but it was only now that the news had been conveyed to his parents, Joseph and Emma, who resided in Stanwick.

"Thanks – Mr and Mrs J Stubbs and Family desire to express thanks to their numerous friends for their heartfelt sympathy in the sad bereavement of their only son, **Philip Ernest Stubbs (113)**, Kings' Royal Rifles, Killed in France – 'Forester's Arms', Raunds."

"Dilemma in the Boot Trade" ran a headline in the Rushden Echo. Apparently, there was a big Army contract in hand, yet more men were to be called up. Conflicting departments in the War Office had issued a circular saying that all Class A and B1 men engaged on Army boot making could be withdrawn from the Industry by 15 January, but simultaneously had stated that the delivery of two and a half million ankle boots for Russia was to commence on 21 January!

At Wellingborough Police Court today, a Raunds motor mechanic was summoned for driving a motor car without a licence at Rushden on 30 December, pleading not guilty. Sgt Brumby said he asked the defendant for his licence, which he failed to produce saying that he had left it at home. The man now produced a renewal certificate and the case was adjourned pending production of the actual licence.

"Wanted – Hand-sewn men on Italian Army boots, full work guaranteed to the end of March – Adams Bros., Raunds."

On Saturday, **6 January**, it was announced that Company Sergeant Major H L G Shelmerdine, Royal Engineers, the second son of Mr and Mrs J Shelmerdine, of "Kirkfields", had been mentioned in Sir Douglas Haig's despatches for gallantry in the field.

Also today, the annual New Year's Tea, given by the Adult Schools to the old people over 65 years of age, was held in the Temperance Hall, when about 120 sat down to the tables. After tea an entertainment was held, when vocal and instrumental music etc was given. The chair was occupied by Miss Pulpher (president of the Women's School) and the following contributed to the programme: songs by Messrs A Tebbutt and W Rands, Misses M Sanders, W Pentelow, M Hasseldine, and Alice Vliegen (one of the Belgian refugees), and three of the Belgian children, and recitations were given by Messrs S Head and W Rands. A violin solo was also given by Miss Louie Pettit, with Miss Lilian Robinson as the accompanist.

A Stanwick correspondent observed an aeroplane passing over the village at about 2pm on Sunday afternoon, **7 January**, heading in the direction of Raunds.

Tuesday, 9 January, the Allies capture another Turkish garrison in Sinai.

Today at the Thrapston Petty Sessions, a Raunds clicker was summoned for disobeying a maintenance order to contribute 5s-0d per week towards the support of his son, an inmate of the Ackbar Reformatory Training Ship. The man explained that he was living apart from his wife in lodgings at 14s-0d per week whilst his average weekly wage was £1-6s-6d. He added that he did not enjoy the best of health and produced a certificate from Dr Mackenzie. He was willing to pay the arrears but only if the Bench would reduce the order. The Bench ordered the defendant to pay the arrears within a fortnight or to go to prison for a fortnight.

At the weekly Thrapston Market, beef was selling at 16s-0d to 17s-0d per stone, mutton at 1s-2d to 1s-3d per pound, pork at 14s-6d to 15s-0d per stone, butter at 1s-10d per pound, and eggs at 4s-3d to 4s-4d per score.

The Temperance Band organised another dance in the Temperance Hall on Wednesday, **10 January**, this time in aid of the Temperance Society's New Building Fund. Again there was a good company present, dancing to the music supplied by band members.

On Thursday afternoon, **11 January**, a very pretty wedding was solemnised in the Wesleyan Church, when Pte W Cyril Groom, of the ASC MT, eldest son of the late Mr Charles Groom, and Mrs Groom of Lawson Street, and Grace, only daughter of Mr and Mrs Walter Lawrence, of "The Poplars", were united.

"Wanted – Reliable Man (ineligible) or strong Girl to go round with milkcart, good wages and permanent position to suitable person – Mr Amos Lawrence, The Hall, Raunds."

On Friday, **12 January**, the parents of **Arthur Clark (35)** inserted a plea in the Rushden Echo for any information of their son who had been posted as "missing" since 18 November 1916.

Also today it was announced that Private, 18305, Nash, D, of the Northamptons and of Raunds, had been wounded the previous Saturday, but no further details of his condition were given.

"Notice to Lads of 18 – It is notified for general information that all Lads, when they attain the age of 18 years and 7 months, should report for Service to the Recruiting Officer of their Sub-Area."

The Brotherhood met on Sunday afternoon, **14 January**, in the Wesleyan Church when the speaker was Mr W L Carter, of Northampton, who gave a very interesting address on the subject "The Postern Gate". Miss Miriam Sanders rendered the solos entitled "Beyond the Dawn" and "A Dream Song" in a very creditable manner. Miss Edith Sanders accompanied at the piano.

The first Urban Council meeting of 1917 took place on Monday, **15 January**, with Messrs John Adams (Chair), Camozzi, James Adams, Smith, Shelmerdine, Gates, Asbery, Agutter, Hodson, Batchelor, and Hazeldine present.

The medical officer, Dr Mackenzie, reported the district to be quite free of notifiable infectious diseases since October. During the month of December there had been five births and five deaths registered. The chairman was then appointed to examine periodically the tuberculosis register in place of the late Mr J Gant, JP.

With regards to the increase of food supply, it was decided to consider applications from persons desirous of keeping pigs in premises which at present contravene the bye-laws. It was also decided to offer land on the reservoir site for cultivation as a whole, and to plough up the Recreation Ground and the surplus land at the Cemetery field and to let it in 10 pole allotments.

The Thrapston Board of Guardians also met today and the Cottage Homes Committee reported that there was an absence of all winter vegetables in the garden, and that they had given the superintendent permission to obtain supplies for present use.

The clerk also reported that the milk contractor to the Children's Home, who had contracted at 1s-2d per gallon, now wrote that he could not continue at this price but could at 1s-4d. The chairman said "I think he ought to be held to his contract. He knew the conditions." He added "If it went the other way we should have to put up with it and if we give way here, other contractors would be encouraged to say the same". It was agreed that the Board would adhere to the contract.

During this afternoon, the annual tea and meeting of the Women's Adult School was held in the Primitive Methodist Schoolroom. There was a good attendance at tea and the annual business meeting was conducted over the tables, when Miss Pulpher presided. The secretary gave a report of the year's work, showing that the sum of £7-12s-6d had been devoted to charitable work during the period.

Appearing this week at the Palace Theatre, Rushden, was Arthur Rehan, the Favourite Comedian, presenting his Novelty Revue "Wait a Minute", with Celia Danvers, Comedienne; Doris May, American Wooden Shoe Dancer; Whitmore & Lingard, Continental Tango Experts; and Lily Austen, the Yorkshire Nightingale.

On Tuesday, **16 January**, the War Savings Committee met at the office of the secretary (Mr W F Corby) with Mr John Adams, JP CC, presiding. The chairman gave a report of the meeting with the Chancellor of the Exchequer in London which he had attended in connection with the New War Loan. The secretary announced that he had been elected a member of the County War Savings Association. The treasurer's report showed that about £500 had been paid in to the end of 1916.

"Operatives To Go – Startling Order for the Shoe Trade" headlined the story that today the Government had announced the alteration of the list of certified occupations resulting in many more men no longer being exempt from call up. It was predicted that this would cause "a great sensation in the trade in the county".

On Wednesday, **17 January**, at a meeting of the Thrapston District Tribunal, a Stanwick clicker, 31 and married, working at Raunds, asked for exemption till 31 March on domestic grounds. When granted one month (final) exemption the man replied "Thank you very much, I am quite willing to join up in a month", to which a Tribunal member responded "A very nice spirit".

A Chelveston boot operative, 29 and married, also employed at Raunds, appealed for temporary exemption on domestic grounds (the state of his wife's health). He had organised a War Savings Club at his factory, there were 128 members, and he was secretary. He was also an ambulance man, and asked to join the R.A.M.C. when his wife's health improved. He was granted two months exemption.

And at the Thrapston Police Court this afternoon, a private in the Royal Defence Corps, recently stationed at Raunds, was charged with stealing a wristlet watch, value 10s-6d, at Raunds on 1 January. Sgt Ellingham gave evidence that he received the prisoner into custody from Shrewsbury police, and read the warrant to him, to which the man replied "Yes, I stole it and sold it". On this evidence the prisoner was remanded to the Petty Sessions on 23 January.

On Thursday, **18 January**, it was announced that the Christmas Day collection in Stanwick in aid of the Belgian school children realised £1-13s-6d, including 101 pennies and 62 halfpennies.

This evening, Local Appeals Tribunal met with Mr John Adams, JP CC, in the chair, assisted by Messrs A Camozzi, G E Smith, W Gates, E Batchelor, W Asbery, J Hodson, W Agutter, W F Corby (clerk), and J Shelmerdine, JP, (military representative). A motor mechanic and agent, appealed for his son, 18, single, who was an instructor in the Flying School at Hendon, and was also finishing his training as a pilot. This was considered for some length, and eventually adjourned for a fortnight. Several other cases were reviewed, the appellants being given exemptions until 31 March or 30 April.

Also this evening, a Juvenile Foreign Missions meeting was held in the Wesleyan Schoolroom, when there was a large company present. Scholars from the Sunday School were dressed in costumes of many nations, and sang native songs to native tunes; recitations, speeches and dialogues were also given. The superintendent minister, the Rev E P Blackburn, gave an excellent address on Mission work. The collection, which was in aid of the Foreign Mission Fund, amounted to £3-10s-0d.

And at this evening's meeting of the Raunds District Old Age Pensions Sub-Committee, a question was raised by the pensions officer with respect to a pensioner who had gone into the Workhouse, and the pension was discontinued. Seven new claims were considered, including six from Raunds. Six were allowed at the full rate of 5s-0d per week, and one Raunds case at 2s-0d per week.

At the Wellingborough Police Court on Friday, **19 January**, a 17 year old shoehand from Westfields was charged with "Failing to soften the lights of acetylene motor vehicle lamps" at Wellingborough on 6 January. The case was adjourned for a week.

The County Tribunal met today at Northampton and Mr J Gribble, a National Union of Boot and Shoe Operatives official, suggested that the new instructions from the War Office, regarding the call up of A and B1 men, should be ignored if "manufacturers showed that the taking of a particular man in to the Army would stop an important machine, and thereby jeopardise the output of the factory".

Frustration on the part of the Allies at the United States' reluctance to join the war was typified in a film currently showing at the Royal Theatre, Rushden: "I'm Glad My Boy Grew Up to be a Soldier" – described as a Great Selig Red-Seal Picturisation of the Popular Song Hit; a stinging reposte to the American ballad "I Didn't Raise My Boy to be a Soldier", currently very popular across the pond.

On Monday evening, **22 January**, the "George Inn" saw the sale by auction of six freehold cottages situated off Marshall's Road, by instructions from the representatives of the late Mr William Litchfield. The houses were all let and bringing in 10s-0d a week. The properties were knocked down to Mr Joseph Webb for £85.

The soldier remanded in custody a week earlier at the Police Court appeared at the Petty Sessions, Thrapston on Tuesday, **23 January**. It was heard that the stolen wristlet watch had been offered for sale in the "Globe Inn" on Monday, 1 January, to a local shoe factory foreman who had paid him 8s-0d, but who then handed it over to Sgt Ellingham. The defendant's Army record was said to be "Very Bad", and the man boasted that he would "keep doing these things so I don't have to go to the front". He was sentenced to three months imprisonment with hard labour.

The Temperance Band arranged yet another dance in the Temperance Hall on Wednesday evening, **24 January**, this time in aid of the Temperance Society Renovation Fund. The music for dancing was supplied by members of the band.

That afternoon, the funeral of the 5 year old son of Mr and Mrs H A Sanders, of Brook Street, who died rather suddenly on Saturday last, took place in the Wesleyan burial ground. The Rev E P Blackburn officiated.

The Hospital Week Fund Committee held their annual meeting on Friday evening, **26 January**. The accounts showed receipts of £278-15s-8d, £136-13s-4d coming from factory collections and £101-8s-5d, the proceeds of the fete. Expenditure totalled £195-17s-6d, of which £195 had been forwarded to the county treasurer. A cheque for a further £80 was ordered to be sent on, making a total for the year of £275, beating the previous record by £25.

"For Sale – A fine curly coat Black Retriever Dog, 13 months old, excellent guard, will retrain, £2 (on approval) – Betts, Chelveston Road, Raunds."

At Wellingborough Police Court this afternoon, a Raunds man was fined 10s-0d for "not shading properly acetylene lamps on a cycle".

And a list published today of Wellingborough School's pupils successful in the Cambridge University local examinations included Raunds scholars S Lawrence, (under 16's) Class 1 Honours in Religious Knowledge and Mathematics, and R Burton, 3rd Class Honours in the Preliminary Examination.

Elsewhere in the county, the first street war shrine to be erected in Rushden was unveiled in Cromwell Road; and in a gruesome accident today, a young girl was scalped in a Rothwell shoe factory through her hair catching in a bottom rolling machine.

At the Ancient Order of Rechabites annual gathering on Saturday, **27 January**, in the Temperance Hall, nearly 200 sat down to a fruit tea. Following the tea was a public initiation service when a number of new members were admitted to the Adult Tent. This was followed by a social, when, in addition to dancing, vocal items were contributed by Mr C Coles, Miss M Lawrence, Miss W Pentelow and Miss M Sanders, and monologues by Mr A Tebbutt and Mr Willis Rands.

The annual dinner given to members of the Woodbine Working Men's Club was held in the large room this evening when about 200 sat down to an excellent spread which necessitated two sittings. A collection was taken for the benefit of members serving with H.M. Forces, to give them a present when home on their final leave before going out to the front, and realised £1-18s-3d.

Among those recommended today to the Board of Agriculture to act as station holders for the current season of the Board's Egg Distribution Scheme was Mr J Allen, of Raunds.

In connection with the Brotherhood, an "open" meeting was held on Sunday afternoon, **28 January**, when a good number of both sexes attended in the Wesleyan Church. The speaker was the Rev H Long of Higham Ferrers, who gave a very interesting address, full of amusing anecdotes, on the subject "Seven Years in the Garden of Eden", reminiscent of his work as a missionary in Ceylon.

Another property sale took place on Monday, **29 January**, at the "George and Dragon" when Messrs Pendered and Son disposed of "All that Freehold Property comprising a comfortable Dwelling House, with good garden, orchard and appurtenances thereto, the Farm Yard adjoining, with the barn, cow house, stables, meal house, piggeries, sheds and rick yard appurtenances thereto, together with the three closes of arable and pasture land extending to the Ringstead Road." Bidding started at £700 and advanced to £965, at which figure Mr N Stanton became the purchaser. The auction was completed by the sale of "All those four closes of Freehold Pasture Land, with the farmyard, barn, stables, and open hovel thereon, situated in the parish of Raunds." Opening at £460, spirited bidding quickly brought it up to £865, at which it was knocked down to Mr John Adams.

In the evening, the 50th half-yearly meeting of the Distributive Co-Operative Society was held in the Temperance Hall. The chairman, in referring to the reduced dividend said that the assessment for excess profit duty for the three periods from the commencement of the war to December 1915 was much higher than anticipated. The sales for the half year amounted to £20,543-6s-10d, an increase of £1,242-6s-4d over last year; the disposable surplus amounted to £1,657-19s-10d; allowing a dividend to all members of 1s-4d in the £.

The severe winter continued and despite there now being 15 miles of safe ice on the famous Cowbit Wash at Spalding, because of the war, there would be no British Ice Skating Championships this year, Mr F W Dix of Raunds still being the holder of the British Amateur Title.

An inquest was held at the "Forester's Arms" on Tuesday, **30 January**, by the Divisional Coroner, Mr J T Parker, touching the sudden death of a six month old child, Jack Bottoms, son of Mr and Mrs John Bottoms. Giving evidence, his mother said the child was given some milk then went to bed, falling soundly asleep. When checked at 5.30am, the baby was found lying on his side dead. A neighbour, Mrs Nunley, was called and sent for the doctor. Dr A McInnes said he saw the child at about 9.30am, lying in bed, having been dead some hours. There were no marks of violence. A verdict of "Misadventure – suffocated by vomiting matter while endeavouring to vomit" was recorded.

"For Sale – Good Cycle Business, also 3¾ Grandex Motor Cycle, recently enamelled, £24 – W Wheatley, 22 High Street, Raunds."

Wednesday, 31 January, Germany announces unrestricted submarine warfare.

A Raunds cinematograph proprietor appeared unsuccessfully on two charges at the Thrapston County Court this afternoon. Firstly, was a claim by the Postmaster General for £1-2s-9d for the rent of a telephone and judgement was made in favour of the plaintiff for that amount and costs; secondly, a claim was made by a film distributor for £2-2s-6d for the hire of film. The defendant admitted only to £1-17s-0d, stating that the remaining 5s-6d related to two nights hire but for which only one night was shown, a claim refuted by the plaintiff. After much exchange of opinion, judgement was again found in favour of the plaintiff.

FEBRUARY – In a fiery editorial in this month's Parish Magazine, the Rev C C Aldred wrote comparing the military no man's land to the spiritual one. "You can't serve two masters – you cannot serve God and mammon!"

He then went on to announce the commencement again of Evening Service at 5.30pm, adding that he hoped to keep to this time for the present, so that services at the Picture Palace would not be needed after Sunday, 25 February.

Congratulations were made to Mr F A Potter, the Church School Headmaster, on his appointment to a larger school at Kettering although at the same time acknowledging the loss to the parish of two real helpers in him and Mrs Potter.

Finally, he asked that anyone who could supply names omitted from the Roll of Honour in the Church, to contact him as he would be glad to hear from them.

Thursday, 1 February, Cornelius Robins (100), died.

On the day that the town's oldest Great War casualty died, the Local Appeals Tribunal met in the clerk's office with Mr John Adams, JP CC, in the chair. No less than eighteen individual appeals were presented and all were successful, receiving exemptions of up to three months.

The Temperance Society held their annual meeting today in the Temperance Hall; re-elected as officers were: president, Mr H W Lawrence; vice-presidents, Mr J P Hall and Miss Pulpher; secretary, Mr A Tebbutt; treasurer, Mr F Lawrence.

The 80th Annual Report of the Directors of the Northamptonshire Union Bank Ltd, sub-branch in Raunds open daily, was released on Friday, **2 February**, showing net profits for the financial year ending 31 December 1916 of £72,385-1s-0d.

"Wanted – a Pressman for cutting insoles and throughs – C E Nicholls, Midland Works, Raunds."

Weatherwise it was reported that last week was the coldest week recorded in any January since the year 1881, while locally it was revealed that diphtheria was still prevalent in the parish of Wollaston.

At a luncheon at the Masonic Hall, Northampton on Saturday, **3 February**, it was revealed that the top subscriber to the Northampton Hospital Week Fund in 1916 was Olney, followed by Earls Barton and Raunds. Representing the town at the festive board was the Rev E P Blackburn, Messrs W F Corby and R Annies, and Captain Fred Adams of the town's fire brigade. Also present was Mr J Gribble, of whom it was observed that "he was still more known for his adventures with Raunds bootmen some 11 years earlier than for being a county representative."

A "Khaki Wedding" took place at Stanwick Parish Church today, the Rev H W Richards officiating. The contracting parties were Corporal E Morris, Northants Regiment, eldest son of Mrs T Craven, and Miss Florence Elizabeth Arnold, second daughter of Mr and Mrs Arnold, of Raunds. The bride was attended by her two sisters and Able Seaman A J Cox, home on leave, acted as best man.

In the evening, the employees of Messrs Tebbutt and Hall Brothers, arranged a tea and social for a fund for sending presents to their fellow employees serving with the forces.

At a meeting of the Joint Board of Conciliation and Arbitration for Northamptonshire on Monday, **5 February**, the following instruction was agreed, no doubt prompted by the tragic incident at Rothwell ten days earlier, "that all females employed in the boot trade be requested to wear munition caps whenever at work and that such caps be provided by the manufacturers", adding that "it is most important that the hair be wholly covered by the cap."

A Raunds smallholder, 27, married, appeared before the County Appeals Tribunal today and was granted a final exemption until 28 February. Two town factory mechanics also appeared and given two months final exemption and their employers advised to train replacements.

Disaster struck Raunds late on the evening of Tuesday, **6 February**, when the "Wellington Works" in Wellington Road, operated by Messrs E W Stanley Ltd, Government boot contractors, caught fire. The building was already an inferno when the alarm was raised at 11.30pm. The premises, the older three-storey portion and the newer single-storey factory, were gutted and the valuable plant of modern machinery and a large stock of boots and leather, utterly destroyed.

The occupants of four adjoining cottages, fearing that their dwellings would share the same fate, hurriedly removed their belongings into the street, but the Raunds Fire Brigade, by a really fine piece of work, succeeded in saving their properties and confining the outbreak to the factory. At about 2.00am the Rushden Brigade arrived to give splendid assistance to their Rance colleagues in getting the situation completely under control. The firemen were greatly hampered in their work by the bitterly cold weather. Although they had a good supply of water from the mains, and despite the great heat, the spray quickly froze and huge icicles hung in fantastic shapes from the building, forming a weird and unique spectacle.

Mr Stanley was in London and ignorant of the awful loss he had sustained until the next day. Mr Grocott, the company secretary, who lived next door, pluckily attempted to force his way into the office to save the books, but was driven back by the smoke and flames. The debris was still smouldering the next morning and the firemen had to continue damping down on the mass for some hours to prevent a further outbreak.

It was also strange to report, but many residents were quite unaware of the fire until they arose on the Wednesday morning and not a few of the employees proceeded to work as usual only to find facing them on arriving, a scene of ruin and desolation. As the loss sustained by the firm, said to be many thousands of pounds, was covered by insurance, it was hoped that arrangements could be made for the 200 to 300 operatives thrown out of work to recommence work as early as practicable. ***(Plate 5)***

Earlier that evening, Mr John H Mason, of Rushden, had offered by auction at the "Globe Hotel": Two enclosures of 15 acres in Brooks Road, sold to Mr John Adams, JP CC, for £420; Twelve acres in Cotton Lane, knocked down to Mr Cobley for £505; and 10 acres in Cotton Lane, sold to Mr Hazeldine for £450.

And in the afternoon, at the Thrapston Licensing Sessions, Sgt Tebbey presented his report for the Thrapston Division for 1916. There were 40 full license houses, 12 beer-on, 3 beer-off, and 2 grocers wine licences, a total of 57. This was a decrease of 4 licences since 1915, including the "Golden Fleece" at Raunds. There were also four registered clubs including two at Raunds. Seven persons, all males, had been prosecuted and convicted for drunkenness, a decrease of one on 1915.

On Wednesday, **7 February**, the Thrapston Rural Appeals Tribunal met at the Workhouse and a Raunds case was the main item of business. The Thrapston man, 36, was cashier and ledger keeper at the Raunds sub-branch of the Northamptonshire Union Bank. He was given conditional exemption until 30 June.

In a headline entitled "Friends of the Wounded – Travel to See Them at the Old Rate", the first concession by the Board of Trade on the tax on travel was announced today. It had been decided that the 50% increase on railway passenger fares was not to apply to tickets issued to relatives desiring to visit wounded soldiers or sailors in hospital and producing the hospital authority to do so.

Friday, 9 February, the Germans withdraw to behind the Hindenberg Line.

Before the County Appeals Tribunal today was a 29 year old, married, Raunds boot operative, cycle agent and repairer of Hill Street. His was a personal appeal, he having been released for service under the agreement with the shoe manufacturers. The grounds for his appeal were of financial hardship and the Raunds Tribunal had given him a fortnight. The County Board extended this for the final time to 28 February.

The Rushden and District United Clubs' Blind and Crippled Children's Association met at Stanwick Working Men's Club on Saturday, **10 February**, and several letters of thanks were read out from parents in Raunds, Ringstead, Stanwick, Higham Ferrers and Rushden.

In the afternoon, the wives of the members of the Woodbine Working Men's Club were entertained to a meat tea, the catering for which was entrusted to the Raunds Distributive Co-Operative Society and about 160 sat down to an excellent spread. After the tea, a social and dance was held, when songs were also given by Mrs W C Lawrence, Mrs F Smith, Miss Mabel Butler, Mr A Mayes, and Mr P Britchford. The music for the dancing was supplied by Mr E Vickers (euphonium) and Mr C W Knighton (piano), the latter also accompanying the singing.

That evening in Stanwick, the old people's tea and entertainment took place at the Church Rooms, and for those unable to attend tea was sent to their homes. Among the host of artistes giving great pleasure were Miss Sanders, Mr Tebbutt, the brothers Coles, and Mr A Rands, all of Raunds.

The usual Brotherhood meeting was held in the Wesleyan Church on Sunday afternoon, **11 February**, when the speaker was the Rev W Wrigley Haughton, of Bedford, who gave a very interesting address on the subject "Some lessons we can learn from our soldiers". A fluegel horn solo was finely contributed by Mr W Groom, Mrs H Ruff accompanying at the piano.

The Thrapston Guardians met at the Workhouse on Tuesday, **13 February**, when Mr Agutter called attention to the case of a girl from the Cottage Homes who had been in the service of Mrs Agutter since September 1915, and who had been allowed by the previous superintendent to spend short visits at the Homes, where her brothers and sisters were. Recently an application had been made to the present superintendent for the girl to be allowed to spend a weekend at the Homes, Mrs Agutter offering to pay all expenses. His reply was that the girl could visit her family any weekend afternoon, but she could not stay overnight, as this would upset the discipline in the Homes. The matter was referred to the Cottage Homes Committee with the desire that the girl be allowed to stay the weekend.

Some alarm was raised just before 7 o'clock that morning when an atmospheric disturbance was noticed throughout the district, many windows rattling violently for some seconds.

Thursday, **15 February**, "Wanted At Once – Nurse-Companion for invalid elderly lady, housekeeper and maid kept; state salary – Horrell, Raunds."

Friday, 16 February, Horace Francis Gunn (57), died of wounds.

Both the Rushden Echo and Northampton Independent ran stories today about Private H Reynolds, 7th Northants, and 54 Marshall's Road. Under the headline "An Example to the Shirkers", it told how he had been at the front for 15 months, and had a family of eight young children back at home.

At the Temperance Hall on Saturday, **17 February**, the members of the Temperance Society arranged a tea and social in aid of their Building Fund. About 140 sat down to the tables. Tea was followed by a social, dancing being interspersed with songs by Mr W Gibbs and Miss W Pentelow, and a monologue by Mr W Rands. Miss E Pack, of Higham Ferrers, supplied the music for dancing.

A packed agenda greeted councillors at Urban District Council meeting on Monday evening, **19 February**. Firstly, it was unanimously decided to send a letter of condolence to the medical officer, Dr Mackenzie, in his illness. A letter was read from the postal authorities at Wellingborough regarding the hour (9am) at which the Raunds Post Office was opened, and stating that the department did not consider a case had been made for an earlier opening. The letter stated that a record had been taken of the business transacted from 9 to 9.20am for a week, revealing that there was no necessity for an earlier opening. However, when one councillor heard that this record was made by the sub-postmaster, who had already openly stated there was no need for a change, he observed that "It's no trouble for a man who conducts his own poll to win the election!" The clerk was instructed to write a further letter to the Wellingborough postmaster.

The acting surveyor reported that there were a large number of burst pipes after the recent frost, and some domestic supplies had been cut off pending repairs. There was also some loose stone on the old building in Brook Street belonging to Mr T G Jervis, which was dangerous to the public. It was decided to call the owner's attention to the same. It was also decided to repair the footpath leading through the churchyard. Finally, a letter was read from Mr W Denton stating that he proposed to make a charge of £2 per annum to the Council for tipping refuse in the Crow Spinney field. This question was deferred to the next meeting.

At Thrapston Police Court on Tuesday, **20 February**, a married Raunds woman, who appeared with a child in her arms, was summoned for "wilfully or negligently causing the water supplied to her to be wasted at Raunds on 1 February." The defendant pleaded not guilty of wilful waste. The temporary surveyor for the Raunds Urban Council said he was passing up the street and noticed that a standpipe was turned on and running full bore. Under the spout there was a vessel, which was running over with water. It was at least five minutes before the water was turned off. The defendant said that she had two children and went in to see them. Mr W F Corby, Clerk to the Council, said that they had no desire to press the case, but to stop the waste. The woman was fined 5s-0d.

Wednesday, 21 February, Frank Pentelow (88), died.

The latest Local Appeals Tribunal took place this evening when there were a number of personal appeals. First, cases adjourned from previous meetings were dealt with as follows: a young man, single, 18, training as an air pilot, asked for his case to be withdrawn; a plumber and painter, married, 22, was exempted to 8 March, and told to go before the Medical Board in the meantime; and a milk vendor, who met with a nasty accident last December, and at present was unable to move without assistance, was given conditional exemption. Twelve other personal appeals were then considered, seven of which were dismissed, the others receiving exemptions of up to three months.

The Raunds Gas Company Ltd held their annual meeting of the shareholders at the Coffee Tavern on Thursday evening, **22 February**. The director's report showed a decrease in gas sold of 1 million cubic feet which was attributed to the Daylight Saving scheme, the restrictions on public lighting, and the early closing of business premises. However, prepayment meter consumption had doubled during the past six years, and the amount of gas sold per ton of coal carbonised had also increased. The company now had 430 cookers and 540 slot meters installed, and had recently branched out into gas fires, but owing to the difficulty in obtaining the same only 20 so far were in use.

A dividened of 10% was recommended, and all the directors were then re-elected. Finally, the chairman reflected on the loss the Company had sustained during the year by the death of the late chairman, Mr J Gant, JP.

Earlier in the day, two Raunds shoehands appeared at St Neots Petty Sessions charged with "trespassing in search of game at Tilbrook on 3 February". Giving evidence, the farmer said he met PC Hitchcock and they saw two men with two dogs leave neighbouring land and work a hedge belonging to him. The PC then accosted them and attempted to search them. One man produced a letter which gave them permission to go on to nearby land. The search produced seven nets and a ferret in a bag. Inspector Tebbey confirmed that one of the men had been convicted 19 times for various offences, including poaching. The "novice" was fined 7s-6d or seven days, the "old hand" £3 or thirteen days – both men then produced gold to pay the fines!

On Friday, **23 February**, the Church School Managers met to interview the applicants for the vacant Headmaster's position. After due deliberation, Mr A D Rawlings was offered the position at £145 per annum, pending Local Education Authority approval.

Saturday, 24 February, the Turks evacuate Kut and the Allies occupy the city. Harry Rice (96), killed in action.

On the day that the fortunes of war continued to flow in favour of the Allies in Mesopotamia and the town suffered another casualty in France, the Temperance Band held their annual tea and business meeting in the Temperance Hall, Mr W F Corby presiding. The chairman congratulated the Band on having been able to keep together, not withstanding the number of members they had lost during the past two years. Mr J H Haynes, the secretary, in his annual report, said nine concerts had been given, and one contest had been entered, in which the band won third prize. Eleven members had joined up during the year, and sixteen altogether were now in the Forces. The financial statement showed an income of £111-4s-7d, and expenditure of £95-14s-0d, raising the balance in hand from £45-7s-10d to £60-18s-5d. Thanks were expressed to Mrs Coggins and Mrs Camozzi for the use of their grounds for concerts, and to Mr C Masters, for the use of his yard for practice. The evening was then spent in a social manner.

For three days commencing Monday, **26 February**, local folk had the opportunity to see some of the Allies' latest exploits on the silver screen as the Royal Theatre, Rushden, showed "The Battle of the Ancre" and "The Advance of the Tanks". As a bonus, the services of the Rushden Rifle Band had been secured to play all accompaniments. Customers were urged to "Book Your Seats at Once to Avoid Disappointment"!

* *

MARCH – In this month's Parish Magazine, the vicar announced the appointment of Mr A D Rawlings, currently headmaster of Carrington School, Boston, to succeed Mr Potter as headmaster of the Raunds Church of England Mixed School. The death of **Cornelius Robins (100)** on 5 February was also confirmed in the "Died in the Service of Their Country" column.

On the financial front, the newly published Church accounts for the period October 1915 to October 1916, included receipts of £15-0s-6d for churchyard fees, £1 for the sale of a tree, and 15s-0d for the sale of grass; expenses included £41-1s-0d for the sexton, £2-10s-0d for chiming, and £3 for tuning the organ. From the Clergy Fund, £155-16s-8d was paid to the curate, the Rev W S Bethway, for 13 months service, of which £100 was paid by the vicar. Of the "Vestry Class War Savings Association", as at 31 December 1916, 25 certificates had been bought, and £19-13s-0d paid in. The vicar urged all to buy more at 15s-6d each.

Finally, the following young folk were recognised as collectors of boxes for the "Waifs and Strays Fund": Gladys Mayes, Millie Coles, George Hales, Edith Bamford, Willie Sharpe, Tet Pound, Gertie Gaunt, Edith Allen, Leslie Smith, Ida Askham, Sydney Nunley, Willie Lawrence, Kenneth Spicer, and Edna White.

Meanwhile, in Brook Street, the Wesleyan Methodist Church's Young Men's Class register for March 1917, included the following entries with subsequent grim appends: **Horace Bugby (29)**, 3, Grove Street, June 1918, Killed in Action; **Arthur Hazeldine (61)**, 11, Park Street, November 1917, Missing at the Front (Name kept on until June 1918); **Herbert Bates (22)**, Coleman Street, Killed in Battle 1918; **Stanley Allen (10)**, 2, Sackville Street, Killed in Action 1917; and **Albert Masters (77)**, 6, Brook Street, Killed in Aeroplane Accident May 1 1918.

The Thrapston Board of Guardians issued the following invitation to tender on Thursday, **1 March**: "To Bakers, Butchers, Grocers, Drapers, Coal Merchants and others – Notice is hereby given that the Guardians at their next meeting to be held on Tuesday, 13 March, will receive Tenders for supplying their Children's Home at Raunds, the following articles: Bread and Flour; Rounds, Rands and Stickings of Beef without bone, Legs and Shins of Beef, bone and all, and fore-quarters of Mutton and Suet; Provisions and Grocery; Coal and Coke; Meal and Oats; New Milk; Drapery Goods; Clothing, Shoes, Brushes and Haircutting. The Guardians do not pledge themselves to accept the lowest or any tender."

The death of Mr Owen Nunley, Wellington Road, who had been unwell for the last few weeks, and was taken to the Northampton Hospital a fortnight ago, occurred today, the cause of death being pneumonia. He left a widow and eight children, including seven sons, four of whom were serving with the colours. Two of these, **Horace (82)** and **Leslie Beman (83)**, were to fall in the coming months.

At the Wellingborough Police Court on Friday, **2 March**, a shoehand from Westfields was summoned for "being in charge of a bicycle without a front light, at Stanwick on 20 February". However, the defendant failed to appear and the case was adjourned for one week.

Controversy reigned in Rushden when some non-conformists questioned the need for Street War Shrines adding that they were unhappy that "certain zealous Anglicans" had decided to erect the shrines without any reference to the Methodists or other Free Churchmen in a town where non-conformists probably represented more than half the population!

The Northants District (No.28) of the Independent Order of Rechabites held their annual meeting in the Temperance Hall on Saturday, **3 March**. Business commenced at 10.30am and closed shortly after 5pm, with a luncheon interval. Raunds delegates attending were Messrs J T L Turner, G Ernest Smith, Harry Wm Lawrence, A Whitney, J P Hall, and G T Brown, who welcomed the delegates to the meeting. The audience heard that there were approximately 800 district members serving in HM Forces, of which 23 had to date been killed. £1,611 had been paid out in full accident and disablement benefit during 1916; £1689 had been paid in sickness and maternity benefit and current funds stood at £23,555.

A report issued on Monday, **5 March**, by the council of the National Union of Boot and Shoe Operatives declared trade to be still good on the whole, and the out of work benefit being paid very low. The factories in all principle districts continued to be very busy, a large proportion of the firms being engaged on Government contracts, but those engaged on civilian work were also well employed. However, the shortage of skilled labour continued to be acute.

The Bishop of Peterborough, making his first visit to Raunds, conducted a confirmation service this evening in the Parish Church. There were 38 candidates for confirmation – 36 from Raunds and 2 from Hargrave – 15 boys and 23 girls.

And in a new campaign to attract customers, the Palace Theatre, Raunds, began advertising its forthcoming programmes in the local newspapers, this week being:

"Mon/Tue/Wed: An Exciting Drama (2 Reels) – 'President's Special', 'Peg 'O The Ring' (8th Episode), 'Hit Him Again' (Charlie Chaplin), 'Circumstantial Scandal' (Vitagraph Co)."

"Thu/Fri/Sat: A Drama in 3 Reels – 'The House of the Lost Court' – A Dramatic Adaption of the Novel by Mrs C M Williamson, 'Mrs Jarr and the Society Circus'."

At the Thrapston Police Court on Tuesday, **6 March**, a Raunds shoehand was summoned for disobeying a maintenance order made on 17 October, 1916, to pay 5s-0d per week towards the support of his son, currently in the Akbar Reformatory School. He was ordered to pay £1-15s-0d of the £2-5s-0d arrears within a month.

While in London today, Mr John Adams, JP CC, representing the Raunds Urban District Council, attended a meeting at Westminster which had been convened to meet the Director-General for National Service. As a follow up, a special meeting of the Council was to be held to consider what could be done locally.

In the evening, a grand entertainment was held in the Palace Cinema, by kind permission of the proprietor, in aid of funds of the Raunds War Charities Committee. The programme included the striking four reel film "Key to Yesterday" featuring Carlyle Blackwell, and the sensational two reel drama "The Master Cracksman". The pictures were interspersed with songs by Mrs J W Hall, Mrs W C Groom, Miss Louie Smith, and Mr W Gibbs, who kindly gave their services. The net proceeds amounted to between £14 and £15.

The special meeting of the Urban Council was held in the Wesleyan Schools on Thursday evening, **8 March**, to discuss the meeting Mr John Adams had attended in London the previous day regarding National Service. There was a long discussion during which opinion was expressed that as the factories were already severely depleted of men, there was very little chance of finding any who were not already doing national service. The chairman and Mr J Shelmerdine strongly advocated that the council should appoint a committee and fall into line with the request of the Director-General; this was eventually agreed and it was further decided to have a circular delivered to each home, and to make arrangements for dealing with any inquiries that might arise.

Friday, 9 March, Arthur Roland Groom (55), died of wounds.

On the day that the town lost another of its young men, the Rushden Echo confirmed the death the previous month of "Another Rushden Victim", that of **Horace Francis Gunn (57)**, describing him as "formerly of Raunds, and married six months ago while on leave." It was also reported that Mrs S Draper, of Marshall's Road, had recently received the news that her brother, Pte John G Stringer, Northamptonshire Regiment, had been severely wounded by a gunshot in his leg and hand, and had been admitted to the 11th Stationary Hospital, Rouen.

At the County Tribunal in Northampton, four Raunds factory foremen made personal appeals; one case was adjourned for a month, the others were dismissed.

Saturday, 10 March, the Czar suspends the Russian parliament.

War Savings – This evening, the vicar and Mr W F Corby paid a visit to the Palace Cinema and, with permission of the proprietor, gave short addresses urging the need for war savings.

"Wanted – Hand Laster on box derbys and chrome bluchers etc; work supplied to own homes, carriage paid, any quantity. Apply: Adams Bros, Raunds."

Sunday, 11 March, General Maude captures Baghdad.

At the Higham Ferrers Police Court on Monday, **12 March**, a married woman from Raunds was summoned for "not properly obscuring her bicycle lamp light at Higham Ferrers". The defendant said her husband was an invalid and was waiting to go to hospital and that she was only wheeling the bicycle. The Bench were lenient and she was ordered to pay only costs and allowed time to pay.

The mortal remains of the late Mr E Mayes were laid to rest in the Wesleyan Burial Ground on Tuesday, **13 March**, the officiating minister being the Rev E P Blackburn. Wreaths included one "With deepest sympathy from all at Kimbolton Grammar School".

Thursday, 15 March, the Czar abdicates. John Brackley Higby (63), died of wounds.

At this evening's Local Appeals Tribunal a question was raised by two members on "why young fellows whose appeals had been dismissed two months previous had not been called up yet?" They added that they, as members of the Tribunal, were continually being confronted with the question "How is it 'so and so' is still here when older men had to go?" They concluded that if the Tribunal had dismissed the cases, but the men had not yet been called up, they ought to know the reason, if there was one.

During the present week, Miss Thirsk, the organiser from the War Savings National Committee, had been at work in the town. On Monday, several of the factories, where associations had been formed, were visited and the workers urged to support the same to the utmost of their ability. One new association was formed and at an evening meeting of the existing association joint committees, it was decided to make a canvass of the town with a view to forming a town association.

A public meeting was held in the Temperance Hall on Friday evening, **16 March**, to consider the advisability of starting a Nursing Association in the town. It was proposed and unanimously decided to form a Nursing Association for the town, to ask each factory and every recognised body to provide a representative, and to include Hargrave. A provisional committee was chosen to make the arrangements.

And today it was announced that Privates S Manning and W Coles, both former members of the Raunds Fire Brigade, had been wounded in France, and that Pte Gerald Tite of Findeon, a former teacher at Raunds, had also been wounded.

The Raunds Wesleyan Circuit quarterly meeting was held on Saturday, **17 March**, and at the commencement of the meeting, the Chairman referred to the death of one of their local preachers – Mr **Arthur Groom (55)** – who had died of wounds in France on 9 March, and by a standing vote the meeting directed a vote of sympathy to be forwarded to his mother and the other members of his family.

Monday, **19 March**, was a red letter day in the history of Raunds Methodism when a special thanksgiving service was held to celebrate the clearance of the debt on the school buildings. The building was originally erected for a day school in 1861, and enlarged on two or three subsequent occasions at the request of the Education Authority. When, in the spring of 1914, the day school was transferred to the new Council School, there remained a debt of £640 on the buildings. Mr W F Corby, referring to the raising of the last £500, recounted how Mr John Horrell had promised to give one half of that sum on the condition that the whole amount was raised. Within a few days nearly the whole sum had been raised in promises.

The Palace Theatre, Raunds – Week Commencing Monday, 19 March 1917:

"Mon/Tue/Wed: 'The World at War" – A Sensational Drama of the War, Splendid Zeppelin Views. 'Peg 'O The Ring' (10th Episode), 'Love and a Savage' Comedy, 'When Two Play a Game' (Comedy), 'Battle of Trafalgar' (October 21, 1805) The Death of Nelson."

"Thu/Fri/Sat: Twice Nightly at 6 and 8 – 'The Battle of Ancre' and 'The Advance of the Tanks'. 'A Mix Up in Black' (Edison Comedy)."

Tuesday, 20 March, the United States War Cabinet votes in favour of declaring war on Germany.

On the day that the U.S. finally decided to throw its cap into the ring, a Raunds shoehand was summoned to Thrapston Police Court to show cause why an order should not be made on him to contribute towards the support of his mother. The deputy clerk of the Thrapston Board of Guardians stated that the mother, of Denford, had been in receipt of 6s-0d per week out-relief from 24 October last. The Guardians made an order upon the defendant to contribute 2s-0d per week on a letter received from the man's employers stating that his earnings for the two months up to 15 December were £2-2s-6d per week. The defendant said that he had two children not earning and refused to pay, but offered 1s-0d per week. The Bench duly ordered him to pay 1s-6d per week.

In the evening, the Urban Council held their monthly meeting and a letter was read from the Postal Authorities at Wellingborough in reply to the council's renewed request saying that the Raunds Sub-Office would in future open at 8.45am instead of 9am. The medical officer reported one case of tuberculosis and one of German measles during February.

The Acting Surveyor reported that the Recreation Ground had been ploughed up and the allotments allocated. It was decided to plant an acre of the Sewage Farm with potatoes instead of mangolds; Messrs Shelmerdine, Smith, John Adams and Hodson were then re-elected as overseers; finally, it was decided to purchase a hand hearse and bier from Mr F Parker, of Higham Ferrers, for £29-10s-0d.

The Church School Managers also met this evening and they decided to ask Mrs Edge if she would come in as a teacher for the period of the war and also to ask the Local Education Authority to send a supply teacher for May until the new headmaster arrived. Finally, they agreed that salary increase applications should be submitted for Mr Potter, Miss Gooding, Miss Lodder, Mr Edge, Miss Hall, Miss Kirk, and Mrs Ash.

"For Sale – Buff Orpington Cockerels, April 1916 hatched, 10s-0d each; eggs, 5s-0d dozen; White Leghorn Cockerels, 5s-0d to 10s-0d each; eggs, 4s-0d dozen – George White, Poultry Farm, Raunds."

"Wanted – In Raunds, Few Hours Work daily – Apply: 4, Streathers Yard."

At the Local Appeals Tribunal on Thursday, **22 March**, a letter was read from the secretary of the National Union of Boot & Shoe Operatives with reference to the release of C2 and C3 men to take the place of the general service men who were being called up. The suggestion was approved. The military representative stated that he had been instructed to press for the release of all men in the boot trade in Classes A and B1, for school teachers in Classes A and B1 under 31, and for those in all other occupations passed in Classes A, B1, B2, C1 and C2.

Twenty-three individual appeals were then considered, and all but one received exemptions ranging from one week to permanent unconditional; the unlucky exception's case was dismissed!

The following stirring item appeared in Friday, **23 March's** Evening Telegraph:
"National Service – The Peril of Delay – The men who 'put off' enrolling for National Service are foolish Canutes defying the waves, or fiddlers while Rome is burning. The fields are waiting for the plough, the Army is waiting for Aeroplanes, the Artillerymen are waiting for big guns, the food stocks are dangerously low. What would you think of a man who delays at this critical time?"

The deaths of Corporal **Arthur Groom (55)** and Private **John Brackley Higby (63)** were confirmed in the local press today. The life-long pals, who were engaged to the Barnes sisters of Woodford, had enlisted together and died within six days of one another, albeit at different locations at the front. Also reported today was news of two more Raunds men wounded in France: Privates J Stringer and Leslie Knighton, both of the Northamptons, the latter being said to be in hospital in Manchester with leg wounds.

"Thanks – Mrs Charles Groom and Family and Miss G Barnes wish to thank all kind friends for the sympathy shown to them in their recent sad bereavement – Lawson Street, Raunds."

On Saturday evening, **24 March**, a social was held in the Temperance Hall, arranged by members of the Temperance Band, who also supplied the music for dancing. There was a good company present and dancing was indulged in from 7.30pm to 10.30pm. Mr J H Haynes acted as MC. The proceeds were in aid of the Temperance Society's Building Fund.

An open meeting of the Brotherhood was held on Sunday afternoon, **25 March**, when a good number of both sexes attended in the Wesleyan Church. The service was conducted by the Rev E P Blackburn who also gave a very interesting address on the subject "A message from our wounded". During the meeting the secretary, Mr W F Corby, read out the names of Brotherhood members who had joined HM Forces. These numbered between 80 and 90. Three members had been killed, Pte **Harry Finding (50)**, Cpl **Arthur R Groom (55)**, and Pte **John B Higby (63)**, two were amongst those missing, Ptes **Cecil Burton (32)** and **Arthur Clark (35)**, and five others were in hospital. Appropriate hymns were sung and the collection taken at the close was in aid of the YMCA Fund.

During the evening service at the Wesleyan Church, the Rev E P Blackburn made reference to the loss that the church had suffered by the death from wounds received in action of **Arthur Groom (55)** and **John B Higby (63)**. Before enlisting they were like David and Jonathan, close personal friends who joined up together. Although serving in different parts of the line both received their wounds and died in the same week. The one was unconscious and the other left a beautiful testimony behind. Their sympathy went out to the family and friends of these two stricken soldiers, but they had not sorrow as those without hope. Their two friends had died a hero's death in the service of their King and Country. Favourite hymns of the deceased were sung during the service.

Monday, 26 March, the First Battle of Gaza. Sidney Smith (107), killed in action.

At the Temperance Hall, a meeting of members of the Urban District Council and the committees of several War Savings Associations was held to consider a circular from the National Association with respect to carrying out a campaign to prevent the wasteful consumption of food. A motion was passed to fall in with the suggestion and for a committee to be formed to carry out the campaign.

Today it was officially announced that the Government had decided to reintroduce Summer Time throughout the United Kingdom and that all clocks were to be altered on 8 April.

At a meeting of the Stanwick War Charities Committee on Tuesday, **27 March**, it was reported that at present 132 officers and men from the village were away with the Forces; that sixteen had already lost their lives and nine had been discharged.

The annual meeting of the Raunds Conservative Bowls Club was held at the club in the evening, with Mr J Shelmerdine, JP, in the chair. The financial statement for last season was submitted and considered satisfactory. The following were elected officers for the coming year: captain – Mr A Lawrence, vice-captain – Mr W Partrick, committee members – Messrs W H Spicer, V S Sykes, J Shelmerdine, T Bailey, A Camozzi, W Asberry, G H Kirk, A Martin, J W Peck, J Curtis, J Sanders, T Haddon, G Mason, and H Bamford.

"For Sale – Eggs for Hatching, White Leghorn, good strain, 4s-6d – White, Poultry Farm, Raunds."

On Wednesday evening, **28 March**, a lecture was given in the Temperance Hall on "Poultry and Egg Production". Mr John Adams, JP CC, presided over a large company. The lecturer was Mr Calthorpe of the Agricultural Organisation Society, who gave a most interesting talk on "How to form an Egg and Poultry Society". It was then decided to form a committee to further consider the matter and the Rev C C Aldred, Mrs White, Mrs A Lawrence, Miss L Coles, Mrs Milligan, and Miss Adams were appointed to serve on it.

Thursday, **29 March** – "Wanted – Organist, Parish Church, Raunds, desires work of national importance – J P Archer."

2 – April to June 1917

The Boys and Girls strike, but at last the Yanks are coming!

APRIL – In the vicar's Parish Magazine editorial this month he postulated that Easter should bring again the message of hope and comfort to all who had been in trouble. He opinioned that the recent visit of the Bishop of Peterborough for the Confirmation had given great pleasure to all and also gave notice that there would be a "Three Hours Service" on Good Friday which would be taken by the Rev P J Richards, of St Peter's, Rushden. Finally he reminded his flock that Summer Time would begin on Easter Day, 8 April.

Meanwhile, the "Died in the Service of Their Country" column reiterated the deaths of **Arthur Groom (55)**, **Horace Gunn (57)**, and **John B Higby (63)**.

Sunday, 1 April, John William Elliot (48), killed in action.

At Monday, **2 April's** meeting of the local branch of the National Union of Boot & Shoe Operatives it was somewhat controversially stated that the high number of women now employed in men's positions meant an increase in the number of accidents and a higher rate of sickness benefit being claimed. However, it was also felt that the women, together with the youths, who had replaced the men called to the Colours, were not receiving fair rates of pay.

The Palace Theatre, Raunds – Week Commencing Monday, 2 April 1917:

"Mon/Tue/Wed: A Fine Drama in 3 Reels 'Idols of Clay', as played at the Drury Lane Theatre, London, featuring Ella Hall and Robert Lenard, 'Peg 'O The Ring' (12th episode), 'Sins on a Sabbath' (Comedy)."

"Thu/Fri/Sat: A Fine Drama in Four Parts 'The Evil Eye', 'Lizzie and the Beauty Contest' (Nestor Comedy), A Fine Drama, One Reel 'The Vagabond'."

"If you want a good laugh, see Lizzie. Time and Prices As Usual."

Two Raunds men appeared at Thrapston Police Court on Tuesday, **3 April**, summoned for "failing to subdue the lights of their houses." The first defendant wrote to say he was very sorry and that it was impossible for him to attend. He was fined 5s-0d. The second man also did not appear but again wrote to explain the facts, saying he was very sorry. He was fined 2s-6d.

In later business, on the application of Mr W F Corby, clerk to the Raunds Urban District Council, the Bench excused (for the fourth time), the rates on the house at Raunds occupied by the Belgian refugees.

The Council School managers met on Wednesday, **4 April** with Mr John Adams, JP CC, in the chair. The usual applications for teacher's annual increase of salary were submitted and agreed to. The clerk reported that Mrs Ruff, of Ringstead, a former teacher in the Infants Department, was on temporary duty in the same in place of Miss Hodder, who had been ill for some weeks.

A meeting of the District Sub-Committee followed when special permits for employment under the relaxed bye-laws were then reported and approved. The attendance report was considered where it was revealed, generally speaking, that attendances were much below the average, due in the Infants Department to the inclemency of the weather, and in the Upper Department to special permits.

In the evening of Thursday, **5 April**, the Local Appeals Tribunal met in the Wesleyan Schoolroom when around twenty personal cases were considered. All received exemptions ranging from 30 April to 30 September. The boot factory cases, of which the military authorities had asked for a review as their current exemptions would expire on 31 March, were all discussed. All the applicants who had not been examined by the Army Medical Board were requested to be so before they made a further appeal.

Good Friday, 6 April, the United States declares war on Germany.

Three town men, all serving with the Northamptons, were today reported as being wounded: Corporal W Coles, and Privates L Knighton and S Manning.

"Deaths – on the 2nd inst at "Roseleigh", Raunds – Horace R Sawford, the dearly loved husband of Eleanor M Sawford, aged 25 years."

Like the rest of the country, the clocks in the town were put forward one hour on Saturday night, **7 April**, or early on Sunday morning, and the longer light evenings to come were much anticipated. Most of the people fell in with the alteration except some farmers, who were keeping to "old time" for a little longer.

Monday, 9 April, the Battle of Vimy Ridge & the Arras Offensive begins. Sidney James Cope MM (43), killed in action.

On the day that another local hero fell, Easter Monday passed off very quietly for holiday making owing to the unsatisfactory weather. During the afternoon snowstorms were frequent, and the weather was more like Christmas than Easter.

At the monthly meeting of the Thrapston Guardians held on Tuesday, **10 April**, it was stated that Raunds parish showed a considerable increase in out-relief funds given out during the quarter ended 31 March, £8-9s-2d!

Wednesday, 11 April, John Henry Bamford (19), killed in action.

At the County Tribunal on Thursday, **12 April**, there was mixed fortune for two Raunds cases: a grocer gained a final exemption until 30 June to enable him to arrange for his business to be carried on in his absence; whereas a 27 year old, lasting room foreman's appeal of being in a reserved occupation was dismissed.

At the Easter Vestry meeting this evening, the vicar re-appointed Mr A Camozzi as his warden, and Mr J Shelmerdine, JP, as the people's warden. Mr Camozzi then presented the vicar with £20, the Easter offering from the congregation. A letter was read from Colonel Stopford Sackville in which he offered to double any contribution up to £100 raised during the year for the endowment of the living. This offer was received with thanks.

An inquest was held by Mr J T Parker at the Thrapston Workhouse today on John Allen Mitchell, aged 74, who, while in the workhouse infirmary, fractured his thigh on 24 March and died on 3 April. The deceased's daughter, Ada Moules, of High Street, Raunds, said her father, an agricultural labourer, lived in Raunds until he became an inmate of the workhouse in January 1915. A verdict of "accidental death sustained by a fall while getting out of bed" was returned.

Also today, it was claimed that by catching moles and selling their skins at the record price of 7d each, many farm labourers were adding 10s-0d a week to their minimum wage of 25s-0d!

Saturday, 14 April, Herbert Richardson (99), died of wounds.

"To Let – Good Furnished Rooms, suit elderly couple or young people – Apply: 35 High Street, Raunds."

Sunday, 15 April, the 5th Anniversary of the Titanic disaster.

Monday, 16 April, the Second Battle of the Aisne.

The Urban Council met this evening for the first assembly of the new administrative year and Mr A Camozzi was unanimously elected chairman for the coming year. The seal of the council was then affixed to a general district rate of 5s-8d in the £ for the new year, this was the highest in the county. The chairman explained that no other council had the length of roads they had. Replying to a question from Mr Hodson, the clerk then advised that the seed potatoes were ready for delivery and that Mr Jeeves had sold no potatoes for eating outside of Raunds.

Dr Mackenzie presented what was to be his last annual health report as medical officer. During 1916, 80 births had been registered, the same as the previous year. The birth rate was 19.2 per 1000 of the population. The death rate was 11.78 per 1000 and three inquests had been held. One case of suicide had taken place, that of a man of 69, who drowned himself in a water barrel in April.

Finally, the clerk submitted the attendances for the past year; five members had attended all meetings: Messrs A Camozzi, J Shelmerdine, W Asbery, G E Smith, and J Hodson, Messrs Camozzi, Asbery and Smith having also attended every committee meeting too.

"To Let – Large Room over shop, suitable for offices or dentists, central position of Raunds – Apply: E W Felce, High Street."

Tuesday, 17 April, the French army uses tanks in battle for the first time.

Two Raunds residents who probably would not have been shouting "Vive Les Tanks" today were the married woman and fifteen year old girl who both appeared at Thrapston Police Court this afternoon. The woman was fined 5s-0d for failing to subdue the lights of her house in Raunds at 11pm on 4 April.

The girl, a lift maker, was summoned for finding and stealing a leather purse, value 1s-0d, containing a 10s-0d Treasury note and two 2s-0d pieces at Raunds on 16 March. The defendant pleaded guilty and admitted spending some of the money in Rushden on a new jacket, two hats, and oranges and sweets. Supt Tebbey said that although this was the first time the girl had been before the Court, there had been instances before where she had been suspected of similar offences but the people had not been willing to prosecute. Her father's conduct in her upbringing was also called into question. A fine of £1-0s-1d, including costs, was imposed. The girl was also placed on probation for one year and her father was bound over for his daughter's good behaviour for the same period.

On Wednesday, **18 April**, The Rev C J Keeler, of Rushden, was the speaker at the Wesley Guild when he spoke on his experiences with the men in France.

Mr John Martin, aged 78, a highly respected inhabitant, died suddenly at his residence in Coleman Street today. The deceased had his tea and returned to work at the back part of his house where he had a workshop. Soon after 6 o'clock, Mrs Martin found him on the floor with an iron in his hand. The deceased, who was an excellent bespoke bootmaker, was just finishing ironing a pair of ladies boots when he had a seizure. He was a loyal Churchman and Conservative.

Thursday, 19 April, the Second Battle of Gaza. Leslie Beman Nunley (83), killed in action.

Many miles away from the Middle East, a capital concert was given to the wounded soldiers at the Auxiliary Hospital, Hinwick, by the Rushden Angelus Quartette Party assisted by Miss Spicer, contralto, of Raunds.

The quarterly meeting of the Hospital Week Fund committee was held in the Temperance Hall on Friday evening, **20 April**. The treasurer reported receipts of £27-11s-7d, expenses of £9s-0d, leaving a balance in hand of £27-2s-7d. It was decided to hold the annual demonstration, as before, and to ask Mrs Coggins for the use of the Hall grounds, Mrs A Camozzi to make the arrangements for the Rose Day, and the Fire Brigade to arrange the Fire Brigade Competitions.

It was stated today that the Temperance Silver Prize Band, with so many young members called up, had been doubtful if it could continue, however, a number of veterans had volunteered to play for the present time.

On Saturday, **21 April**, a very pretty wedding was solemnised at the Roman Catholic Church, Rushden, the contracting parties being Monsieur Jean Joseph H Desherhaut, Adjutant to the Belgian Army, of Chotelineun, Belgium, and Madamoiselle Mitge Vliegan, a Belgian refugee, of Antwerp, a resident of Raunds since the autumn of 1915. Later in the day, the wedding party, including the whole of the Belgians at present in Raunds, sat down to an excellent tea in the Wesleyan Schoolroom, the catering for which was admirably carried out by the Raunds Distributive Co-operative Society. ***(Plate 6)***

Another meeting of the Raunds Appeals Tribunal was held at the Council School on Monday evening, **23 April**. The chairman, Mr John Adams, JP CC, first referred to one of the appeals to the County Tribunal made against their local decision. He said that neither he nor his firm, *Messrs Adams Bros Ltd*, had had anything to do with it. When the appellant asked him about it he told him that he was released according to age, and that he would be no party to the breaking of the agreement. He wished the members to know this, because he (the chairman) had heard it was said that he was at the back of the man's appeal, which was without foundation, as they had taken no steps whatever.

A "Khaki" wedding took place on Tuesday, **24 April**, at the Parish Church, when Pte Jack Roland Freeman, Royal Irish Fusiliers, stationed at Rockstown, Ireland, the fourth son of Mrs Freeman, of Higham Ferrers, was married to Miss Phoebe Hall, of Raunds. The bridegroom had seen service in France and Salonica. The bride had five brothers and the bridegroom four brothers serving with the Forces.

The Church School managers met in the evening and discussed the matter of a child of over 5 having been entered by its mother into the school on 23 April, but then on 24 April, wanting to move the child to the Council School.

A meeting was held on Thursday evening, **26 April**, to explain the working of a Nursing Association, the speaker being Miss Harrington, of Northampton. After much discussion, it was proposed and carried unanimously that a Nursing Association be formed for Raunds and district.

Friday, **27 April's** newspapers brought news of yet another Raunds death at the Front; that of L-Cpl **John Henry Bamford (19)**, RAMC, on 11th of this month.

On the recommendation of Earl Spencer, KG, the Lord Lieutenant of Northamptonshire, the addition by the Lord Chancellor of Mr John Adams, CC, of "Darsdale", to the Commission of the Peace for the County was announced today.

"In Memoriam" – a tribute to the late Mr John Martin penned by Mr S Head:

God has been pleased to call away, A Worker from our side,
But while he lived, all men will say, To do his best he tried,
The young and old who came to him, He nobly strove to please,
The swollen bunions to reduce, To painful corns give ease,
All kinds of boots, both thin and thick, Were made with equal skill,
He knew just howe to do the trick, And did it with a will,
John Martin was a busy man, And will be missed by all,
But only those who knew him can, His estimate recall.

Saturday, 28 April, Arthur Revitt (94), killed in action.

Sunday, 29 April, the French army mutinies, Charles A Major (74), died.

On Monday evening, **30 April**, after a weekend that saw the loss of two more town men and trouble in the ranks "en France", the Local Tribunal met at the Council School. The lists were gone through and forty-one men were released.

MAY – The vicar opened his notes in this month's Parish Magazine with thanks to all who contributed to the Easter offering and attended the various services. He was especially pleased with the turnout for Holy Communion, with over 300 "communicating".

The valued offer of Mr S G Stopford Sackville to double any sum raised between £50 and £100 towards the endowment of the parish was also reviewed. It was pointed out that many parishes were not too well endowed and Raunds was one of them. At present the gross income of the vicar was £263, and the net income £177. In 1916, the £263 was made up of: Rent of Land, £180-10s-0d; Tithe, £7-15s-0d; Ecclesiastical Commissioners, £30; Railway Co, £27-15s-0d; Fees, £7; Easter Offering, £10. The 1916 outgoings were: Rates and Taxes, £36-3s-7d; Land Tax, £3-2s-5d; Tithe, £1-1s-3d; Collection of Rents, £6-13s-6d; Five years Average of Repairs, £25; Insurance of Buildings, £2-13s-0d; Tenths, £1-3s-5d; Queen Anne Bounty, £2-4s-3d; Quit Rents, £1-3s-9d; Nene Valley Taxes, £6-16s-2d.

He said all were grieved to hear of the death of **John Henry Bamford (19)**, of the RAMC, observing that he was the second Sunday School teacher and member of the choir to have laid down his life, following on from **Phillip Stubbs (113)** in November last.

A very pleasing little ceremony was noted to have taken place on the last Friday in April, after school was over, in the form of a small presentation to Mr and Mrs Potter – a teapot, milk jug, sugar basin and tray, given by the children, Day and Sunday School teachers, managers and friends. The girls of Mrs Potter's class, past and present, gave her a salad bowl at their last Sunday class meeting.

Finally, three more names appeared in the "Died in the Service of Their Country" column: **John "Jack" Elliot (48)**, **John Henry Bamford (19)**, and **Herbert Richardson (99)**.

On Tuesday, **1 May**, Mr A J Mayes, deputation secretary, paid a visit to Raunds with some of the boys from Dr Barnardo's Homes, arranged by the Young Helpers' League. The Palace Theatre was kindly placed at their disposal by the proprietor, Mr J W Hall. Two "shows" were given and the boys gave fine performances on various instruments and were greatly applauded. Mr Mayes gave an account of the work done by the Homes, and votes of thanks were accorded. The building was crowded on both occasions, the gross takings being £31-10s-3d.

May-Day was celebrated at Chelveston on the village green by the children of the school and their efforts were so successful that £2-18s-6d was raised, to be devoted to the comforts for "Chelson" lads on active service. Little Kitty Barker was chosen as May Queen and among the various songs and dances performed around the Maypole the infants were congratulated on their Sir Roger dance.

Speaking in the House of Commons on Wednesday, **2 May**, the Chancellor of the Exchequer reported that the total national expenditure during the war had been £4,318,000,000, of which no less than £1,137,000,000 had been raised by taxation.

Thursday, 3 May, the British break through the Hindenberg Line. Stanley Oswyn George (53), Ralph Higby (64), & George Pettitt (92), all killed in action.

On another black day for the town, and several thousand miles away, the Toronto Star published a report on **Sidney James Cope, MM (43)**. This Raunds old boy had emigrated to Canada before the war and found work with a firm of Toronto builders and contractors. He had enlisted in the Royal Canadian Regiment in August 1915 and by January 1917 had been awarded the Military Medal. He was killed in action three months later on the first day of the Battle of Vimy Ridge.

The Temperance Silver Band gave a concert on "The Hill" on Sunday afternoon, **6 May**, conducted by Mr Owen Pentelow.

Disappointing news for locals on Monday, **7 May**, was that the Kaiser had narrowly escaped being assassinated while motoring in Berlin. The culprit, who was later arrested, had fired three revolver shots, two of which hit the car.

The Palace Theatre, Raunds – Week Commencing Monday, 7 May 1917:

"Mon/Tue/Wed – A First Class Drama by the Famous Players (4 Reels), 'The Straight Road', 'The Girl of Lost Island', (3rd episode), Those American Comedians in a Comedy 'Pressing Business'."

"Thu/Fri/Sat: A Drama by the Famous Players 'Aftermath' (4 Reels), 'Love, Pepper, Sweets' (Comedy), By Those American Comedians, 'Luke and the Mermaids' (Pathe Comedy)."

"Coming Shortly : 'The Eternal City'."

"Always The Best of Pictures Shown – Cycles Stored Free."

News of two Raunds soldiers featured in the newspapers of Wednesday, **9 May**. Mr and Mrs B Mayes, Mill House, had received an official communication that their son, Pte Ronald Mayes, Suffolk Regiment, was missing, and believed to be a prisoner of war. The nineteen year old had previously worked for Messrs T Wingell, butchers. Reports had also arrived that Lance-Corporal J W Edwards, Northants Regiment, had been wounded in action in Palestine three weeks earlier. The Terrier had joined up in November 1914 and served in the Dardanelles in 1915. After bouts of dysentery, during which he was hospitalised in Alexandria, and enteritis, which required a period of convalescence in Cairo, he rejoined his unit which was stationed near the Pyramids. He then described how "we wandered about like the Israelites of old, marching in the same direction, eventually reaching Palestine", where he was subsequently wounded.

The Local Tribunal met on Thursday evening, **10 May**, and the clerk reported that the military had appealed to the County Tribunal against all those exempted in Classes A and B1, and the manufacturers had appealed for those they agreed to give up if the military authorities did not appeal against the others, a total of 181. Mr Camozzi said that it was not fair for them to sit for hours, only for the military authorities to appeal wholesale, after they had considered the cases on their merits.

A Raunds farmhand appeared before the County Appeals Tribunal at Northampton on Friday, **11 May**. He was described as the only man left on the Glebe Farm and having suffered from consumption. As his employer was leaving the farm at Michaelmas, he was granted final exemption to 29 September.

Examples of the widespread shortage of all manner of commodities were shown on Saturday, **12 May**, when it was announced that the use of paste for paper-hanging or bill posting was now prohibited and that local grocers were appealing to the public to voluntarily reduce their ration of sugar to eight ounces per week.

Salvation Army – Captain Marden, of Whittlesey, who used to be stationed at Raunds, conducted the Army meetings in the town on Sunday, **13 May**, changing places with Captain Phillips, who led the meetings at Whittlesey.

Monday, **14 May**, and Mr and Mrs W Higby, High Street, received news this morning that their youngest son, Pte **Ralph Higby (64)**, Bedfordshire Regiment, had been missing since 3 May and was believed killed. This was the second son they had lost on the Western Front and their two other sons were also serving.

The Palace Theatre, Raunds – Week Commencing Monday, 14 May 1917:

"Mon/Tue/Wed – 'Wildflower', Drama featuring Marguerite Clarke, 'Mashers and Splashers' (Comedy) – Those American Comedians, 'The Girl of Lost Island' (4th episode)."

"Thu/Fri/Sat: Secured At Enormous Cost – Hall Caine's Famous Novel:
'The Eternal City' – Supreme Dramatic Triumph – Eight Reels.
Scenes laid in Rome and London were actually filmed in Rome and London!
Such Magnificent Scenes as are shown here have seldom been seen on any Film."

"(TWICE NIGHTLY SATURDAY), Cycles Stored Free."

On Tuesday, **15 May**, it was announced that the town's shoe manufacturers would close on the Monday, Tuesday and Wednesday of Whit Week for the annual Whitsuntide holidays; that Earl Spencer, Lord Lieutenant of the County, had promised to attend the town's Hospital Week Demonstration on 21 June; and rather more bizarrely, Mr and Mrs Hodges, of Wellingborough, wished it known that they would prosecute "anyone reporting scandalous statements about them!"

This afternoon at the Thrapston Police Court, a soldier from Raunds was charged with assaulting his neighbour, a shoehand on 6 April, while home on leave. The Complainant said that the defendant hit him between the eyes, knocking him down, half blinding him, then picking him up and hitting him again. The soldier said his neighbour had called his wife a liar and a bad lot. The case was dismissed.

At the same session, a Raunds clicker was summoned for disobeying a maintenance order to pay 5s-0d per week towards the support of his son, leaving arrears of £2-10s-0d. Supt Tebbey said that the accused had sent 10s-0d that morning leaving £2 due. An order was made for payment of the arrears within a month (with costs of 8s-6d), and if in default, one month's imprisonment.

A public meeting was held in the Temperance Hall this evening to discuss "food control". Mrs Tippett, from the Ministry of Food, explained that the situation was a serious one, more serious than they understood for the following reasons: the harvest last year being a failure the world over; the U-boats; and not enough ships to carry food, troops and munitions for the various fronts. However, she added that there were many ways to help: be thrifty and not to waste; see that food was cooked properly; cut down what you have been used to having; and for grown ups to sacrifice a little for the children. She closed with the ominous message that the Government urged the country to adopt these voluntary measures otherwise they would introduce compulsory rationing!

"Notice – Ringstead Soldiers' Comforts Fund – The Draw set for 14 May is unavoidably postponed until the 31st. The Winning Numbers will be published in the "Evening Telegraph" on Saturday, 2 June; T W Johnson, Hon Sec."

Friday, 18 May, the United States conscription lottery chooses the first 687,000 men to serve.

The local Boot and Shoe Operatives' Union made two important announcements today: *National War Bonus* – The Northamptonshire County Board and Joint Standing Committee have agreed to pay all piece workers (male and female), a War Bonus on their earnings of 3 pence in the shilling for one month. *Roumanian Boot Clicking Prices* – The National Joint Standing Committee for fixing prices of all Government boots and shoes that are to be made in future have decided that 3d per dozen extra is to be paid over and above that of the Russian ankle boot. Members who have been working under protest should now make their demands on their respective firms.

"Boys and Girls out at Raunds – More War Bonus Demanded" ran the headlines on Saturday, **19 May**. The report told how, following an undesirable example of other towns, the boys and girls employed in Raunds shoe factories this morning came out on strike. Last night they had been offered an addition to the bonus which would make it up to 15% on their wages, the same as at Kettering, but this they refused, and demanded 3s-6d bonus up to 16, and 5s-6d up to 18. So far they had been acting entirely on their own responsibility, and without consulting the local branch of the Operatives' Union. And although the strike had not greatly dislocated the work of the factories so far, it was feared that if it continued into next week it would cause many adult workers to "stand off".

The fate of the "Barber's Arms", a beer-on-line public house on The Square, was decided by the County Licensing Committee at Northampton on Monday, **21 May**. In evidence given against the renewal of its licence, it was said to be not so well situated as others in the town, and both structurally and in accommodation, compared unfavourably. In its defence, the landlords and tenant claimed that recent business had been higher than others in the town granted licences, up from £837 in 1913-14 to £1,223 during the last twelve months. However, their plea was to no avail and the renewal was refused.

The good news spread this morning was that the strike of boy and girl shoe factory workers had been satisfactorily settled late on Saturday and that they all returned to work today. An emergency court of enquiry held later during the day confirmed that they would receive a bonus of 22½% on their wages, an increase of 12%.

The Urban Council met this evening in the Council School and the first item on the agenda was to agree to affix the seal of the council to the petition to the Bishop of Peterborough to consecrate a portion of the new cemetery. The medical officer, Dr Mackenzie, wrote reporting one case of spinal meningitis, and giving the vital statistics for April as six births and three deaths. Owing to continued ill-health, he asked that Dr McInnes be appointed as deputy medical officer and this was agreed to. On the motion of the chairman, the members congratulated Mr John Adams on his appointment as a county magistrate.

Mr Adams then called attention to the prospect of a plentiful supply of fruit this summer, and asked if anything could be done so that people could get sugar for preserving. After some discussion, it was decided to write to the Local Government Board, and to point out the great wastage of fruit there would be during the summer unless sugar was forthcoming for the purpose of making jam.

A special court of Quarter Sessions for Northamptonshire was held on Thursday, **24 May**, for the swearing in of the new magistrates, including Mr John Adams.

The results of the Adult School examinations in Pitman's Shorthand were announced today. Those successful were: Speed (60 words per minute) - Winifred Abbott and Deborah Jackson; Theory - Lottie Hall, Leah Childs, and Walter Corby; Elementary - Stanley Dickerson, Winifred Betts, Eleanor Newberry, and Albert Bass. Only two students failed in their respective classes.

The local papers of Friday, **25 May**, reported two more town war casualties today. Mrs S O George, Park Road, had received news that her husband, Sgt **Stanley O George (53)**, of the Bedfords, had been missing since 3 May. They told how Sgt George had been an assistant master at Deal School before enlisting, and centre forward for Raunds Town and Peterborough City FCs.

And Mr and Mrs George Elliot, Chelveston Road, had been advised by the Infantry Record Office, Dublin, that their son, Pte **John William Elliot (48)**, Royal Inniskilling Fusiliers, had been killed in action on 1 April. The twenty-one year old had joined up in September 1916, going out to France in January. His two brothers were also serving at the Front.

Saturday, 26 May, the first United States troops arrive in France.

Not wishing to be outdone by the "Doughboys" and miss out on their share of waging war on the enemy, the farmers of Raunds today announced that they had formed a "Sparrow Club", with Mr A E Wingell, of "Southlands", as secretary.

A "Pansy Day", in aid of the Stanwick War Charities Fund, was held in the village today and the very attractive flowers offered by the energetic sellers were sold out by the evening. The sum of £6 was handed over to the fund.

A United Service of all the denominations was held in Thrapston Market Place on Sunday evening, **27 May**, when Mr H Hazeldine, of Raunds, represented the Wesleyans in the good company that was present.

The Temperance Silver Prize Band, conducted by Mr Owen Pentelow, gave a concert on The Square this afternoon when there was a large company present. A collection was taken in aid of the Band funds.

On Monday, **28 May**, Mr and Mrs Bellamy, who had been to Brigstock, were returning home at about 7pm, accompanied by Miss Bellamy (sister) when at Lowick the horse shied and fell down, throwing the occupants of the trap heavily to the ground. The couple received cuts about the head and face, and were very much bruised. Miss Bellamy escaped with a severe shaking. The horse was uninjured, and the cart was only slightly damaged. It was later found that Mrs Bellamy had a broken rib.

The Palace Theatre, Raunds – Week Commencing Monday, 28 May 1917:

"Special Holiday Attraction:"

"Mon/Tue – Monday Performances 3pm, 7 & 9 – Powerful Drama (4,000 Feet), 'A Woman's Triumph', A Novel by Sir Walter Scott, 'Two For a Quarter' (Comedy), 'Girl of Lost Island' (6th episode)."

"Wed/Thu – A Drama (5,500 Feet), 'What's His Name', Carpentier, The French Boxer v Sullivan, 'Juggling Truth' (Comedy)."

"Fri/Sat – A Fine Cowboy Drama (4,000 Feet) 'Where the Trail Divides', 'Pokers and Jabbs' (Comedy), 'Luke Joins the Navy' (Pathe Comedy)."

"Note – Programme Changed Monday, Wednesday and Friday, Prices As Usual."

"Spare the rod" didn't apply at the Thrapston Police Court on Tuesday, **29 May**, when five Woodford boys were summoned for stealing peas from a drill. Three had been before the Bench before and were ordered to be whipped, receiving four strokes each. The two first-offenders were each fined 5s-0d.

That afternoon, a violent and freakish thunderstorm burst over the county. At Raunds, a storm of "exceptional violence" passed over the town. Heavy rain, thunder and lightning were accompanied by hailstones "as big as 2s-0d pieces". They were the largest and most plentiful hailstones seen in the town for a very long time. Water was quickly running down the streets in considerable quantities.

Elsewhere in the county, several houses were struck by lightning, and chimney pots and roof slates brought down and a plot of onions near Oundle was so severely pulped up that they could be smelled a mile away!

The Rushden and Irthlingborough Salvation Army Corps paid a visit to Raunds today, tea was provided in the Temperance Hall, followed by a musical festival, over which Mr George Bayes, of Rushden, presided. Previous to the meeting the band paraded the town. An open air meeting had also been arranged, to be held between the tea and the festival, but unfortunately the thunderstorm struck, and the open air gathering was held over until after the musication.

The Church School Managers met in the evening and reviewed an application for the vacancy in the Upper Department from Miss Vera Tompkins, an uncertified teacher at Newbottle School. It was confirmed that Miss Tether had accepted the post offered her in the Upper School at £70 per annum and would start on 1 July, subject to the approval of the Local Education Authority.

The resignation of Miss W E Gooding, with effect from the end of September, was received and accepted with regret. During the meeting, Mr Rawlings, the new headmaster, having arrived in the town, came in to see the managers.

Wednesday, **30 May** – "For Sale – Strong Pony Trap, polished oak, cord cushions, back seat, sound order, £4-10s-0d. Apply – 24 Spencer Street, Raunds."

"To be Sold or Let – Compact House, bath (hot and cold water), office attached, good garden. Apply – T Yorke, "Hillside", Raunds."

The final Local Appeals Tribunal for the month was held this evening, Thursday, **31 May**, in the Council School, when another parade of appellants took place.

The highlight of the evening was a frank exchange of views on "substitution" between the military representative, Mr J Shelmerdine, who said it was for the employer to apply for substitutes; and the agricultural representative, Mr T H Warth, who said that it was for the military to find them. After this brief "contretemps", Mr Warth added that 700 acres were to be ploughed up in Raunds, and they needed some men to cultivate it.

Prior to the close of the hearing, Mr Gates asked the Tribunal to accept his resignation as a member. On hearing this, the chairman remarked that he was just about to lay before the members a letter he had received from Mr G E Smith, another one of their number. The letter explained that, in view of the latest pronouncement respecting the enlistment of men of his own age, and considerably over, he felt he could no longer retain his seat on the Tribunal. The chairman observed that at the time of the formation of the Tribunal he held very strongly that no one of military age ought to be a member of it. He felt that he must, to be consistent, resign also. The crisis escalated when several other members also remarked that they should not remain as members when the age of conscription was raised. After much discussion, it resolved that the resignations be sent on to the Urban Council for their consideration and advice.

Bearing in mind that nearly all the members of the Tribunal were also councillors, the outcome of this referral would be interesting!

JUNE – The vicar began his June notes in the Parish Magazine with a welcome extended to the new headmaster, Mr A D Rawlings, and his wife, who had now come to live in the town. He hoped their stay in Raunds would be long and that they found their work here very happy.

Next was the important news that the recent town meeting had decided to start a Nursing Association, and it was expected that a nurse would commence her work here at the end of summer. Subscriptions were being asked from 1 July, the lowest being 1s-0d per quarter. A subscription would secure the services of the nurse for a husband, wife and all children under 16.

Confirmation was given that an Egg Collecting Depot for Raunds and District was being started here, the receiving office being at 18, North Street. The aim being to provide members with a good market for their eggs at all times of the year.

Finally, came a strong plea from Bishop Gwynne, Assistant Chaplain General for the Forces in France, to all Diocese for magazines, light literature and games for the Church Huts, most of which were in advanced positions.

Appearing on the "Wounded" list on Friday, **1 June**, was Pte C H Clarke, 43113, of the Bedfordshire Regiment.

"Italians, British and French Defeated" ran a small item in the local papers on Saturday, **2 June**, telling how a boastful Kaiser had recently sent telegrams of congratulations to his Army generals after the latest military engagements.

At home, the annual treat of the members of the Distributive Co-operative Society was held, but owing to the shortage of provisions it was decided not to have a tea as in other years, but to give each child a present instead. Unfortunately it came on to rain and sports for the youngsters had to be postponed. The public meeting, also due to be held outdoors, was diverted to the Wesleyan Schoolroom, where Mr C W Anderson, MP, gave an address on "Co-operation and the food problem".

Monday, **4 June**, saw the announcement of the awarding of the Military Medal to Corporal L Eady. The 34 year old former Raunds postman, of the Garrison Artillery, had originally enlisted in the Army as a young man and served in the South African War. When the Great War broke out he was in the Reserve and was called up. He had last been home on leave in January 1916.

In the afternoon, in glorious summer weather, the Lord Bishop of Peterborough consecrated a portion of the new cemetery, "pleasantly situated adjoining the Ringstead Road, on high ground, about a mile from the church." The council had purchased over five acres from Mrs A M Sharpe, of Brighton, at a cost of about £280, but they were restricted by the Local Government Board to "war-time" expenditure for the present. Over an acre had been fenced off with iron rails, and there were gravel walks, and iron entrance gates in the centre, opening on to the road, but the erection of the chapel, planting of trees etc, had been deferred.

That morning, the Bishop had also consecrated an extension to Hargrave Churchyard, obtained by the inclusion of a piece of glebe land.

Meanwhile at Rothwell, the first "dry" proclamation of Rowell Fair took place at 6am when a crowd of several hundred gathered in front of the Manor House. The first operation of "No Treating" took place in glorious June sunshine although old timers lamented the lack of beer!

The Palace Theatre, Raunds – Week Commencing Monday, 4 June 1917:

"Variety, Variety – Starring and Expensive Engagement of the 'Les Bons Bons' – The Finest Musical Act in Vaudeville, featuring the only Giant Twin Xylophone in the world."

"These artistes also play, in addition to their own instruments, a wonderful novel instrument, which is their own patent, and played with the feet only!"

"Prices As Usual."

The end of an era loomed at the monthly meeting of the Thrapston Guardians on Tuesday, **5 June**, when a letter was read from Dr Mackenzie, resigning with regret, as from 30 June, owing to indisposition, his positions as medical officer and vaccination officer for the Board's 'C' District, and medical officer to the Children's Home at Raunds.

The local press congratulated Miss Elsie Willmott, daughter of the Stanwick newsagent, upon the high sense of patriotism which had prompted her to relinquish her post as assistant teacher at Raunds Council School for the purpose of undertaking nursing duties in France. It pointed out that for some considerable time past Miss Willmott had been giving practically the whole of her spare time to the discharge of similar duties at the Wellingborough VAD Hospital where her work was greatly valued.

Today, at the Thrapston weekly market, butter sold for 1s-8d per pound, eggs for 3s-0d per score, beef for 16s-0d to 16s-6d per stone, mutton for 1s-6d to 1s-8d per stone, and pork for 16s-0d to 16s-6d per stone.

In a lively critique of the special entertainment currently on stage at The Palace Theatre, the Evening Telegraph on Wednesday, **6 June**, enthused that "The proprietor of the theatre (Mr J W Hall) has provided another first class programme this week, the principle feature being 'Les Bons Bons', a first class musical act, which took the audience by storm on Monday evening."

Thursday, 7 June, the Battle of Messines Ridge.

A special "crisis" meeting of the Urban Council was held in the Council School this evening, convened to consider the resignations of Messrs Walter Gates and G E Smith as members of the local Tribunal and the intimation of the other members within the proposed extended age limit for military service of their intention to follow suit. The chairman, Mr A Camozzi, JP, explained that he had personally come to the meeting with an open mind, although if the military age was extended to 50 by conscription he should most certainly not continue to sit on a Tribunal to deal with men of his own age.

Mr J Shelmerdine, JP, the military representative on the Tribunal, expressed the opinion that if the members who had handed in their resignations would consider the best interests of the town they would allow them to be withdrawn. However, neither Mr Gates nor Mr Smith could see their way to continue to act as members of the Tribunal, the long meetings were too much for the former, whilst the latter had not wanted to be a member from the outset, but had been persuaded to do so.

Repeated requests to Messrs Gates and Smith to withdraw proved unavailing and their resignations were reluctantly accepted. Messrs James Adams and Hazeldine then declined the invitation to fill the two vacant places on the Tribunal so it was decided to leave the matter over until the next council meeting.

On Monday, **11 June**, it was announced that at the end of 1916, there were 521,237 paupers in England and Wales, 115,000 fewer than in 1914.

At the County Appeals Tribunal on Tuesday, **12 June**, two single brothers, 21 and 23, employed as horsekeepers on their father's farm, pleaded their cases. After some discussion, the younger son was ordered to join up on 15 July. The elder's case was adjourned for a month, with a view to the provision of a substitute. Also appearing was the 32 year old, married, foreman clicker and pattern cutter employed by Messrs Adams Brothers, and a technical instructor in clicking under the County Council. The case was dismissed.

One of the town's Belgian refugees was summoned to appear at the Thrapston Police Court this afternoon on charges of failing to notify a change of address, as required by Regulation 20c(b) of the Alien Restrictions (Consolidation) Order, 1916, at Raunds on 19 May. The defendant, who sobbed throughout the hearing, was told by the superintendent that she need not cry, there was nothing to worry about. As she did not understand much English, she was talked to in French by Lord Lilford. She said that she went for a holiday and did not know that under those conditions it was necessary to notify the change of address. The police sergeant said that she had been warned before and that they had had a great deal of trouble with some of the Belgians going off without giving notice. He did not wish to press the charge, but had brought it forward as a warning to others. The accused was ordered to pay 2s-0d.

Wednesday, 13 June, the first German heavy bomber daylight raid on London kills 162 civilians.

"Northamptonshire War Agricultural Executive Committee – Agricultural Labour".

German Prisoners for Farmwork, Skilled in Agriculture, will shortly be available at the Camp near Rothwell for work in the district, within a 3 mile radius, or at a greater distance on arrangements being made for their conveyance.

Wages: 4½d per hour; Apply to: Food Production Office, The Drapery, N'pton."

It was reported on Thursday, **14 June**, that farmers in Raunds had commenced cutting clover this week, and if the fine weather continued, the harvest would be pretty general next week.

This evening, the first of a series of demonstrations in war cookery was given in the Council School. The demonstration, given by Miss Hunter, a Northamptonshire Education Committee domestic service teacher, was of a very practical and interesting character and very much appreciated by those present.

"Wanted – Manageress for the Raunds Hotel and Coffee Tavern, assistance provided. For particulars, apply to F W Miller, The Manse, Raunds."

A question of policy in boot cases was raised at the County Appeals Tribunal, Northampton, on Friday, **15 June**. In response to the greater than ever need of men, the Tribunal met exclusively to consider 554 appeals from the boot and shoe trade. Of this total, Raunds cases were submitted by: Tebbutt and Hall (12), Owen Smith (15), Adams Brothers (48), St Crispins (19), R Coggins (28), John Horrell and Son (9), Neal and Gates (4), Walter Lawrence (14), C E Nichols (13), and the Regulation Boot Co (20). J J Peck, of Stanwick (2), and the Unity Boot Society, Ringstead (8), also put forward appeals. The manufacturers were, in general, agreeable to the terms put forward and the cases were all dealt with on these lines.

Among those listed as "Missing" in today's Rushden Echo was Private, 200689, **Leslie B Nunley (83)**, of the Northamptons. We now know that he was killed in action during the Second Battle of Gaza on 19 April.

On Saturday evening, **16 June**, the postponed treat of the members' children of the Distributive Co-operative Society was held in the field adjoining "Thorpe House". The children assembled at 5 o'clock when a programme of sports etc was gone through, and some interesting events were witnessed. During the event each child was given a present, those under 6 receiving a ball, and those between 6 and 14 a lovely handkerchief. The Temperance Band marched to the field and played selections. Unfortunately at 8 o'clock came a thunderstorm, and caused the company to beat a hasty retreat and upset the dancing arrangements.

Monday, 18 June, Arthur Burton (31), killed in action.

On the day that another town Army veteran was lost, the Urban Council held their monthly meeting in the Central Hall of the Council School. First on the agenda was Dr McInnes, the deputy medical officer, who reported that four births and three deaths had been registered during May, and four cases of notifiable infectious diseases had been confirmed, but on the whole the health of the district was good. Next, a letter was read from Sgt L G H Lee in answer to one authorised to be sent to him at the last meeting. It read:

"My dear Mr Corby, will you convey to the council my thanks for their kindness in remembering me at the annual meeting? I had hoped to be home again by the annual meeting of 1918, but I am doubtful now. I have, however, learned an authentic bit of news – we are to be discharged from the Army on reaching our 70th birthday, whether the war is finshed or not, so that I shall be able to attend the annual meeting in April, 1953. I trust that all existing members will be there. What a patriarchal lot we shall be –Yours sincerely, L G H Lee."

A letter was read from the Local Government Board approving the appointment of Dr McInnes as deputy medical officer of health for the district during the illness of Dr Mackenzie. However, a letter was then read from Dr Mackenzie resigning his post to take effect from 30 June owing to his continued ill-health. The resignation was accepted with regret and it was further proposed and carried unanimously "That Dr McInnes be appointed medical officer of health for the Urban District of Raunds at a salary of £25 per annum from the 1st day of July, 1917, subject to the regulations and approval of the LGB."

On the question of filling the vacancies on the local Tribunal, it was decided that the Boot and Shoe Trade Union be asked to submit two names, from whom one might be selected, and that the clerk interview some others whose names were suggested as to their willingness to accept the office.

News of a Raunds involvement in the Battle of Messines Ridge was reported on Tuesday, **19 June**. Mr F W March, High Street, had received a letter from his son, L-Cpl **Arthur March (75)**, from a Rouen Hospital. He wrote: "Just about dawn a big shell burst in the trench, I did not hear it coming, but I had an impression of yellow smoke and flames, dust and stones, and most horrible fumes, and then found myself deposited several yards from where I had been sitting. I waited a little while until my nerves had steadied, and then walked down to the aid post!"

Also today, a Raunds ex-soldier, formerly of Kettering, appeared at the Thrapston Police Court charged with stealing, between 3 January and 28 April, 1917: one pair of boots, one pair of lasts, 6lbs of brass rivets, 4 lasting tacks, a quantity of mixed nails and sprigs, one piece of finishing wax, 50 pairs of soles, 5½ pairs of insoles, 9 pairs of middle soles, one pair of clumps, 6½ pairs of stiffenings, 4 pairs of lifts, one pair of heel pieces, 5½ pairs of piece soles, 5 pairs of split lifts, 2½ pairs of puffs, 7 pairs of tips, 2 pairs of tip fittings, 4 pairs of toe plates, and 103 pairs of top pieces, together having a value of £10-8s-9d, the property of Messrs Adams Brothers, Army boot contractors. After hearing appropriate statements, the prisoner was remanded in custody until the Petty Sessions on Tuesday, 26 June.

The annual convention of the Raunds Wesleyan Circuit was held at the Brook Street Church on Wednesday, **20 June**. In the afternoon there was a good congregation, including a number from the villages in the circuit, however, owing to the Food Control there was no public tea this year, the visitors being entertained to tea by the members of the congregation. In the evening a public meeting was held in the Church, when the Rev G H McNeal gave a stirring address in which he noted that an earlier minister in the circuit had been the Rev Robert T Rundle, the first white man to penetrate beyond the Rocky Mountains.

Moving on to the current military conflict he expounded that "The crimes of Germany make it very difficult for those who are living to forgive them, when they think of Belgium, Serbia, the Lusitania, Nurse Cavell, Capt Fryatt, and the murder of women and children by air raids." He closed with an attack on the liquor traffic, saying it would be no use smashing Germany unless they destroyed the drink traffic – they must all work for a sober England – all cheered!

The second cookery demonstration of the series was given in the Council School on Thursday evening, **21 June**, when further recipes in the use of "substitutes" were demonstrated in a very thorough and practical manner by Miss Hunter.

Included in the casualty lists of Friday, **22 June**, was one **Corporal Sidney Smith (107)**, Essex Regiment, reported as "missing" in Palestine since the First Battle of Gaza on 26 March. This status was later changed to "presumed killed".

"Official Notice – The Thrapston Board of Guardians invite applications from qualified medical practitioners for the posts of District Medical Officer and Public Vaccinator for the "C" District of the Union, comprising the parishes of Little Addington, Chelveston, Hargrave, Raunds and Stanwick.

The salary as Medical Officer will be £50 pa, and subject to the deductions under the Poor Law Office Superannuation Act, 1896, and as Public Vaccinator at the fees sanctioned by the Local Government Board. The gentleman will also act as the Medical Officer of the Children's Home at Raunds at a salary of £10 pa.

Applications must reach me not later than Monday, 2 July 1917 – By Order, Gerald Hunnybun, Clerk to the Guardians, Union Offices, Thrapston."

The annual demonstration on behalf of Northampton Hospital was held on Saturday, **23 June**, and was a great success. The weather, although at times somewhat threatening, held fine for the well-marshalled parade which was found by the crowds who assembled to be a varied and interesting spectacle worth seeing, and for the open-air meeting in the ideal grounds of "The Hall".

In the grounds of "The Hall", the Right Hon Earl Spencer, KG, Lord Lieutenant of the County, Sir Robert W Perks, Bart (London), Mr J H C Crockett, Chairman of the Northampton Hospital Week Fund Committee, and Alderman Thomas Patenall, Mayor of Higham Ferrers, gave enthusiastic speeches.

The fancy dress competition brought success for Kathleen Richards (South African Girl) and Eleanor Newberry (Britannia) in the *"Children's individual get-up"* class; Marguerite and Elsa Pfienschneider (Fairies) in the *"Children's best get-up"* class; and Walter Lawrence's employees' tableau "Germany Submissive to the Allies" in the *"Factory Challenge Shield"*.

Winners in the sports events were: Harry Webb, *100 Yards Handicap for boys 10 to 14*; Edward Gates, *boys 14 to 15*; and R Dix, *Veterans' 80 Yards Handicap*. Raunds No.1 won the Fire Brigade Hose Cart Competition; the winning quartette receiving the Challenge Cup, a silver medal each, and a £1 cash prize.

The Palace Theatre, Raunds – Week Commencing Monday, **25 June** 1917:

"Entire Change of Programme – PRICES AS USUAL."

This was the last advertisement featuring the town's cinema to appear in the local press during the Great War period. Maybe the manager's attentions were directed elsewhere towards ongoing "extra-curricula activities"!

A Raunds baker appeared before Thrapston Petty Sessions on Tuesday, **26 June**, summoned for exposing for sale a loaf of bread which did not weigh 1lb, or an even number of pounds, in the town on 7 June. In his defence, the man said that the small loaf placed in the window of his shop was never intended to be sold. It had never been weighed and was intended for consumption in his own home. The defendant's wife and temporary assistant corroborated his story. The chairman said that he believed there had been a mistake, but still fined the man 2s-6d!

The Raunds ex-soldier, who had been remanded in custody the previous week, charged with stealing leather and boot making accessories from Messrs Adams Bros, was found guilty and sentenced to one month's hard labour.

Finally an order to pay poor rates of £4-13s-5d and district rates of £5-5s-0d was made against a Raunds fruiterer, who was serving in the Army.

The town's Appeals Tribunal met in the Council School on Wednesday evening, **27 June**, when the military representative, Mr J Shelmerdine, JP, asked them to give their decisions some degree of finality, as some of those who would be before them that night had been before them a number of times, and it was becoming a regular promenade! The Army wanted men more than ever.

Mr Hodson, who came in late, was asked by the chairman if he did not notice the time of the meeting. Mr Hodson replied that he had noticed how the Tribunals throughout the county had been treated, and he did not think that it was worth losing half an hour from work to attend at the commencement!

The review of more than forty cases then took place, and as Mr Shelmerdine had predicted, most of these were "regular visitors". The majority were successful in gaining exemption until the end of August or September although a small number were ordered to go before the Central Medical Board for examination.

"For Sale – 6 pure bred Black Leghorn Pullets, 13 months old, laying; 6 cross-bred Black Leghorn Pullets, 13 months old, laying; one White Leghorn Cockerel; also hen's pen 6 x 1 and 6 x 5, nearly new, comes apart in five pieces; and a quantity of nearly new wire netting – W H Maiment, Church Street, Stanwick."

The Hospital Week Committee and workers met in the Temperance Hall on Thursday evening, **28 June**, in connection with the recent demonstration. The secretary, Mr W F Corby, submitted the account of the Factory Challenge Shield, showing that the manufacturers had subscribed £16-12s-0d and the cost of the shield to be £12-13s-0d, leaving a balance of £3-19s-0d. It was decided to thank the subscribers for their gift. The treasurer, Mr W H Lawrence, submitted the accounts of the demonstration showing receipts of £178-11s-7d and expenditure of £27-11s-8d, leaving the net proceeds of £150-19s-11d. The result was considered to be in every way highly satisfactory and hearty thanks were accorded to all who had contributed to so excellent a result.

Also this evening, the third demonstration of economical cookery was given in the Council School when Miss Hunter dealt with the use of "meat substitutes".

News broke on Friday, **29 June**, that Pte **Roland Archer (15)**, Northamptonshire Regiment, who was posted as missing on 17 August 1916, was now officially considered to have been killed on that date. He had worked for E W Stanley Ltd before enlisting, and had previously been wounded at the Battle of Loos in September 1915, returning to France after recuperation in April 1916.

Better news arrived in the town today with the announcement of the promotion of 2nd Air Mechanic Harold W Holmes, Royal Flying Corps, to the rank of 1st Air Mechanic in recognition of his skill in advanced mechanics. It was said that for the past few months 1AM Holmes had been working under high pressure within shell fire. His brother, 2nd Air Mechanic Walter Holmes, also RFC, was currently undergoing an aviation course in the north of England.

Fifty-three boot and shoe companies appeared before the County Tribunal at Northampton today, including from Raunds: Tebbutt and Hall Bros, Owen Smith, Adams Bros, St Crispin Productive Society, R Coggins and Sons, John Horrell and Son, Neal and Gates, Walter Lawrence, C E Nichols, and the Regulation Boot Company. Each firm came before the committee separately and of the employer's lists, slightly more than a third of the eligible men were designated as "indispensable" to the business and given 6 month open exemptions.

On Saturday, **30 June**, it was reported that Mr and Mrs B Mayes, of Mill House, had received news from their son, Pte R Mayes, Suffolk Regiment, who had been reported wounded and missing, that he was a prisoner of war in Germany, and that he was being well treated. He also told his parents to keep smiling and that he would let them know his address as soon as possible.

Some months ago the trustees and committee of the Temperance Society decided to make some structural alterations and additions to the Temperance Hall at a cost of £300 and the opening ceremony was held this afternoon. At 2.30pm the members of the Temperance and Band of Hope Societies, the Independent Order of Rechabites, a number of the youngest members of the latter being taken round on a truck, and members of the Salvation Army, headed by the Temperance Band, paraded the town, after which the meeting was held in the Temperance Hall.

A platform had been erected on the ground adjoining the new building, but the weather conditions were not favourable for an open-air meeting. Mr John Claridge, JP CC, of Rushden, declared the building open and the company marched through the new room to the hall where the meeting was held. After the meeting a tea was provided in the Primitive School, when about 90 sat down. Sports were then gone through in Carter Hill Field and selections were given by the Temperance Band. A total of £53 was raised during the day.

In the concert room of the Stanwick Working Men's Club this evening, a very enjoyable time was had celebrating the coming of age of Arthur, eldest son of the late Mr W Hall and Mrs Hall. A musical soiree followed the excellent tea, the dance music being supplied by Mr Knighton, of Raunds, on piano and Mr A Gates on violin.

3 – July to September 1917

"Farewell" to the good doctor and death in the mud.

JULY – The Rev C C Aldred began his notes in the Parish Magazine with the reminder that on the first Sunday, the Patronal Festival would be celebrated, the Church being dedicated to St Mary and the Chantry Chapel to St Peter.

He then noted that the Sunday School Treat would be held on Saturday the 7th, adding that all understood why no tea was being given to the children this year. The children were to meet at the schools at 4.15pm, a service would be held in the Church at 4.30pm, then sports in the Vicarage paddock at 5pm. Admission to the Vicarage grounds would be 3d, with dancing on the lawn after the sports. The Vestry Class Marathon would be run and there would also be other amusements.

Lastly, he looked back on the glorious day in June when part of the new cemetery was consecrated by the Bishop of Peterborough. He then explained that the fees for the consecration were made up as follows: Chancellor, £2-2s-0d; Registrar or official performing the duty, £6-6s-0d; Secretary to the Bishop, £1-1s-0d; Apparitor, £1-1s-0d; Registrar expenses, £1-5s-0d; W L Carter (Plans), £2-12s-6d; G Hunnybun, 10s-0d; Motor Car, 12s-6d.

On Feast Sunday, **1 July**, the Temperance Silver Band gave two sacred concerts which were well attended. The first was held on "The Hill" at 4.30pm, and the second on The Square at 7.30pm. Collections were taken in aid of Band funds.

Also today, the Wesleyan Church anniversary services were held, when the preacher, both morning and evening, was Mr Milner Gray, of Luton. There were good congregations, especially at the evening service. The collection, in aid of Trust funds, amounted to nearly £14. During the announcements, it was made known that it had been decided at the recent circuit quarterly meeting to try and arrange for a day to wipe out all the debts in the circuit, including those related to the Tilbrook Chapel Renovation and the Ringstead Chapel Debt Schemes.

Anger was expressed at the Boot and Shoe Operative's Union meeting on Monday, **2 July**, against the further calling up of more men out of the trade, the members feeling that it had already contributed considerably more than its quota when compared with many other trades.

At the monthly meeting of the Thrapston Guardians on Tuesday, **3 July**, the Rev C C Aldred reported that the Children's Home committee had received an application from the master and matron of the Home for an increase of their salary. At present the master received £35 and the matron £25 per annum. The master had done all the gardening himself and the matron had saved altogether the expenses of a sewing woman, and also saved on one charwoman. The couple had also voluntarily reduced their rations for the last 20 weeks, which had saved the Guardians 9s-3d a week, a total of £9-5s-0d. The committee recommended an increase in the salary of £5 each and the Board accepted this recommendation.

A special meeting of the Urban Council was held in the Council School on Thursday evening, **5 July**. The meeting had been specially convened to consider a circular from the Local Government Board with respect to the proposed reconstitution of the Parliamentary boundaries in the county. After some consideration, it was unanimously decided "That the Council make a strong application to be included in the Eastern Division of the county".

The Church School managers met this afternoon to interview Miss Darby for the vacancy of headmistress in the Infants Department and decided to appoint her to the post at £85 per annum, subject to Local Education Authority approval.

The fourth cookery demonstration was given by Miss Hunter in the Council School this evening. The subject was "Fruit bottling and jam making" and it was treated in a very practical manner, and much appreciated by those present.

On Friday, **6 July**, there was a contentious utterance from the powers that be when the Ministry of Food proclaimed that "no one ought to keep a horse that is beyond serviceable age" – so much for being a nation of animal lovers!

"Business Notice – Prudential Assurance Co Ltd – Personal Insurance, covering the risks of Death or Disablement caused by or resulting from AIRCRAFT: Benefit - £250 in the event of Death of Loss of Limbs; 30s-0d per week during Total Disablement (52 weeks); for an Annual Premium of 5s-0d. Contact your local agent today."

Saturday, 7 July, the second German heavy bomber daylight raid on London kills 57 civilians.

In the light of the above, it was surely no coincidence when today it was announced that arrangements had been made "for the priceless pictures in the National Gallery to be made secure against the heaviest bomb!"

The annual treat of the scholars attending the Church Sunday School was held this afternoon, but owing to the food controls there was no tea. The children, accompanied by the teachers and friends, marched in a procession headed by the Temperance Band via the Church, where a short service was held, to the Vicarage paddock, where a programme of sports was carried out. During the evening a Marathon race was held for members of the Vestry Class; the course was from the Vicarage paddock, up the Slade and down the road by the Red House, and return. The winners were: 1st, A Mayes; 2nd, R Holmes; 3rd, E Gates. The Temperance Band played selections during the sports and for dancing until dusk.

Sunday, 8 July, the Battle of the Dunes, many British soldiers taken prisoner.

On Moday, **9 July**, Messrs G E Smith and W F Corby represented the town at the Commissioner's Enquiry at Northampton, in connection with the Representation and Redistribution Bill now before Parliament, to discuss the re-division of the county into four constituencies. The Conservatives and Liberals had proposed the transfer of the Raunds urban district from the North to the East Division and Labour, and the shoe trade and farmer's unions took the same view.

Two town men received their come-uppance at the Thrapston Police Court on Tuesday, **10 July**. A shoehand was summoned for using obscene language to the annoyance of the passengers on the public highway at Raunds on 23 June. Although the defendant pleaded not guilty, he said he was very sorry it occurred and that it was the first time he had been in a police court for this kind of thing, a statement confirmed by Supt Tebbey. The man was fined 15s-0d.

A farmer then appeared, summoned for being the owner of a dog not kept under effective control, at 3am at Raunds, on 4 July. The man pleaded guilty. PC Newberry said it was a sheep dog and there had been one or two bad cases of sheep worrying lately. The farmer was fined 10s-0d.

Another County Tribunal was held on Wednesday, **11 July**, when fourteen cases from Rushden were referred to and adjourned. The Rushden Tribunal had recently had some "communication" with the Local Government Board and War Office and were presently "on strike" for reasons unpublished!

The Council School managers met this evening and a letter was read from Miss M E Lawrence notifying the managers of her intended marriage during the harvest holidays, and intimating that for the present she would be prepared to continue her work in the school. The managers agreed that Miss Lawrence should continue on the staff under present war conditions.

A meeting of the Education District Sub-Committee followed and the latest quarterly attendance report was reviewed. This showed the number on the register to be 1,112 as against 1,137 the previous year, a decrease of 25, with a percentage attendance of 89.1 as against 88.7, a slight increase of 0.4. The total number of special permits in existence was 28, 22 being for agriculture and six for other employment. Several parents appeared before the committee with respect to the irregular attendance of their children, and in each case a pledge was given to meet the requirements of the committee.

The town was dealt a hammer blow on the evening of Thursday, **12 July**, when Dr Mackenzie, who had recently resigned the position of medical officer of health for the Urban District Council, passed away at his residence, "Aberlour House", just before midnight. The doctor, who was 67 years of age, had been suffering for the past two years from an internal complaint.

An LRCPS of Edinburgh and LRSPS of Glasgow, he had first come to Raunds 39 years previously as assistant to the late Dr J Crew of Higham Ferrers. After a stay of five years he went to Ceylon, where he resided for the next three and a half years. Then, at the request of the town's Friendly Societies, he returned to Raunds, and established a practice of his own, which he had kept up till quite recently.

In the early days of his practice he was assisted by Dr Ramsey, who, it was remembered, had contracted blood poisoning whilst attending a case and died as a result. The good doctor then conducted his practice alone till two years ago, when he was joined by Dr McInnes.

He was popular with all classes, and would be missed by a wide circle. In the early days of the war he took a keen and practical part in the provision of cigarettes and other comforts for the soldiers. He was never married, his sister residing with him as housekeeper, and with her deep sympathy was felt. The funeral was set to take place on Monday afternoon at 3 o'clock.

Despite this setback, it was business as usual for the Local Tribunal and the clerk reported that the military authorities had appealed against a decision given at the last meeting, and that six men to whom were granted conditional exemptions to 31 August (final) had all appealed to the County Tribunal, and that four out of twelve to whom they granted exemption to 31 July (final) had also appealed. The military representative said that most of the appeals before them that night had been from men whom the manufacturers had released, and had now made a personal appeal. He added that he would like to impress upon them that there was room for every man in the Army who was fit for civilian work.

On a lighter note, the last of the series of cookery demonstrations was given by Miss Hunter in the Council School this evening. The subject was "Sugar substitutes" and a number of "summer recipes" were dealt with. Miss Hunter also gave a short talk on "Infant Welfare", dealing especially with the food aspect.

A Raunds man appeared at Wellingborough Police Court on Friday, **13 July**, charged with allowing a motor car to be out on the highway at night without lighted lamps at Finedon. The defendant said that he was neither the owner nor the driver of the car. He then refused to say who was driving, though pressed several times. The chairman told the man he had not done his case any good by refusing to answer questions and imposed a fine of 10s-0d and costs. On hearing that his licence would be endorsed, the defendant gave notice of appeal.

Also at the same session, three Raunds lads were fined 7s-6d each for riding bicycles at night without lights.

Saturday, 14 July, Horace Nunley (82), killed in action.

Wesleyan Church services in aid of the Foreign Missions were held over this weekend, when the Rev W Goudie, general secretary, London (late of India), paid a visit. On Saturday a fete was held in the grounds of "Ashfields" and a meeting was held on the lawn, Mr J C Horrell presiding. Mr Goudie gave an address and the children of the Sunday School, dressed in foreign costumes, sang native music and gave short speeches. On Sunday, Mr Goudie preached to good congregations.

Monday, 16 July, T E Lawrence and his Arab forces take Aqaba from the Turks.

Although the actions taking place in the Middle East today would later inspire a film, the thoughts of Rance folk were totally focussed on the funeral of the late Dr William Mackenzie, his mortal remains being the first to be laid to rest (and by his dying request) in the new town cemetery.

The obsequies, of a public character, were a striking manifestation of esteem and affection: factories and shops were closed for the afternoon till four o'clock, flags were lowered at the Church and schools, blinds were everywhere drawn, and the inhabitants in very large numbers, and with a most reverential demeanour, paid their last tribute to one who had gone in and out among them as their doctor and friend for more than a generation.

A procession formed outside the doctor's residence near The Square, and included the Temperance Band, Urban Councillors, the Fire Brigade, and members of the Freemasons and Friendly Societies, as well as the principle mourners: Miss Mackenzie (his sister) and Mrs Kenneth Mackenzie (cousin), and Dr A McInnes. The Church of England Schoolyard, commanding a view of the procession on its way to the Church, was filled with school children.

After the service in the Church, the procession re-formed and proceeded to the cemetery, where many hundreds had assembled (inside and out) and the committal sentences were pronounced by the Vicar. The grave had been lined by Mr J Copperwheat with sweet-peas, lilies, roses, and ivy. The coffin, of plain oak, with brass fittings, bore the breastplate:

"Dr William Mackenzie, Born May 17th, 1850, Died July 12th, 1917."

As the deceased's brother Freemasons filed past the grave they dropped in their sprigs of acacia, and on the coffin there was a bunch of flowers. The route had been well kept by PS Ellingham, PC Newberry, and Special Constables.

The Urban Council held their monthly meeting this evening with a lengthy agenda to go through. The clerk reported that he and Mr G E Smith had attended before the Boundary Commissioner on 9 July and presented their petition asking for the inclusion of Raunds in the Eastern Parliamentary Division. Their request was supported by all the political parties so they had not needed to say more.

A letter was read from Mr H Thurston offering to pay the balance, according to his agreement, if the council would let him The Square for the Feast, 1918, on the same conditions as last year, and he would pay the deposit when sending the balance. This was unanimously agreed.

The chairman, in very suitable remarks, then moved a vote of sympathy be sent to Miss Mackenzie on the loss of her brother, Dr Mackenzie, their late medical officer. There followed a string of personal tributes from individual members.

The medical officer's report for June showed that there had been five cases of notifiable diseases but there were no epidemic diseases. Two deaths and six births, four girls and two boys, had been registered, making a total for the first half of the year of 33 births, 23 girls and 10 boys. He added that the town did not help the belief that the birth rate, during periods of war, showed an excess of male children!

The acting surveyor then reported that the water supply had been well maintained and that a house had been disinfected following a case of tuberculosis.

Tuesday, 17 July, King George V changes the family name to Windsor.

As the King lost his Saxe-Coburg and Gotha, Mr Bonar Law announced in the House of Commons that an extra half-crown (2s-6d) would be paid to all old age pensioners entitled to receive 5s-0d or a lower rate per week. The additional half-crown was already being paid to those showing "special necessity".

Stanwick celebrated "Baby Week" on the afternoon of Wednesday, **18 July**, with a picnic tea in the grounds of the Manor House for all mothers and children under seven. Tea and milk were provided free and a large number of maters and offspring from Raunds joined in the most enjoyable party.

Thursday, 19 July, Arthur Clarke (37), killed in action.

Today, Mr and Mrs William Higby, of High Street, received news that their son, Pte Arthur Higby, Northamptonshire Regiment, was a prisoner of war. All four sons of Mr and Mrs Higby had served with the Colours. The two youngest, Privates **John B Higby (63)** and **Ralph Higby (64)**, of the Bedfords, had been killed, and their eldest son, Pte Walter Higby, Army Service Corps, had not been heard of for nearly a month.

This afternoon, Mrs Sarah Lawrence, wife of Mr Alfred Lawrence, Marshall's Road, died at the ripe old age of 78. Mrs Lawrence left her husband, three sons, Mr Amos, Mr Jethro, and Mr Horace, and four daughters to mourn their loss.

"Wanted – Experienced Nurse for holiday duties to elderly (sick) lady, from 28 July to 1 September – Apply, stating terms, to Horrell, "The Maples", Raunds."

There were a number of Raunds cases appearing before the County Tribunal on Friday, **20 July**. Half of the appellants were successful in obtaining extensions to their exemptions, the other half, however, had their cases dismissed.

The Church School managers also met today and learned that Miss Darby had accepted the offer of the post of headmistress in the Infants Department. It was also reported that Mr Samuels had "gone home" because of his brother's death.

Today, the Ministry of Food claimed that "war bread", if properly baked and stored, would keep in good condition for a week. The ministry also stated that the scarcity of potatoes was at an end. Not in abundant supply, however, was leather, with some shoe manufacturers experiencing such great difficulty in securing material for Army requirements that they were having to give their men extra holidays because of the lack of sole leather of the requisite substance.

"Thanks – Miss Mackenzie wishes to thank all kind friends for their expressions of sympathy, and the beautiful floral tributes, sent on the death of her brother, Dr William Mackenzie, Aberlour House, Raunds, 19 July 1917."

A garden party in connection with the Temperance Society was held in the grounds of "Ashfields" on Saturday, **21 July**. Various attractions were provided and the Temperance Band played for dancing.

Mrs Ann Stubbs (*see page 86 of Volume 1*) died on Sunday, **22 July**, at the age of 93, at the residence of her grand-daughter, Mrs P Bates of Hargrave. The funeral took place on Tuesday, 24 July, the Rev C C Aldred officiating.

A meeting of the Raunds and District Nursing Association was held in the Temperance Hall on Monday evening, **23 July**, when Mr A Camozzi, JP, presided over a good attendance. The secretary reported that about 500 members had now joined the association, and that Nurse Pym, who had had four years training at St George's Hospital, London, would commence her duties at the end of September.

A town shoehand made an unwelcome return appearance before the Thrapston Bench on Tuesday, **24 July**, once more summoned for using abusive language to the annoyance of passengers on the public highway and for subsequently using the most filthy language to PC Newberry, who was attempting to serve the summons, and "inviting" the constable into a field to fight. As there were previous similar convictions against the defendant, he was fined £1 or 14 days, with the advice from Supt Tebbey to "stop these little Saturday night episodes!"

Meanwhile, at the County Tribunal today, a 32 year old Raunds heel-builder, producing 8,000 pairs a week for Army contracts and marine boots, was given a three month final exemption.

News reached Mrs Owen Nunley, Wellington Road, on Wednesday, **25 July**, that her eldest son, Pte **Horace Nunley (82)**, of the Northamptons, had been killed in action in France on 14 July. He had joined up in January of this year having worked for the Thrapston Co-operative Society for the previous twelve months.

There was happier news from Southport, Lancashire, today, when Dr Archibald McInnes wed Miss Ruth A Rose, just nine days after saying his final farewell to his mentor, Dr Mackenzie. The young doctor, a native of Campbelltown, Scotland, had come to Raunds in October, 1915, as assistant to "Dr Mack" and had since succeeded him as medical officer of health to both Raunds Urban District Council and the Raunds section of Thrapston Rural District Council. After the service and wedding breakfast the newly-weds left for their honeymoon in north Wales before returning to the town and their new residence at "Hillside".

Thursday, 26 July, Luther William Coles (41), killed in action.

The annual show of the Thrapston and District Shire Horse Society was held in a field off Chancery Lane today. Mr W Denton, of Raunds, was one of the stewards and also enjoyed considerable success in the competitions, securing a first, three seconds, a commendation and winning the "President's Prize" of £5.

In the evening, the Local Tribunal met again in the Council School and a fair number of personal appeals were then presented, the most interesting being that of a hand laster, married, 38, with eight children. He said he had an allotment and produced all his own vegetables and thought it was of more benefit to the country for him to stay at home and keep his wife and family, than that the country should keep the ten of them; the Tribunal agreed, granting an unconditional exemption!

The Hospital Week Fund committee met for their quarterly meeting in the Temperance Hall on Friday evening, **27 July** and a cheque for £175 was ordered to be paid to the county treasurer, making £200 for the half-year. Among other topics discussed was the question of collecting waste paper, and it was decided to get particulars as to the sale of the same and submit them to the next meeting.

Meanwhile, at the County Appeals Tribunal, the Northamptonshire Union Bank appealed against the finality given by the Thrapston Tribunal to the three months exemption of Percy F Rushton, 37, married, the cashier looking after the Raunds branch five days a week. It was argued that ladies were able to do clerical work, but could not substitute for cashiers, highlighting the difficulty attending the identification of signatures. The "finality" was duly removed.

Today the Ministry of Munitions announced an urgent requirement for horse chestnuts, and hoped that "chestnut clubs" would be arranged throughout the country for children to collect the fruit in the autumn.

At Denford on Saturday, **28 July**, another productive effort for the Soldiers' and Sailors' Comforts Fund, held in charming weather in the Vicarage grounds, saw Rance folk prominent in their attendance. The St Crispin's Lady Pierrots stood out with their vivacity and tuneful songs, and Andrew's Ragtime Band caused considerable amusement. Among the judges for the fancy dress competition was Mrs A Camozzi, who, with her colleagues, rewarded the Pierrots and Ragtime Band first prizes in their respective classes. F Beeby, "Italian", Kitty Kirk, "Reaper", and M Andrews, "Drummer Boy", were also successful.

A most successful birthday party was held at the Wesleyan School today to celebrate the coming of age of Gladys, youngest child of Mr and Mrs C York, 32, Hill Street. A reception began at 6 o'clock, after which, by kind permission of Mr and Mrs Lee, a very enjoyable and pleasant evening was spent in their beautiful garden at "Kingswood". The elderly guests and young friends enjoyed themselves exceedingly; croquet and other games were indulged in until dusk.

The Parish Church held a flower, fruit, toy, and egg service on Sunday afternoon, **29 July**, when the address was given by the vicar, Rev C C Aldred. There was a good company present, and the gifts taken by the scholars were sent to the Northampton General Hospital the next day.

Raunds Distributive Co-operative Society held its half-yearly meeting in the Temperance Hall on Monday, **30 July**, Mr T Pentelow presiding. The secretary, Mr R Lawrence, reported sales for the half-year to be £23,472, an increase of £3,017 on the corresponding period in 1916. The disposable surplus amounted to £797-4s-6d, which was disposed of as follows: dividend to members, including coal, 1s-0d in the £; to non-members, 6d in the £.

Tuesday, 31 July, the Third Battle of Ypres (Passchendaele) begins. Jasper Sydney Gilbert (54), and Lieutenant-Colonel Edgar Mobbs, killed in action.

AUGUST – The vicar's monthly parish magazine editorial began in strident fashion, he wrote: "We did not enter on this struggle for gain or glory. It was the attack on those whom we were pledged to defend, it was the open violation of a solemn compact between the nations, and the cruel invasion of a small and neutral state, that stirred the spirit of our people and made us with one voice declare war on the aggressor!"

Calming down a little he referred to Dr Mackenzie's funeral in the new cemetery, adding that no words could express the very great respect and esteem people felt for him. The loss of Mrs Ann Stubbs was also recorded. She had been born during the reign of George III, and had lived through the reigns of six sovereigns.

Looking forward, he drew attention to a meeting to be held in the Institute on Tuesday, 21 August, for all interested in the formation of a company of the Church Lad's Brigade. Mr Rawlings had promised to undertake the training of the new company, observing that "Mind, belonging to the Brigade is not all jam. It means real business and not playing the tom-fool. There is plenty of good fun about it, but you must play the game and take the kicks with the halfpence!"

The Sunday School Treat was pronounced a great success; the races both for girls and boys were up for entries, and as usual the pillow fights had proved a great attraction. The Vestry Class Marathon had found out some new racers whom he thought would probably be heard of again. He observed that the sideshows did well and that the number of cherries eaten had beat all records.

Finally, **Horace Nunley (82)** was noted as "Died in the Service of His Country".

The local papers of Thursday, **2 August**, reported that Mr and Mrs C H Hunt, of Brooks Road, had received news that their son, Pte G W Hunt, Northamptonshire Regiment, was posted as "missing" after an engagement in France on 10 July. Nineteen year old Pte Hunt had previously worked on Mr A E Wingell's farm.

At the monthly meeting of the Stanwick Parish Council this evening it was decided that the clerk (Mr W F Corby) should write to the Thrapston Rural District Council stating that the Parish Council were not at all satisfied with their ruling that improvements to Church Hill corner would be delayed until after the war. He would draw to their attention that accidents were continually occurring at that point and that the Rural District Council would have to take the blame if there should be a fatal one! It was also decided to proceed with the purchase of the necessary land for £50 and take down part of the offending high wall.

Friday, 3 August, Cyril James Clarke (38), died of wounds & Albert Webb (120), killed in action.

As two more town men were lost, the local branch of the Shoe Operative's Union reported that "trade was good, but some departments are losing time through unbalanced labour owing to members being called up for military service, and that the 'combing out' for July would aggravate the difficulty very much indeed." It closed lamenting "When will it all end, and how?"

Extracts from the late Dr Mackenzie's will appeared in today's newspapers. He left all his property to his sister, Miss E Mackenzie, for her life. On her death, £250 would be paid to the Raunds Urban Council to be invested and the income divided every Christmas between twenty or more of the aged poor of the town, preference being given to those in receipt of poor relief. "Dr Mack" also left two sums of £100 to the council to be invested and the income used annually in giving prizes for the boys and girls of the Church of England and Council Schools.

"In Memoriam: In ever loving memory of **Oliver John Barritt (21)**, Seaforth Highlanders, who died in France, July 13, 1916. Also of Arthur, brother of the above, Northants Regiment, who was killed at Aubers Ridge, May 9, 1915.

Forget them, no, we never will, we loved them then, we love them still.
Their memory is as dear today, as in the hour they passed away.

From their brothers and sisters."

Saturday, 4 August, Robert William Richards (97), killed in action.

Todays columns made grim reading: "Raunds Co-operative's Death" told of Pte **Arthur Clarke (37)**, Middlesex Regiment, being killed in action on 19 July; "Raunds Family's Patriotic Record" recounted the contribution the combined Coles-Parker family had made to date, losing Pte **Ernest Parker (86)**, of the Gloucesters, in 1915 and now Pte **Luther W Coles (41)**, Royal Garrison Artillery, killed in action on 26 July; finally "Raunds Man Wounded" gave the slightly better news that Pte Herbert Stubbs, Northamptons, had been severely wounded!

A United Service of Intercession, to commemorate the third anniversary of the war, was held on The Square on Sunday, **5 August**. A wagonette was used as a platform on which were the Rev C C Aldred (Vicar), Mr G T Brown (Wesleyan), Mr A F Wright (Primitive Methodist), and Mr Fuller, of Chatteris (Baptist). The service was very impressive; the Vicar gave an address, and a collection in aid of the town's War Charities was taken.

Monday, **6 August**, saw reports of extraordinary scenes at local railway stations over the weekend. Neither the likelihood of all the trains being more or less uncomfortably crowded, nor the unpromising character of the weather, deterred many Northants folk from setting out for the holidays they had so long and so eagerly anticipated, and of which the majority of them were more in need, perhaps, than they had ever been before.

A local death saw the passing of Mrs John Horrell, of "The Maples", on Tuesday, **7 August**, after a long and painful illness, at the age of 76. For the last ten years she had been blind, and of late had also suffered from an acute internal complaint.

On Thursday, **9 August**, it was announced that a meeting of the creditors of E W Stanley Ltd, boot manufacturers, had been called for Friday, 17 August by Mr A C Palmer, the liquidator, at Northampton. Folk were informed that the company was in voluntary liquidation and that the meeting would be of a quite formal character for the purposes of complying with the Companies' Act.

Friday, 10 August, William James Askham Smith (109), killed in action.

Results of the year's theoretical and practical examinations in boot and shoe manufacture were released today, and successes from the Raunds Centre were: *Advanced Stage*, 2nd Class Certificate and pass in practical machine finishing – Alfred York; County Council prize for practical rough-stuff cutting – Arthur H Ward; *Elementary Stage*, Pass – Ewart O R Archer and Horace R Mayes.

The Northamptonshire Health Report for 1916 was published today, showing the county death rate of 14.0 per 1,000 of the population; Raunds was 11.7. The county birth rate was 26.6 per 1,000; with Raunds achieving 18.5. The county "infants under 12 month death rate" was 91 per 1,000 births; Raunds was 61.7. Deaths through tuberculosis in Raunds was 1.74 per 1,000.

"In Memoriam – In loving memory of Ptes **S Brayfield (27)** and **P Watson (119)**, East Anglian Casualty Clearing Station, RAMC, who lost their lives on board the "Royal Edward" which was torpedoed in the Aegean Sea on 13 August, 1915.

'At the call of duty they left everything that men hold dear'; CWW."

Ringstead held another successful effort for their Soldier's and Sailor's Comforts Fund on Saturday, **11 August**, and the Raunds presence was noticeable. Amongst the judges for the fancy dress competition was Mrs Wells of "The Crossways" and there was reward for the following townsfolk: *Class 4, Fancy Dress, individual under 16 years of age*: 1st, "BDV Cigarette Girl", Ruth Denton, 2nd, "Italian", Frances Beeby; *Class 8, Best Ragtime Band*: 1st, Budgett's Mixed Band.

"Wanted – Manager for Branch Grocery Store; trade about £170 per week; male (ineligible) or female; Applications to be made by Tuesday, 14 August, stating age and experience, to: Co-operative Society, Grove Street, Raunds."

While the Temperance Band were playing at St Neots on Sunday, **12 August**, the conductor, Mr Owen Pentelow, bought a 6d ticket for a competition. This turned out to be the winning ticket and the lucky bandsman received a gold watch.

"Deaths: On the 12th inst, Ellen Draycott, Primrose Hill, Raunds, aged 66 years."

Industrial action took place on the morning of Monday, **13 August**, when the lads employed by Mr Nichols, Regulation Boot Co, ceased work after breakfast demanding the payment of holiday wages. This action naturally rendered a number of men unable to work. The town cryer was sent round calling for a mass meeting during the dinner hour, but the local union president intervened and the meeting was called off. Mr Nichols said he would not close the factory and the employees could return when they pleased, there was no lock out of any kind, but he had no intention of paying the boys holiday money. In response to claims that foremen received the payment, Mr Nichols explained that they received a regular wage, not piece rates, so were entitled to holiday pay. However, some other members of the local Manufacturer's Federation said they regarded the payment of holiday wages as a trick to entice labour from other factories. The boys returned to work the following morning.

A Raunds shoehand was summoned to appear before Higham Ferrers Police Court today, charged with driving a horse attached to a wagon without proper lights attached at Higham Ferrers on 14 July. The defendant said he had borrowed the trap for his wounded son. He was fined 6s-0d.

Wednesday, 15 August, the Allies capture Hill 70 overlooking Lens.

At Thrapston Police Court today, a Raunds labourer was charged with wilfully neglecting to maintain his four children, whereby they became chargeable to the common fund of the Thrapston Union. It was said that his wife had died, he had broken his home up, and had tried to get someone to look after the children but had failed. The children had been removed to the Raunds Children's Home, but if the man took them out and found a home for them, the Guardians would be satisfied – but the Union was not a boarding house! He was bound over in £5 to appear at the next Petty Sessions, and allowed bail to go back to work.

Thursday, 16 August, Thomas William Bamford (20), killed in action.

A very pretty wedding was solemnised at the Wesleyan Church this afternoon, the contracting parties being Mr Lloyd W Sheffield, youngest son of Mr and Mrs W Sheffield, of Earls Barton, and Miss May Ellen Lawrence, youngest daughter of Mr and Mrs William Lawrence, of Wellington Road.

On Friday, **17 August**, it was reported that Pte **Thomas H Keeley (66)**, Northumberland Fusiliers, missing since 7 July, 1916, was now "presumed killed on that date". The Reading-born man, nicknamed "Snowie", had worked for Mr S Woolley, of "Friendly Lodge", for a number of years.

Also today, it was announced that the Rev Harry Shaw, having done excellent service in the Raunds Wesleyan Circuit and a former missionary in Southern Rhodesia, had been appointed to the Park Road Wesleyan Church, Rushden.

On Saturday, **18 August**, the headline "Sport in the Army" led into the story today that Mrs William Whiteman, Thorpe Street, had received news from her son, Pte Joe Butler, ASC, Salonika, saying that he was in good health and that it was still very hot. It then told how he had entered the Anglo-French Sports in the 100 metre race, and was presented with a silver illuminated watch; he was congratulated by the commanding officer in front of the French and English troops, and also that at a sports event a week previously he had won a first prize.

The Wesleyan Sunday School's 105th anniversary was held on Sunday, **19 August**. In the afternoon a flower service was held when hymn books and Bibles were presented by Sgt L G H Lee to 32 scholars who had reached the age of 15 years during the year. Sgt Lee, home on leave from the front, remarked on how most of the young folk were his scholars before he joined the Forces. There was also an egg collection for wounded soldiers when no less than 883 eggs were taken by the children, other gifts included a packet of chocolate, seven bananas, a writing pad, and three hampers of fruit. This bounty was divided and sent the following day to the Military Hospital at Duston, and the VAD at Higham Ferrers.

Monday, 20 August, the Third Battle of Verdun begins.

It was revealed today that Mr and Mrs Thomas Clarke, of Rotton Row, had received the news that their son, Pte **Cyril Clarke (38)**, Northants Regiment, had died of his wounds in France. In a letter dated 10 August from the 32nd Casualty Clearing Station, the Church Army Chaplain told how Cyril had been "buried in our cemetery in sure and certain hope of Resurrection".

Also today, the Food Controller announced that jam and jelly were to be brought into the widening sphere of fixed prices to take effect on 1 September. The retail price for a 7lb jar would range from 6s-5d for apricot, cherry, blackcurrant, pineapple, and strawberry jams, to 4s-8d for plum and apple. The price of jellies, other than black or red-currant, would be fixed at ½d per lb more than that of jam.

A Raunds shoehand made an unwelcome return visit to Thrapston Police Court on Tuesday, **21 August**. He was summoned once again for disobeying a justice's order to pay 5s-0d per week towards the support of his son, an inmate of the Akbar Reformatory Ship. The order had been made on 17 October, 1916. When he was ordered to pay the arrears of £2 with costs within 14 days, the defendant said that he would appeal under the Poor Persons Act of 1903.

At this evening's council meeting, with respect to the appointment of a Food Control Committee, the members were reminded that representatives on other committees could be released if necessary to serve. At this point, Sgt L G H Lee, home on leave, humorously asked if he could serve and be released from his other duties; the clerk replied "I'm afraid it only means civilian duties!" A letter was then read from the Friendly Society Council asking the council to appoint representatives for the committee for getting up a memorial to the late Dr Mackenzie. Mr Camozzi and Mr John Adams agreed to represent the council.

Wednesday, **22 August's** newspapers featured the story that Pte **Harry Rice (96)**, Royal West Surreys, youngest son of Mr and Mrs John Rice, Marshalls Road, had been missing since 24 February and nothing had been heard of him since.

The Local Tribunal met on Thursday evening, **23 August**, and a large number of personal appeals were presented. Six men produced doctor's certificates and were recommended to be examined by the Central Medical Board. A group of boot factory men appealed on domestic grounds or asked for time to get their produce off their allotments. The committee were reasonably sympathetic and gave final exemptions until 30 September or 31 October depending on the circumstances. Finally, a conscientious objector appealed on the grounds that he did not believe in fighting and would not take part in combatant service. He said, however, that he was prepared to join the remounts as he had been used to horses, or do any work of national importance; his case was dismissed.

News of the death of Pte **Robert W Richards (97)**, of Marshall's Road and the Norfolk Regiment, reached Raunds on Friday, **24 August**. The twenty-one year old had been killed in action on 4 August, and before joining up in June 1916, had worked for the St Crispin Productive Society.

At the first meeting of the Raunds Food Control Committee today, Mr W F Corby acted as provisional chairman pending the permanent appointment. Mr Hodson moved that Mr Camozzi take the chair, however, Mr Camozzi declined on the grounds that he was actively engaged in the distribution of food (*as owner of Palmer's Stores*). Mr Hodson then moved Mr Batchelor for the post, but he also declined. Finally, Mr John Adams was unanimously elected. With regard to the appointment of an executive officer, Mr Camozzi remarked that they could think of no-one better than Mr Corby. This proposal was also carried unanimously.

It was "Thrapston's Day" on Saturday, **25 August**, when the town put on another fine effort for their Soldier's and Sailor's Comforts Fund. Once again the St Crispin Lady Pierrots and Budgett's Mixed Band successfully flew the flag for Rance, winning prizes in their respective classes.

Berry Brothers and Bagshaw held a property auction at the "George and Dragon Hotel" on Monday evening, **27 August**; the main sale being that of the freehold "Glebe Farm". The bidding started at £1,500 and was secured for £2,225 by Mr T Warth, of "Raunds Grange", who also purchased 13 acres of meadow for £450.

At the Thrapston Board of Guardians meeting on Tuesday, **28 August**, Mr J Shelmerdine said that the Homes Committee desired that the minimum age of admission should be fixed; he proposed 3 years and this was agreed.

Another name was added to the town's list of war dead on Wednesday, **29 August**, with the news that the War Office had now uprated their status of "missing" on Pte **Arthur Clark (35)**, Queen's Royal West Surrey's, to "missing, presumed killed in action on 18 November, 1916". His brother was currently recovering from wounds received at Vimy Ridge in April.

Thursday, 30 August, Henry Price (93), killed in action.

At the Local Tribunal today the military representative asked about men who lived in other districts making personal appeals to this Tribunal because they worked in the town. The clerk reminded him that this had been raised before and that men had the right to appeal to the Tribunal in the district where they worked; "men in the boot trade from the villages who worked in Raunds would be better served by our Tribunal than by the Thrapston Rural one", he added.

It was announced on Friday, **31 August**, that the Rev J L Gillians had been appointed to Thrapston as Assistant Wesleyan Minister in the Raunds Circuit.

The casualty lists released today included that of Pte E Morris, 7869, Northants Regiment, reported wounded on Saturday, 25 August.

And it seems that the Western Front was not the only place to witness horrible deaths as today it was also reported that a 53 year old farm labourer in Essex had been killed by wasps! He had accidently cut through a wasp's nest while harvesting and the angry insects then swarmed all over him, stinging him so badly that he fell to the ground and died just three minutes later.

SEPTEMBER – In the Parish Magazine this month, the vicar announced that the Town's Hospital Week Committee would be making a collection of all kinds of paper on Saturday, 15 September, with proceeds going to hospital funds. There was also good news on the response to the "Endowment of the Living" appeal, which had been most encouraging; and the Church hoped to send a good amount in answer to Mr Stopford Sackville's generous offer to the Diocesan Committee.

There were cheery tidings of a Vestry Class old boy; William Darlow, now serving with the Australian Light Horse in the Middle East, was reported to be keeping up the reputation of Raunds on the football field, his team having recently won cups in the YMCA Football League. However, the sadder military news was the listing of five more town men to have "Died in the Service of Their Country": **Arthur Clarke (37)**, **Cyril Clarke (38)**, **Luther Coles (41)**, **Jasper Gilbert (54)**, and **(Robert) William Richards (97)**.

Finally, readers were advised that applications for graves in the new cemetery should be made to the clerk of the council, not to the vicar; when the service was held at the Church, the time had to be arranged with the Vicar at least 24 hours previous; and that the fee for tolling the bell would be 1s-0d for all funerals.

A joint-meeting of the town's National Relief Fund Committee, Belgian Relief Fund Committee, and War Charities Committee was held in the Temperance Hall on Monday evening, **3 September**. Mr W F Corby reported National Relief Fund receipts of £717-4s-2d, expenditure of £630, a balance in hand of £87-4s-2d. He also reported the Belgian Relief Fund receipts to have been £390-7s-9d, and expenditure of the same amount. He went on to say that all of the Belgians under the care of the committee had now left the town, and proposed thanks to the Co-operative Society for the free loan of the house for the whole of the period.

The monthly meeting of the Boot and Shoe Operatives Union local branch today discussed the actions of some Appeals Tribunals giving exemptions on the condition that the men joined the Voluntary Training Corps, the members arguing that it could not be a voluntary corps if men were forced to join it!

At the Thrapston Police Court on Tuesday, **4 September**, a number of Raunds transgressors made appearance. Leading the way, the proprietor of the Raunds Picture Palace had two pieces of business to transact: firstly to successfully apply for the renewal of licence to theatre for a further period of six months under the usual conditions (interestingly, when questioned he stated that his age was 38 and that he was a Portugese!). He was then charged with driving a motorcycle to the danger of the public at Raunds on 19 August. Found guilty, he was fined £1.

A carrier was summoned for allowing a horse to stray on the public highway on 17 August. The defendant said that someone must have opened the gate; a fine of 10s-0d was imposed. A shoehand was summoned for a breach of the Poaching Prevention Act by having in his possession, 11 rabbits unlawfully obtained and one net used for taking them on the public footpath on 26 August. Pleading guilty, the defendant, a previous offender, was fined 16s-0d with 4s-0d costs.

Finally, a Rotton Row man was brought up in custody, charged with failing to report himself under the Military Service Act. After presentation of the facts, the man was fined £2 and handed over to the military.

Wednesday, **5 September** – "In Memoriam – In loving memory of our dear son, **George B Flavell (51)**, killed in France, 4 September, 1916, aged 27 years.

You are always in our thoughts, dear one, It is sweet to breathe your name;
In life we loved you dearly, In death we do the same.
God will link the broken chain, Closer when we meet again.

From father, mother, brother, sisters and Mary, his fiancée, 87, Marshall's Road."

Thursday, **6 September**: "Wanted – At Once, good Sacks or Bags, any quantity – Apply, stating quantity and price, to the Regulation Boot Co (Raunds) Ltd."

More military misery for the town was reported in the local newspapers on Friday, **7 September** with the news that Mrs Bamford, 12, Scotland Street, Kettering, had been officially informed that her husband, Pte **T W Bamford (20)**, Northants Regiment, had been killed by a shell whilst in the trenches on 16 August. Pte Bamford was formerly employed in the signal department of the Midland Railway. Two other Raunds casualties announced today were LCpl J Robinson and Pte L Esscom, also of the Northamptons, who had been wounded the previous Saturday.

Lepidopteran horror emerged from Burghfield, Berks today with the announcement that 10,214 white butterflies had been caught by the children of the village during August; with Master A Selwood alone exterminating 2,200 of them!

"Wanted – For Chelveston CE School, a Supplementary Teacher; salary £30 pa with £5 war bonus added – Apply: Correspondent, Higham Ferrers Vicarage."

In a special sitting of Thrapston Police Court on Saturday, **8 September**, Lt-Col Benyon in the chair, a 22 year old single woman was charged with concealing the birth of her newly born child at Raunds during the month of July. The prisoner was remanded to the Workhouse until the following Tuesday.

At Stanwick's Hospital Fete today, their Raunds neighbours joined in the fun and fancy dress with some success: Messrs Bugbys came second in the *"Decorated Vehicle"* class; Messrs A and M King won the *"Comic"* class as "Derby and Joan", with a commendation for A Knight's "Scarecrow"; whilst in the *"Fancy Dress"* class, Miss C Richardson secured second place as a "Japanese Girl", with A Webb's "Page Boy" and H Webb's "Soldier" also being commended.

Over at Titchmarsh, a Parade and Fete was held in aid of their Soldier's and Sailor's Comforts Fund and Rance provided several victors or runners-up. St Crispin's Pierrots won the *"Pierrots and Jesters"* class; Olive Denton, "Oranges and Lemons", won the *"Girls"* class; "The Raunds Ragtime Band" took second place in the *"Ragtime Bands"* class, generously donating half their prize money to the fund; and in the sports, S York was runner-up in the *"Boys Under 18's"* race.

On Sunday, **9 September**, an open-air baptismal service was held at The Mill, Stanwick at 3.30pm, followed by a gospel meeting in the Gospel Hall at 6pm. The speaker was Pte H Murray Rankin, of Aberdeen, whose subject was "Beyond the grave, the battlefield, and the depths of the sea – what?" Meanwhile, at the mainstream churches, the Rev J Lewis Gillians, the newly appointed minister at Thrapston, preached at the Wesleyan Church; the curate, the Rev W S Bethway, home on leave from France where he was an Army chaplain, led the worship at the Parish Church; and Harvest Services were celebrated by the Primitive Methodists when Sister Isobel, of the South East London Mission, preached.

A Raunds chemist was summoned to the Higham Ferrers Police Court on Monday, **10 September**, for riding a bicycle at Higham without a light on 13 August. The defendant claimed that he had a rear and front light combined, but this was denied by PC Powell who said there was only a rear lamp, which showed very little light. A fine of 6s-0d was duly imposed.

"Official Notice – Local Food Control Committee – Registration for Sugar – Householders are requested to register for their supply of Sugar at the shop or store where they have previously obtained their Sugar, but they can only register at one shop or store. Any forms or cards already signed are useless. By order, Executive Officer, G L Renshaw."

The "concealment of birth" case came up for a full hearing before Thrapston Police Court on Tuesday, **11 September**. Giving evidence, a neighbour deposed that in the afternoon of the last Wednesday in July, she saw the prisoner in her garden and she was smoothing a mound in the garden where she stood; she looked very ill. The defendant's landlady said that she believed her lodger had had a baby but this was denied by the prisoner.

PC Newberry deposed that he and Sgt Ellingham were called to the house in Rotton Row and they went into the garden. There they dug up what appeared to be the partly decomposed body of a child. When he told the woman what they had found, she replied, "Yes, I gave birth to a child about six weeks ago. It was dead, and I thought the best thing to do was to bury it and say nothing." The prisoner was remanded back to the Workhouse for another week pending further enquiries.

On Thursday, **13 September**, the Government announced that the 9d loaf would be on sale from the following Monday, but emphasised that the reduction in price must not lead to an increase in consumption; "Bread is only cheaper because it is necessary, not because it is plentiful!" The subsidy of £20 million per annum required to produce the cheaper loaf would be met by taxpayers.

That afternoon, a youth named Mabbutt, who was employed at Messrs Adams factory, had his left hand crushed while working a bottom levelling machine. He was conveyed in a motor to the Northampton General Hospital for treatment.

At the County Appeals Tribunal on Friday, **14 September**, three Raunds men made unsuccessful personal appearances as their cases were dismissed, although the military were asked not to call them up until 15 October.

Young Reggie Holmes featured in Cousin Claude's column today when his letter entitled "Jolly Days – Fishing in the Ouse", was printed, telling of his August holiday at Olney. "Altogether, I had a splendid holiday", enthused Master H.

"Coming shortly to the Royal Theatre, Rushden, the Ideal Wonder Production: 'Masks and Faces'. In the matter of cost nothing like it ever has been seen before, and nothing approaching it is ever likely to be seen again. Starring 55 of the Leaders of the English Stage, including: Gladys Cooper, Viola Tree, Lottie Venne, Sir Johnstone Forbes-Robertson and Weedon Grossmith."

Today it was announced that LCpl Bernard Cody, MGC, the grandson of Buffalo Bill, had been killed in action in France; and that 100 years ago, a sweeping machine had been invented to obviate the practice of sending boys up chimneys.

Saturday, 15 September, Kerensky declares the first Russian Republic.

A varied agenda was dealt with at the monthly Urban Council meeting on Monday, **17 September**: the clerk reported that the balance for hire of The Square for Feast Week, 1917, had been received from Mr H Thurston, and also a deposit of 10s-0d for hire of the area for the same period in 1918.

Dissatisfaction with recent sugar distribution for jam making then occupied the gathering for some time. It was said that in many cases, people with a large quantity of home-grown fruit had got smaller amounts of sugar allotted to them compared to those with only one or two fruit trees. It was decided that the clerk should write to the authorities inquiring how the varying amounts were arrived at.

A letter was read from Mr S G Busby's solicitors with respect to the accident he met with owing to some loose stones on the highway on 15 December last, asking the council what they intended to do in the matter. The clerk was instructed to write back saying that the council admitted no liability in the matter.

It was then decided to appoint a Coal Control Committee and it was agreed that this should comprise of the chairman, vice-chairman, and Messrs John Adams, J Shelmerdine, JP, and W Gates. Next, it resolved that the Farm Committee should make arrangements for the sale of the Sewage Farm produce.

Finally, the medical officer, Dr McInnes, reported that for July and August, there had been five and nine births, and four and three deaths respectively. Excepting for cases of tuberculosis, the district was clear of infectious disease.

The next episode in the "alleged concealment of birth" case took place at Thrapston Police Court on Tuesday, **18 September**, when the accused 22 year old, single woman, of Rotton Row, appeared before the Bench once more. The facts of the case were gone through again, including new testimony from the local doctor who confirmed that the remains brought to him by the police were that of a small infant. The prisoner, who did not wish to say anything, was then committed for trial at the next Assizes. As no one was willing to stand bail, she was sent back to the Workhouse until the hearing.

Friday, 21 September, Jack Spicer (110), killed in action.

The Rushden Echo printed several letters today from "Rushden's Soldier Sons" including one from Pte **Charles H Spriggs (111)**, of the Royal Inniskilling Fusiliers, in which he said that he was "longing to be back home with some of his old friends". There was news too of Pte George Hunt, Northants Regiment, missing since 10 July, 1917; he was now known to be a POW in Germany.

Today marked the start of the special effort weekend in aid of the Blind and Crippled Children's Fund. This evening a concert was held in the Palace Theatre, by kind permission of the proprietor, Mr J W Hall, when there was a good attendance. In addition to the film (5,000 feet) "The Fighting Forces of Europe", a comedy picture was also shown. The vocalists were Mr J Shalford and Miss E Harlow, of Rushden, whose singing was much appreciated by the audience.

At the County Appeals Tribunal, a Raunds conscientious objector was due to appear but a member of the Raunds Tribunal advised that the man had been arrested in the town that morning on a charge of stealing leather. When the defendant's appeal to the Local Tribunal was dismissed, he had said that he would not join the Army, but would "clink it" instead; the appeal was dismissed.

"Notice of Sale – on Monday, 8 October, Arthur G Brown and Son will sell by auction at Glebe Farm, Raunds, Live and Dead Farming Stock, by instructions from Mr E G Gaunt, who is leaving."

On Saturday, **22 September**, it was "Forget-me-not" Day. A large number of young girls were about selling the flower in aid of the funds. The proceeds of the concert amounted to £15-3s-0d, and the "Forget-me-not" Day £12-2s-0d, making the excellent total of £27-5s-0d for the two efforts.

Also today, the Woodbine Working Men's Club held their annual Members Show when some very good specimens of fruit and vegetables were exhibited. The show had been arranged in aid of the Tobacco Fund for the soldier members serving at home or abroad. The prize winners were: *"Round Potatoes"* and *"Six Heaviest Potatoes"*, Mr H Shaw; *"Kidney Potatoes"*, *"Cabbages"* and *"Carrots and Parsnips"*, Mr A Burton; *"Spring Onions"*, Mr J Hodson; *"Large Eschalots and Pickle Eschalots"*, *"Cauliflowers and Pair of Marrows"* and *"Potatoes (freaks) and Pears"*, Mr E Batchelor; *"Kidney Beans"*, Mr M Cuthbert; *"Collection of Vegetables"*, Mr C E Nunley; *"Beetroot"*, Mr Jas Smith; *"Turnips"*, Mr A Attley; *"Apples"*, Mr W Attley; *"Tomatoes"*, Mr G Hall; *"Bunch of Flowers"*, Mr Jas Lack; and *"Asters"*, Mr E Vickers.

At the close of the show the exhibits were sold and the proceeds of this sale, together with donations, entrance fees, and skittles competition takings, realised £12 for the Tobacco Fund.

"Wanted – Stove, in good condition, for warming large room; Apply: March, Printer, Raunds."

"Messrs Pendered and Son Ltd will sell by auction at the 'Grange Farm', Stanwick, on Monday, 24 September, by order of Mr Robinson Burton, who is leaving, items including: a Tinckler's Churn, Three Beehives, a Four-Wheeled Dog Cart, and Three Owls in Cases."

The Harvest Thanksgiving services of the Salvation Army were held on Sunday, **23 September**, in the Club Room in Rotton Row, the services being conducted by Captain G Chapman, who drew some spiritual lessons from vegetables!

The Wesleyans also held similar Harvest Festival services this weekend when the Rev John Williams, of Pateley Bridge, was the guest preacher. At the Sunday afternoon musical service, the lesson was read by Mr Charles Wicksteed, JP, of Kettering, and the choir contributed the choruses "Gloria" and "Hallelujah". On Monday, a welcome was given to the new minister, The Rev J Lewis Gillians.

The Raunds Food Control Committee met in the Council School on Monday evening, **24 September**, when a list of meat prices was submitted, signed by the butchers. It was decided to send an intimation to each butcher that the weight as well as the price, should be shown on the ticket sent to the customer.

At Thrapston Police Court today, a Raunds clicker was charged with stealing top pieces, calf marine fronts, box calf marine quarters, box calf marine tongues, and other leather goods, valued £16-2s-3d, property of Messrs Adams Bros, Boot Manufacturers. Supt Tebbey said that the prisoner and a Rushden man were only arrested on Friday, and there was a good deal of inquiry to be made respecting some other stuff. On this evidence, the prisoner was remanded in custody until the Petty Sessions on 2 October; the Rushden man was similarly remanded.

On Tuesday, **25 September**, it was reported that during the year the Raunds Red Cross workers had sent to Northampton the following: 99 mufflers, 35 property bags, 83 pairs mittens, 86 pairs slippers, 66 pairs day socks, 6 pairs bed socks, 2 hand-knitted vests, 2 helmets, 21 blankets, 6 hospital rugs, 3 small pillows, 24 pillow cases, 4 face washers, 24 handkerchiefs, 12 bed jackets, 5 pairs operation stockings, 12 bath and 12 huckaback towels, 24 dusters, and 14 tea cloths.

Some positive news at last from the Western Front reached Raunds on Wednesday, **26 September**, with the award of the Military Medal to Pte George W Agutter, a company runner in the Middlesex Regiment, the son of Mr and Mrs William Agutter, Harcourt Street, for gallantry and good service in the field. Writing to his parents he said that he won it in the first week August, when he usually had his seaside holiday, so now he would have something to show for a change! ***(Plate 23)***

"For Sale – Two commodious and well built houses in Marshalls Road, Raunds; house and orchard and four cottages, Bottom End, Stanwick; also three cottages and garden, Bottom End, Stanwick; Apply – W F Corby, Raunds."

On Saturday afternoon, **29 September**, the members of the Temperance Band paraded the town and collected on behalf of one of their old members, Mr Fred Haynes, who had been ill for a long time. The amount realised was over £12.

4 – October to December 1917

The justice of a miscarriage and Albert's tragic mishap.

OCTOBER – At the start of what would prove to be a costly month in terms of town war casualties, the vicar's Parish Notes opened with advance notice that the Lord Bishop of the Diocese would be holding a Confirmation Service at Higham Ferrers on Saturday, 8 December. He thanked all who had responded so well to the Endowment Fund appeal. The Glebe had sold well and the proceeds were being invested by the Board of Agriculture; the sale would relieve the Raunds clergy of a great deal of anxiety.

Looking back at the Harvest Thanksgiving Services, there was an abundance of fruit and vegetables and the sale on the Monday night must have satisfied all buyers, for they got both quality and quantity. The proceeds realised £8-0s-8d, and collections £13-18s-1d, a grand total of £21-18s-9d from the proceedings.

He advised that the Raunds Company of the Church Lads' Brigade was now being enrolled, after having done the preliminary six weekly drills. The next step would be in about seven or eight weeks when the khaki uniforms arrived. "We do not mean to be beaten by any other Company for smartness and keenness when we attend the anniversary meeting in Northampton in November" he enthused.

Finally, regret was expressed at the appearance in the "Died in the Service of Their Country" list of **Thomas W Bamford (20)**, a member of the old Church Lads' Brigade, and two former Vestry Class members, **Henry Price (93)** and **William J A Smith (109)**.

A sale of work in connection with the Raunds Temperance Society was held on Monday, **1 October**, towards a fund for renovating and furnishing the Temperance Hall. Mrs W H Lovell, of Stanwick, presided and the sale was formally opened by Mrs George Bass, who was over 80 years of age. Two of the youngest members, Master Kenneth Hall and Miss Gladys Lawrence, presented bouquets to Mrs Bass and Mrs Lovell. Tea was served, and various stalls were well patronised. A good programme was given by a Pierrot Troupe, and there were numerous competitions. The proceeds were £52.

At the Thrapston Petty Sessions on Tuesday, **2 October**, the Raunds clicker and his Rushden accomplice made return appearances and, after lengthy depositions from factory owner Mr John Adams, JP CC, a fifteen year old clicker in his employ, Sgt Ellingham and PC Newberry, both men were committed to come before the next Assizes. To add to the town man's woes, he was also committed for the additional charge of receiving from a person unknown, well knowing the same to have been stolen, nine pairs of leather soles, valued at 45s-0d, the property of Walter Lawrence, boot and shoe manufacturer of Raunds.

Today, the Boot Operatives Union made public the recently agreed terms on the employment of females on work normally performed by male labour:

"Females may be employed upon any operation in the Lasting and Finishing Departments except the following, namely: Pulling-over machines, Consul Lasting machines, Bed Lasting machines, Pounding Up machines, Revolution Press, for the Cutting of Butts, Bends and Sides, Slipping Solid Block Lasts, Welt Sewing, Rough Pounding, Edge Trimming, and Edge Setting.

Before a Female is engaged to operate the Screwing Machine, Heel Parer, or Auto Edge Setter, 48 hours notice must be given to local Trade Union Officials to give them an opportunity of finding a male operative. Men unfit for military service shall have first choice, and females shall not be employed in any Department, except the Closing and Shoe Rooms, where short time is being worked."

Also today, it was sadly reported that Mr Fred Haynes, the beneficiary of a collection made by the Temperance Band just three days earlier, had died. He left a wife and two children to mourn their loss.

The marriage took place at the Independent Wesleyan Church, Rushden, on Wednesday, **3 October**, of Miss Lilly Ellen Bates, of Rushden, and Gunner Horace Walker, Royal Garrison Artillery, the second son of Mr and Mrs T Walker, of Marshall's Road, Raunds. The Rev C J Keeler officiated. The bridegroom was well known in Rance as a footballer, having played as goalkeeper for the town team. He had enlisted in early 1915 and had been in France since January 1916.

Thursday, 4 October, Leonard Walter Minkley (79), died of wounds & Herbert Leonard Robinson (101), killed in action.

On the day that the casualty list claimed two more town men, Messrs C and H Thurston, the amusement caterers, located their attractions on The Square, where they would remain in evidence until Saturday, 13 October.

Good news from the front emerged on Friday, **5 October**, with the announcement that Sgt H Pell, Sussex Regiment, the youngest son of Mr John Pell, had been awarded the Military Medal for conspicuous gallantry and devotion to duty during the Battle of Ypres. ***(Plate 24)***

Several thousand miles away, the Toronto Star today reported on a letter recently received in Canada from an unknown comrade of Pte **Sidney J Cope MM (43)**. He related how he had visited his friend's grave, describing it as "one of the most beautiful cemeteries in France." Pte Cope's decoration had since been sent home to his friends in Toronto.

Figures announced today showed that Australia had to date recruited 306,227 men for the war effort, with New South Wales leading the way with 111,970, followed by Victoria with 86,648.

Closer to home, the children of Chelveston Day School were being praised for gathering over 400 lbs of blackberries for jam for the soldiers and sailors.

Saturday, 6 October, John Stanley Allen (10), died of wounds.

The town's War Charities Committee held an auction sale this afternoon in the playground of the Church School. Prior to the sale the Temperance Band had paraded the town. In connection with the auction Mrs A Camozzi had also arranged a Red Cross flag day, a morning jumble sale, and various sideshows. The numerous gifts donated for auction included fruit, vegetables, poultry, butter, eggs, two store pigs, an Old English sheepdog, and various items of furniture. Three partridges were the first lot to be offered up and were in turn knocked down to no less than eight different successful bidders, realising in total £8-16s-6d!

In Stanwick this afternoon and evening, concerts were given for the County Red Cross effort and Miss Louie Smith, of Raunds, was one of the artistes. The wounded boys from the Higham Ferrers and Hinwick VAD's were entertained to tea, and in all £15-2s-6d was raised.

Sunday, 7 October, Ernest Stringer MM (112), killed in action.

The Urban Council's Coal Distribution Committee met for the first time on Monday evening, **8 October**, in the Council School. A letter was read from the Distributive Co-operative Society stating that, in view of the danger of being cut off from the supplies of coal altogether, they could not see their way to approach the collieries for a revision of pit prices.

A meeting of the town's Food Control Committee also took place this evening when a letter was read from the Food Controller stating that sugar for the purpose of sweetening alcoholic drinks could not be allowed. The whole of the applications made, therefore, for this purpose were not entertained.

Tuesday, 9 October, Arthur Llewellyn Fairy (49), killed in action.

A mass meeting of boot and shoe workers was held in the Woodbine Club today when the large hall was crowded. Making his first appearance at a town meeting since he led the famous strike and march 13 years earlier, was Councillor James Gribble. He addressed the gathering on the subject of workers wages and conditions. He also ventured the opinion that, as there were now millions of men in the Army who had never previously worn such heavy footwear, they would, to a large extent, continue to wear these heavy boots when they left the Army and so the industry, Raunds included, must be prepared for this demand.

Today it was claimed that 25 tons of blackberries had been collected in the county by school children to make jam for the troops.

The town's War Charities committee met in the Temperance Hall on Wednesday evening, **10 October**. The Treasurer announced that the proceeds of the auction sale the previous Saturday, together with that of a concert arranged by Mrs A Camozzi, and some other items still to come in, was expected to raise no less than £700. As a result, it was decided to allocate the following amounts to the following funds: County Red Cross, £500; Y.M.C.A., £25; Blind Soldiers and Sailors, £25; Armenian Red Cross and Refugees, £20; Northants Prisoners of War, £20; and to send 5s-0d to each Raunds man serving with the Forces at Christmas.

A very pretty wedding took place at the Parish Church on Thursday, **11 October**, between Miss Ida Adams and Pte E Walden. The bride looked very charming in a dress of cream alpaca and white silk trimmed with pillow-lace, and carried a sheaf of white lilies, and also wore a gold bracelet, a gift of the bridegroom.

At the Peterborough Bankruptcy Court today, three brothers, from Raunds, Stanwick and Caldecote, previously trading as boot manufacturers from the "Wellington Works", applied for discharge from bankruptcy. After an exchange of views between Judge Wheeler, KC, the Official Receiver, and the brothers' solicitor, His Honour announced his great pleasure in finding in favour of the applicants and granted them immediate discharge on the grounds that they had acted at all times in good faith but circumstances had arisen out of their control.

The Local Tribunal met again this evening in the Council School when several appeals were given exemptions ranging from 31 October to conditional exemption.

Also this evening, offered for sale at the "George and Dragon" Inn were 55 acres of superior arable and pasture land situated on the Stanwick Road, by order of the executors of the late Mr Samuel Brown. However, the lots were withdrawn after no suitable offers were made. Perhaps the presence of an existing right of way of the Urban Council across this land to their Sewage Farm deterred would be buyers!

Friday, 12 October, Richard Cobley (39), died of wounds & Ralph Driver (46), killed in action.

Today, the Boundary Commission accepted the recommendations of the local political parties and agreed to the transfer of Raunds, Stanwick, Chelveston, and Hargrave to the East Northants Division (Wellingborough), which would now have a total population of 62,712.

"Raunds Town War Charities Committee – Corresponding Number Competitions: Competition No.1 – 1921, No.2 – 8126, No.3 – 8594. All prizes to be claimed within seven days – W F Corby, 'Hawarden House', Raunds."

On Saturday, **13 October**, it was disclosed that Nurse Pym, who had recently been engaged by the Raunds Nursing Association, had commenced her duties in the town and was residing at 80, High Street.

The Kettering and Wellingborough District of Co-operative Societies met today at Desborough with its president, Mr F Miller, of Raunds, in the chair. The main topic discussed was proper Parliamentary representation for the 3 million Co-operators in the country. On this subject, one delegate colourfully expounded: "The average House of Commons is a mere combination of landlords, lawyers, captains, stockbrokers and betting men, animated with every class prejudice imaginable. Political life must no longer be a fanciful field for the careers of the incapable! Twelve thousand Co-operative societies in Russia had been a mighty force in the downfall of Czarism!" – Tea was then provided.

"Notice of Sale – By order of the Raunds Urban Council, Arthur G Brown will sell at 3 o'clock prompt today at the Sewage Works Field: four acres of Mangold Wurtzel, one acre of potatoes, and 50 perch of carrots, in convenient lots."

Monday, 15 October, the Allies execute Mata Hari as a German spy.

Or "What's the matter Harry?" as my old grandma used to say!

At this evening's Urban Council meeting another letter from Messrs Darnell and Price, solicitors, of Northampton, was read out with respect to the accident that Mr S G Busby had met with on 16 December. After some consideration it was unanimously resolved to reply that the Council had nothing to add to their previous communication. The one tender received for lighting and cleaning the street lamps, viz Mr John Finding at 15s-6d per week, was accepted. Then a letter was read from the police authorities giving permission for the lighting of the 13 lamps agreed at the previous meeting.

Dr McInnes reported one death and three births registered during September and there was one case of a notifiable infectious disease. Finally, a circular was read from the Royal Commission on Paper with respect to the collection of waste paper, and it was decided to point out what was already being done in the town.

"Three Raunds Men Lay Down Their Lives" was a headline that would have grabbed local attentions on Tuesday, **16 October**. It led into brief descriptions of the demise of Pte **John Stanley Allen (10)**, Royal Dublin Fusiliers, Pte **Jack Spicer (110)**, Machine Gun Corps, and Cpl **Ernest Stringer MM (112)**, of the Northamptons, the latter having died before he could receive his decoration.

Thrapston Magistrates today considered the case of a Raunds machine operator, who was charged with failing to report at Kettering on 29 September under the Military Service Act. The recruiting officer said that the prisoner should have reported himself, and further notices had been sent. The Bench were informed that on being arrested while at work at a Raunds boot factory, the prisoner dirtied the officer's uniform, which had to be cleaned. The man was fined £2 and ordered to pay all costs, and to be handed over to a military escort.

A more amusing tale appearing in today's newspapers was that of an Army officer's wife who was fined £5 for sending a live German hand grenade by post from Hove to Newcastle-on-Tyne!

At the County Appeals Tribunal on Wednesday, **17 October**, a Raunds boot foreman in a rough leather department made a personal appeal. He explained that he had formerly been a manufacturer who had been burnt out, so he had gone into a Rushden factory. He was given exemption until 17 November.

"Wanted – a reliable man as Caretaker and Sexton of the Cemetery, and to fill up spare time in general Council work – Apply, stating wages required, to: W F Corby, Clerk, Raunds Urban District Council."

This evening, the first of two concerts was given in the Wesleyan Schoolroom, the second taking place on Saturday, 20 October, both being performed to full audiences. The programme consisted of varied items by the St Crispin Pierrot Troupe, with additional songs and dances by eight tiny tots under five years of age, from the Church of England School's infants department. The "Tiny Tots" were Mary Sanders, Mary Baker, Mary Wilmott, Winnie Smith, Bertha Mitchell, Violett Cuthbert, Evelyn Scrivener, and Nina Lack, their singing and dancing giving evidence of very careful training by their teachers. The total proceeds, for the Town War Charities' Fund, amounted to the excellent sum of £29.

A special Court was convened at Thrapston on Thursday, **18 October**, to hear the case of a Raunds cinema proprietor, a married man, who was charged that he did, between 1 January and 6 August, 1917, in the parish of Raunds, unlawfully procure and supply a certain noxious drug, knowing that the same was intended to be unlawfully used by a 22 year old, single woman, of Raunds.

Mr Harker, prosecuting, said that at the time of the prisoner's arrest there was found in his possession a letter which had been written by the woman, also on remand charged with concealment of birth; this stated: "Just a few lines to let you know that I am not all right yet. There is a woman at Rushden who says she can get me all right; but it is £3, and I have not got the money. It must be done at once, as it is terrible, I can tell you. Something must be done, or you will get into great trouble. Don't come up to our house, or mother will know."

The woman, of Ekin's Yard, Rotton Row, then deposed that she was employed at the Picture Palace at Raunds for about twelve months, and left last Whitsuntide. She was confined of a child on the Thursday before the last August Bank Holiday and the prisoner was the father. She then gave details of the drugs supplied to her by the defendant. Another witness, a married woman in the accused's employ, then described how the prisoner had given her small parcels on several occasions with the instruction to pass them on to the young woman.

Finally, Sgt Ellingham deposed that he and PC Newberry went to the prisoner's house on 7 September and told him "We have just found a baby up there in the young woman's yard; she has told us you were the cause of her trouble and that you gave her something to take." At this point the defendant had admitted intimacy and buying her something at Bedford. In answer to the charge the prisoner pleaded not guilty and reserved his defence. He was committed for trial at the Assizes at Northampton on Monday, 22 October.

The Food Control Committee met this evening at the Council School when the question of the price of milk for the winter months was discussed at length. Ultimately, it was decided to form a sub-committee to meet the milk producers to consider the question, and Messrs John Adams, JP CC, E Batchelor, and Miss Beeby were appointed. The question of the recent increase in the price of butter at the local markets was also discussed and finally, another sub-committee, comprising of Messrs A Camozzi, A Hazeldine and G E Smith, was formed to resolve the issue of some butchers charging prices in excess of the approved list.

"Wanted – Live rats and frogs" was reported to be a notice in a shop window in Oundle's market place!

Friday, 19 October, the last German airship raid on Britain results in all five ships being shot down.

"Auction Sales – Without Reserve, by order of A C Palmer, Esq. (the Liquidator), Re E W Stanley (Raunds) Ltd, in liquidation, Army Boot Contractor: 'Wellington Works', Raunds, Northants, Sale of the Factory Site, Buildings, 4 Cottages, and Land Adjoining. All that desirable Freehold Site situated in Wellington Street or Stanwick Road, Raunds, comprising Portions of Premises not destroyed by fire, Four excellent Semi-Detached Cottages abutting on the main road, and a vacant Piece of Land adjoining, suitable for the erection of cottages; The Whole of the Salvage, Comprising Fifteen Tons of Leather etc; The Contents (mostly undamaged) of the existing Buildings, Boiler and Engine Houses. The Whole of the above will be Sold by Auction on Thursday Next, 25 October, 1917, Upon the Premises at Raunds, Commencing at 11 o'clock sharp."

Monday, 22 October, Jack Herbert Haxley (60), killed in action.

Two Raunds residents appeared at the Northampton Assizes today. First was the 22 year old clicker charged with receiving nine pairs of leather soles, the property of Walter Lawrence, knowing them to be stolen. He was further charged with stealing a large quantity of top pieces and upper leathers, buckles, and other goods, the property of Messrs Adams Bros. The defendant pleaded guilty to the theft, but not guilty to the charge of receiving; he was sentenced to six months hard labour. However, his Rushden accomplice in the theft case, charged with receiving the ill-gotten goods, showed remorse "more than words could express" before the court and escaped with being bound over to be of good behaviour.

The 22 year old single woman, charged with concealment of birth, then appeared and pleaded guilty. Her father insisted that his daughter was a good girl at home. His Lordship then announced that he would not pass sentence today as a connected case would be tried tomorrow. The woman was then liberated on her own recognisances to appear the following day.

Tuesday, 23 October, Gerald Lansom (69), killed in action.

Back at Assizes, the Raunds Picture Palace proprietor pleaded not guilty to the charge of supplying or procuring a quantity of "certain noxious things, namely, alloes and lead, knowing that they would be used with the intent to procure the miscarriage of a 22 year old single woman of Raunds, during the month of July."

The young woman gave evidence that she had been employed at the prisoner's picture palace and that he had taken liberties with her, and fetched her some gin, which she had drunk. He later had told her not to worry and gave her some powders and tablets, some of which she took. On another occasion he had brought her some "black things" and liquid in a skin case. She had taken some of them and they had made her very ill. A week later the child was born dead at the end of July.

The prisoner then explained that the only things he had supplied to the woman were some white pills, bitter apple, and backache pills. He had done this because she had said that if he did nothing she would tell his wife. He had given her nothing except what was harmless. The Official Analyst confirmed this claim. When the prisoner was asked about the letter from the woman in which she asked him for £3 to enable her "to see a woman at Rushden", he replied that he had totally ignored it, however, he had offered her £5 or £10 if she would marry her young man, but she had said that she would rather die first!

The evidence of other witnesses supported the defendant's insistence that he was the victim of the woman's blackmail and His Lordship directed the jury to return a verdict of not guilty, discharging the man. As for the woman, His Lordship said he could not apportion the blame between her and her married man friend. He felt that justice would be met if she were bound over in her own recognisances for 12 months and he hoped that this period would result in her entirely wiping out the circumstances which had led to her being in the dock. She was then discharged.

On a lighter note, at their meeting today, the Thrapston Board of Guardians appointed Dr McInnes as vaccination officer for the Children's Home at Raunds.

Wednesday, 24 October, the Italians are defeated by the Central Powers at the Battle of Caporetto.

The accounts for the recent special effort put forth by the Town War Charities Committee were published on Thursday, **25 October**. Receipts were: Subscriptions, £557-15s-0d; house to house collection, £28-15s-0d; proceeds of sales, £49-17s-4d; sale of flags (by Mrs Camozzi), £17-2s-11d; hoop-la and skittles (per Rev C C Aldred), £3-2s-0d; competitions, £6-13s-0d; corresponding number competition (per Mr G Winsor), £13-9s-0d; concerts (per Mrs Camozzi), £29-3s-9d; total, £705-18s-0d. The expenses totalled £3-18s-9d, leaving net proceeds of £701-19s-3d.

Some remarkable prices were paid at the auction of the property salvaged from the fire at Messrs E W Stanley's "Wellington Works" earlier in the year. The freehold site, including the portion of the premises not destroyed by the fire, four substantial cottages, and a piece of vacant land, was sold for £1,700 to Messrs Lane and Hulett, of Kettering. The salvaged leather sold exceptionally well and other lots to realise high prices were: a 60hp steam engine, £120; a 120lb pressure steam boiler, £70; a 60hp gas engine, £200; and a quantity of brass rivets, £80.

The auction also included Mr F W Dix's disposal of his contractor and laundryman "stock-in-trade" on joining up for military service. His two ton motor lorry fetched £260; a smaller motor lorry £116; and a 5½hp gas engine £28. His carts and vans also sold readily at big figures.

Friday, 26 October, Frederick William Bailey (17), Herbert Lawrence (72) & James William Skelly (104), all killed in action.

On the day that the town suffered a triple loss it was announced that Miss Alice Maud Gant, youngest daughter of the late Mr J Gant JP, chemist of Raunds, had passed the qualifying examinations of the Pharmaceutical Society, after studying at the Northampton Technical School and the South of England College of Pharmacy. She was now qualified to take full control of her late father's business.

It was "Daisy Day" in the town on Saturday, **27 October**, and a large number of young ladies assisted as sellers of the "daisies", and the sum of £11-3s-2d was taken in aid of the National Children's Home and Orphanage Fund.

"Teeth – Bertram Allen, 26 Brook Street, Raunds, Will Attend in Future Every Other Thursday, 4-15pm to 7-15pm, instead of every Thursday."

The President of the Methodist Conference had previously asked for collections to be taken on Sunday, **28 October**, in aid of the Methodist War Emergency Fund, and Mr W F Corby had urged that "the effort be made a special one so as to ensure a good result". And a good result it proved to be as £13-16s-8d was raised.

At the County Tribunal on Monday, **29 October**: a 41 year old, married, hand-laster's case was dismissed, however, the military were told not to call the man up until 31 November; and an 18 year old, single, apprentice motor engineer, with deformed feet, had his case adjourned pending a medical examination.

The newspapers on Tuesday, **30 October**, reported that Mrs Fairy, Thorpe Street, had received official news that her youngest son, Pte **Arthur Fairy (49)**, Norfolk Regiment, had been killed. The 24 year old was a former employee of Messrs R Coggins and Sons and had been a strong Churchman and one of the bellringers.

The funeral took place this afternoon in the Wesleyan Burial Ground of Miss Dora Pentelow, youngest daughter of Mr and Mrs George Pentelow, of Marshall's Road. At the most impressive service the choir (of which the deceased was a member) sang the hymn "How bright these precious spirits shine". Miss Pentelow had been ill for five months and had bore her suffering very bravely.

It was announced today that ten million letters were being sent from England to the troops in France every week!

Wednesday, 31 October, the Third Battle of Gaza, the Allies break the Turkish line in south Palestine. The Australian Light Horse captures Beersheba.

At the Raunds District Education Sub-Committee meeting this evening, it was reported that the attendance register showed the average number for the previous period to be 1,116 as against 1,138 for 1916; the percentage attendance had been 87.4 as against 87; and 13 agricultural special permits were currently in existence.

And at this evening's Food Control Committee meeting a Transport Sub-Committee was formed comprising of Messrs R Lawrence, A Camozzi, M C Bellamy, W E Eady, J Hodson, and E Batchelor.

"Lost – Between Raunds and Wellingborough, Plumber's Kit; Reward on returning to Police Station, Wellingborough."

NOVEMBER – In his opening notes in this month's Parish Magazine, the vicar observed that amongst the names of the fallen during the last month was another member of the choir, **Arthur Fairy (49)**, and **Jack Spicer (110)**, a former Scout and member of the Vestry Class. Their names also appeared in the "Died in the Service of Their Country" column, alongside those of **Stanley Allen (10)**, **Richard Cobley (39)**, and **Ernest Stringer (112)**.

Thursday, **1 November**, on the domestic front the month began with a Government warning that tea would continue to be in very short supply for another four weeks, but there was the prospect of an improvement in December.

There was some good news at last for the Higby family on Friday, **2 November**, when it was confirmed that Pte Arthur Higby, previously listed as "missing", was now known to be a prisoner of war in Germany. Arthur's two younger brothers, **John (63)** and **Ralph (64)** had both become war casualties earlier in the year.

"Perfect Attendance" proclaimed the local newspapers today as they told of Ernest Hall, aged 12, the son of Mr T Hall, Harcourt Street, who had received a medal for five years perfect attendance at school. He had attended the Wesleyan School until it closed three and a half years ago, and since then had been a pupil at the Council School without a single break.

Also today, Earl Spencer KG acknowledged a cheque for £500 from Raunds towards the County Red Cross Fund saying "It is indeed a very generous contribution, and I am deeply grateful for it. Please convey my most sincere thanks to all who have contributed to this splendid cheque."

Saturday, 3 November, the first United States troops are killed in battle.

Today, the captain and members of the Fire Brigade arranged a flag day on behalf of the Widows and Orphans Fund of the National Fire Brigade's Union. During the afternoon the Temperance Band paraded the town and, accompanied by the members of the brigade, made a collection. The flag selling was carried out by a number of willing young ladies under the supervision of Mrs A Camozzi. The amounts collected were: from flags, £14-1s-9½d; collection by firemen and band, £1-13s-0d; special donation, 5s-2½d, a grand total of £16.

This afternoon, a football match was staged between Raunds United and Wellingborough Corinthians, as a result of which £4-8s-0d was handed over to the Treasurer of the local War Charities Committee.

Also today, in a bold demonstration that it was willing to do its bit, Eton College announced that its beagles were to be dispersed for the duration of the war!

It was Foreign Missions weekend at the Wesleyan Church on Sunday and Monday, **4 and 5 November**, and the Rev G Lester, a missionary home on furlough from the Lagos District of West Africa, preached sermons in the morning and evening, and conducted a special afternoon service for young people in which a number of curios he had brought home from the foreign field, were exhibited and explained.

The following evening, the annual Foreign Missions meeting was held and the Rev J L Gillians announced that the total contributions for the year from the Circuit were £100-17s-3d, of which Raunds itself had contributed over £53. The Rev Lester followed with an eloquent description of his work in West Africa.

"Lost, between Woodford, Ringstead, and Raunds on Sunday evening, a gold-mounted Waterman Fountain Pen – Reward on returning to J H Nichols, Raunds."

Tuesday, 6 November, the end of the Third Battle of Ypres, Passchendaele is captured by the Allies. Charles Bradlaugh Reynolds (95), died of wounds.

The news of the death of two more town men made the headlines today. Mr and Mrs Owen Cobley, Marshall's Road, had received a letter from the sister in charge of the 41st Casualty Clearing Station in France informing them of the death of their son, Pte **Richard Cobley (39)**, on 12 October. Meanwhile, Mrs W Walters, Chelveston Road, had received a letter from the Chaplain of the 6th Battalion, Australian Expeditionary Force, containing the sad news of the demise of her nephew, Pte **Herbert Robinson (101)**, on 4 October.

Also meeting this evening were the town's Food Control Committee, to whom a circular was read from the Food Controller asking the committee to appoint a Food Economy Committee. After due consideration, in which the general opinion expressed was that very little good would result from a campaign of voluntary food rationing, it was decided to take no action on the matter. The committee then proceeded to fix maximum retail prices in the district for butter; these included dairy butter at 2s-5d per pound and "Golden Meadow" at 2s-3½d.

Wednesday, 7 November, the Allies capture Gaza.

"Raunds Soldier Suffering from Burns" headed a story today that Mrs C Bailey, Clare Street, had received official news that her husband, Gunner Cecil Bailey, Royal Field Artillery, had been admitted to the 6th General Hospital, Rouen, France, suffering from severe burns to his face and hands.

In today's "Shoe and Leather Record", it was stated that Messrs Lane and Hulett, who had purchased the "Wellington Works" site and property of Messrs E W Stanley Ltd for £1,700, intended to establish leather currying on the premises.

Thursday, 8 November, the Bolshevik revolution in Russia, Lenin and the communists depose Kerensky.

A minor revolution also took place at this evening's Local Appeals Tribunal when the military authorities challenged exemption certificates granted to two members of the Distributive Co-operative Society. A whole rack of low-category shoe trade cases received conditional exemptions, although surprisingly, a hand laster, 41, married, with nine children, and a pressman, 36, married, with six children under 14, and a delicate wife, were only given exemption until 31 December. Finally, our old friend Strangward appeared, the 37 year old farmer presenting a certificate from the Board of Agriculture which earned him conditional exemption.

The awarding of the Military Medal to Rance's Pte E J Elliott, Northants Regiment, was announced on Friday, **9 November**, and elsewhere, the cup that cheers was truly running over today with the news that a vessel loaded with 40,000 chests, containing 3,500,000 lbs of tea, had arrived at a "British port".

"Family's Splendid Record" introduced the story of the three Lansom brothers of Burton Latimer, two of whom were Raunds-born, and one of whom, Sgt **Gerald Lansom (69)**, had been killed in action at Passchendaele on 23 October 1917.

The annual meeting of the Trustees of Peap's and Blaizes Charities was held at the clerk's office on Monday, **12 November**, with Mr Enos Smith, JP, in the chair, supported by Messrs A Camozzi, JP, J Hodson, and W F Corby. The accounts of Blaizes Charity were presented showing the receipts to have been £11-4s-10d, and the expenditure 12s-10d, leaving a balance in hand of £10-12s-0d. It was decided to distribute the balance in coal, as in previous years, if coal could be obtained. The accounts of Peap's Charity were then presented, showing receipts to have been £14-9s-0d, and expenditure £1-8-11½d, leaving a balance in hand of £13-0s-0½d. It was decided to distribute the balance equally amongst those parents whose children were attending secondary schools.

A meeting of the Coal Control Committee also took place this evening, when the merchants complained that the prices they were currently having to pay for coal made it impossible for them to sell at the prices fixed for the district without making a loss. The chairman replied that the committee were only empowered to approve certain defined increases on pre-war prices and that the merchants should take their grievances to the Controller. However, pending investigations, it was agreed that they could charge 36s-0d per ton for coal from the Swanwick Colliery and a rate of 1s-10d per cwt for all kinds delivered in lots of 2 cwts of less.

"Notice of Sale – by Arthur G Brown – Pony, Cob, Trap, Harness, Two Poultry Houses, Implements, Tools, and sundry Household Furniture, by instructions of Mr Ernest Spicer. Sale to commence at 1 o'clock."

In the "Children's Court" at Thrapston on Tuesday, **13 November**, a 12 year old Raunds schoolboy was charged with housebreaking and stealing 3s-6d in money on 8 November. Sgt Ellingham deposed that he saw the lad, who said "I got through the grating into the cellar. I went into the shop and took some money out of the till, but I don't know how much." The defendant (his mother standing by him) pleaded guilty and was ordered to receive six strokes of the birch!

At the "Adult Court" which followed, a Raunds shopkeeper was summoned for failing to subdue the lights of his house at 7.55pm on 31 October. The defendant, who did not appear, was fined 2s-6d after evidence was given by PC Newberry.

On Wednesday, **14 November**, it was reported that Mrs R Gaunt, High Street, had received official news from the Record Office, Shrewsbury, that her nephew, Pte Percy Adams, of the Cheshires, had been admitted to the 11th (Harvard, USA) General Hospital, France, on 24 October, suffering from severe gunshot wounds to his leg and upper thigh. The wounds resulted in his left leg being broken.

At Thursday, **15 November's** meeting of the Food Control Committee, Mr E Spicer reminded the members that the Co-operative Society had refused to supply him with sugar because he had not deposited his sugar card with them. The executive officer reported that he had discovered that the household had been in the habit of having 3lbs per week from the Society and also 2lbs from a private trader. The chairman observed that this was a violation of the orders of the Food Controller and that the Co-operative Society should be asked for an explanation.

The names of **H Allen (9)**, Middlesex Regt, and G Coles, Royal Fusiliers, appeared in the newspapers on Friday, **16 November**. Both men had been listed as wounded during the past week.

A Raunds labourer appeared at the Wellingborough Police Court today, charged with riding a bicycle on the footpath at Stanwick on 3 November. PC Powell gave evidence that the defendant claimed there was no distinction between the path and road at the place he was riding. The Bench disagreed and fined him 7s-6d.

The monthly meeting of the Urban Council on Monday evening, **19 November**, a letter was read from Mr A W Hollis stating that the amount offered by the Council as compensation for damage to his fence in Manor Street was not sufficient. It was decided to allow the offer to remain and take no further action.

The medical officer reported three births and ten deaths registered during October. There had been a number of cases of contagious skin disease which had in nearly every case been suffered by soldiers home on leave. The sanitation officer reported that he had on two occasions sprayed and fumigated the rooms after deaths from notifiable infectious disease.

Tuesday, 20 November, the Battle of Cambrai begins, the first massed tank attack by the Allies.

Two Raunds fitters appeared at the Bedford Petty Sessions today on charges that, with a view to preventing the call up of themselves for military service, they made statements which were misleading in a material particular, on 21 August and 14 September respectively. Both men pleaded guilty and their defence counsel appealed to the Bench to give them an opportunity to redeem their characters, and not to impose a crushing penalty. This request, however, appears to have fallen on deaf ears as both defendants were fined £15 with £5 costs!

The Thrapston Board of Guardians today discussed an application received from the Raunds Nursing Association for a subscription from the Guardians to ensure help from the nurse for poor law cases. The chairman remarked that the subscription of one guinea hitherto given by the Board seemed of a very low grade and hoped that they would soon enlarge their liberality in that direction.

On this very same evening, a meeting of the Raunds District Nursing Association was held in the Temperance Hall, Mr A Camozzi, JP, presiding. The secretary (Mr J V Spicer) reported that 540 members had joined the association, and at the present time they had about £65 in hand.

The Food Control Committee also met this evening and a letter was read from the Distributive Co-operative Society which stated that instructions had now been given to their store managers to supply customers who had been in the habit of getting their sugar from the stores, except where they had reason to believe they were being fully supplied elsewhere.

"In Memoriam – In loving memory of our dear son, **Arthur Clark (35)**, of Raunds, Pte, Queen's Royal West Surreys, who was killed in action, 18 November, 1916:

Not dead to those who loved him, Not lost, but gone before;
He lives with us in memory still, And will for evermore.
Oh for the touch of the loving hand, And the sound of the voice that is still.

From his loving Father, Mother, and Brothers, 86, High Street, Raunds."

On Wednesday, **21 November**, the Government announced that over 5,000 prisoners of war were now employed in agriculture in Britain.

This evening, a successful whist drive and dance, arranged by Mrs A Camozzi and Mrs J V Spicer, was held in the Church Institute in aid of the Church Lads' Brigade Equipment Fund.

"Wanted – Immediately, a Good Plasterer, used to firapite and cornice work. Apply: Smith and Son, Raunds."

Thursday, 22 November, Arthur Hazeldine (61), killed in action.

Mrs William Warwick, Thorpe Street, received news today from the Record Office, Warley, that her grandson, who used to live with her, Pte A C Horner, Essex Regiment, was wounded in Palestine on the 3 November.

"General Notice – Raunds – Teeth – Bertram Allen, owing to his increasing practice at Kettering, will not attend at 26, Brook Street, until further notice, but can be seen daily at Kettering, or at Mr Orrell's, Chemist, Rushden, Tuesdays, 11.15 am to 12.30 pm or Saturdays, 2.15 pm to 5.15 pm."

Mr W Minkley, Marshall's Road, was reported to have received official news on Friday, **23 November**, that his eldest son, Pte **Leonard Minkley (79)**, was listed as "missing" since 4 October. Twenty year old Pte Minkley had joined up soon after the outbreak of war, and sent to France in August 1916, having previously worked for Messrs R Coggins and Son.

Three more Raunds "Victims of the War" were included in the wounded lists published today: Ptes H Jones, Essex Regiment, H Payne, Yorks and Lancs Regt, and J Allen, Royal Dublin Fusiliers, having suffered their injuries two days earlier.

At a special meeting at the Wesleyan Church on Sunday, **25 November**, the Rev C J Keeler spoke on "Donald Hankey – a student in arms", and a collection was taken in aid of the Homeless French Protestants.

A "War Wedding" took place at St Peter's Church on the afternoon of Monday, **26 November**, between Miss Florence Vorley, youngest daughter of Mr John Vorley, Midland Road, and Pte A N Edwards, ASC, of Winchester. ***(Plate 8)***

John S Mason, Auctioneer, held a sale at the "Globe Inn" this evening when a number of houses and cottages, and some freehold building land were disposed of. Mr Hall paid £475 for two well built, newly erected freehold dwelling houses in Marshall's Road, and Mr W F Corby acquired three copyhold dwelling houses and workshops in Rotton Row for £150. Miss Black was also successful in selling off two houses on the corner of Primrose Hill and Thorpe Street, known as Aiden and Primrose Cottages. Also at the sale, twenty £1 shares in the Raunds Hotel and Coffee Tavern Co Ltd were sold to Mr J Vorley at 10s-0d each.

News of two more town war casualties was reported on Tuesday, **27 November**. Pte Cyril Mayes, of the Yorkshires, was now in a Birmingham hospital recovering from head wounds sustained in France. Gunner John Hasseldine, MGC, had been admitted to the 23rd Stationary Hospital, Baghdad, with slight wounds.

Having kept out of the public eye for many months, dear old Strangward featured in a newspaper report for the second time in a month, thanks to his latest appearance at today's Thrapston Petty Sessions. Again it was his poor rover that got him into trouble; the "farmer and dealer" being fined 10s-0d as the owner of a dog found on a public highway and not having his name inscribed on its collar!

"Wanted – Mother's Help to take charge of girl 7 years of age; light duties only; middle aged person preferred. Apply to: Mrs Amos Lawrence, The Hall, Raunds."

A meeting of local War Savings Associations was held in the Council School on Wednesday, **28 November**. It was agreed that the four magic lantern lectures prepared by the National Committee be arranged for, and a sub-committee was appointed to make the arrangements. It was further decided to obtain a number of War Savings Christmas Cards and advertise them in the district.

An accident befell eight year old Ernest Cobley in the playground of Raunds Council School today. The lad, the son of a soldier who was currently in hospital having been gassed, fractured his right thigh in the fall and was rushed to Northampton Hospital for treatment.

Some rather alarming news emerged on Thursday, **29 November**, regarding Company Runner George Agutter, Middlesex Regiment, a recent recipient of the Military Medal. His father had received a letter informing him that his son had failed to return from a mission to deliver a message at the front on 13 November.

Friday, 30 November, Arthur March (75), killed in action.

"Thanks – Mr and Mrs Lansom, of Burton Latimer, and Miss Connie Middleton, Kettering, desire to express their sincere thanks for the many kind expressions of sympathy they have received since their bereavement, the loss of Sgt **Gerald Lansom (69)**, killed in action."

DECEMBER – The vicar, the Rev C C Aldred, began his Parish Magazine notes this month with the news that on Saturday, 17 November, 24 members of the Church Lad's Brigade Company, under Lieutenant Rawlings, had journeyed to Northampton for the inspection by Field Marshall Lord Grenfell. Although still uniform-less, the only unit in civilian dress, the Field Marshall congratulated the lads for starting the company and for being brave and turning up not in uniform.

The very enjoyable whist drive and dance arranged by Mrs Camozzi on Wednesday, 21 November, in aid of the Lad's equipment fund, had raised about £10. The tireless Mrs Camozzi was then said to be arranging another dance at the Institute on Tuesday, 20 December; and a Fancy Dress Dance at the Infant's School on Friday, 28 December, again in aid of the CLB Equipment Fund.

The Christmas Day collections would be given to the Northants Prisoner of War Fund; £450 was required weekly to enable parcels of food and other comforts to be sent to our captive men. And a plea was made on behalf of the Parish Nurse, who would be very glad to receive parcels of linen suitable for use in sick cases. The Vicar urged all to "look out what you have to spare and send it to the Nurse".

Finally, another name was added to those who had "Died in the Service of Their Country", that of Gunner **Charles Reynolds (95)**, another Church Choir member.

Monday, 3 December, the Bolsheviks arrange a unilateral armistice with Germany. Arthur James Knighton (68), killed in action.

"Raunds St Mary's Church Lad's Brigade Corresponding Number Competition – Winning Number: 2967; Prize to be claimed from Mrs A Camozzi, 'The Manor House', Raunds, within seven days."

Thursday, 6 December, an ammunition ship collision in Halifax, Nova Scotia, kills over 1,900 people.

Newspapers of Friday, **7 December**, carried the story that Mr and Mrs George Haxley, of Gladstone Street, had received official news that their youngest son, Gunner **J H Haxley (60)**, Machine Gun Corps, had been posted missing six weeks earlier, on 22 October. Gunner Haxley had joined up in January of this year, going out to France in May and was a former captain of Raunds Town Football Club.

There was happier news today, however, with the announcement of the engagement of the Rev Thomas Greatorex Shelmerdine, Vicar of St Thomas', Derby, son of Mr and Mrs J Shelmerdine, JP, and Eileen, only daughter of Sir Henry and Lady Lunn, of "Oldfield House", Harrow-on-the-Hill, and niece of Miss Lunn of the Northampton Queen Victoria Nursing Institution.

This evening, a largely attended whist drive and dance was held in the Church Institute, arranged by the employees of Messrs Tebbutt and Hall Bros, in aid of a fund to send Christmas presents to their fellow workmen who were serving with the Colours. Mr W Gibbs acted as MC and music for dancing was provided by Messrs J H Stubbs, piano, and Bert Clarke, violin.

On Saturday afternoon, **8 December**, under the auspices of the Kettering and District Shoe Trade Managers' and Foremen's Provident Society, an organising meeting was held at the Temperance Hall when it was proposed that a branch in Raunds be formed; carried unanimously, nineteen members were enrolled.

A thanksgiving day was held in the Wesleyan Schoolrooms this evening, when at 5.30pm, the Rev E P Blackburn, Mrs Blackburn, and other officers of the church, were in attendance to receive the gifts from the members of the congregation. A silver Christmas tree was provided for the children, vocal and instrumental music being rendered by the Young Ladies' Pierette Troupe. Recitations were also given by Miss C Freeman, of Denford. The contributions amounted to over £40.

Meanwhile in the Stanwick Church Rooms, a concert was given by the Raunds St Crispin's Pierrot Troupe and "Eight Tiny Tots". The event was in aid of the Stanwick Soldiers and Sailors Christmas Present Fund and raised upwards of £8.

Over at Kettering, two town fanciers won prizes at the Kettering and District Fanciers Association's 7th Annual Show of poultry, cage birds and rabbits. J Cheadle nested two firsts and a third, and A Tansley hatched a second and a third.

Sunday, 9 December, Jerusalem is captured by the Allies ending 673 years of Turkish rule.

Over this weekend, the Rothwell Salvation Army Band accompanied Major and Mrs Vickers to Raunds for the purpose of dedicating the new Hall. On Saturday evening the Band rendered a grand musical concert and on Sunday, special meetings were held; crowds attended both the outside and inside meetings. On Sunday evening on The Square the Band played the "Dead March" and "Saul" in memory of those men who had fallen in battle. The new premises were situated in Rotton Row, with Captain Cecil Chapman the resident officer-in-charge.

On Tuesday evening, **11 December**, the town's Food Control Committee agreed to accept a suggestion from the Northampton committee to revise slightly the list of meat maximum prices. It was also decided to press the Food Controller to fix the wholesale prices of beef and mutton.

The newspapers of Wednesday, **12 December**, reported another Rance man missing at the Front. Mr Charles Bailey, of Marshall's Road, had been officially notified that his third son, Pte **Fred Bailey (17)**, South Staffs Regiment, was posted as missing on 26 October, but the news had only just filtered through. Fred had joined up on 17 February and gone out to France on 10 October with Pte **Herbert Lawrence (72)**, who had also been missing since the same date. However, unlike Herbert, Fred's body was later recovered and buried in a Belgian Commonwealth War Graves cemetery.

News was also published today that Pte A Horner, Essex Regiment, grandson of Mrs W Warwick, of Thorpe Street, had sustained wounds to his right ankle and was now in Alexandria Hospital, Egypt. Prior to the war he had been employed as a pressman at Messrs J Horrell and Son's boot factory.

In the evening the Bishop of Peterborough paid a visit to the town when he gave an address in the Church on "The Re-building of Britain's Life"; a good number of Nonconformists were noticed amongst the large congregation. The Bishop briefly referred to the arrival of the troops on the borders of the Promised Land, and observed that that country had been full of difficulties from Moses right down to General Allenby! During the singing of the final hymn a collection was taken in aid of the Northamptonshire Prisoners of War Fund, which amounted to £8-6s-6d.

Another old inhabitant of the town passed away on Thursday, **13 December**, in the person of 80 year old Mrs Mary Knighton, of Spencer Street, widow of the late Mr John Knighton.

The Local Appeals Tribunal met this evening at the Council Schools and quickly dealt with the two cases presented before them with contrasting outcomes. A 40 year old, married, hand laster's application for exemption was refused, whereas, the Co-operative Society's 42 year old, married, horsekeeper was granted conditional exemption on the motion of the Chairman.

The Master Butchers of East Northamptonshire, at a meeting at the "Hind Hotel", Wellingborough, today, passed a resolution that "unless an alteration is made in the existing conditions under which beef and mutton are sold, they would close their places of business on the opening day of 1918!" This was in reaction to the maximum prices imposed by the Food Controller which would result in all sales being at a loss. Representing Raunds were Messrs Bellamy and Webster.

News of the death of L-Cpl **Arthur March (75)** on 30 November reached his parents and the local press on Friday, **14 December**. Writing to Mr and Mrs F W March, of High Street, Arthur's commanding officer, Capt Middleton, explained that their son had been "standing to in a trench ready to repel an attack which the enemy were making, when a shell fell just beside him and killed him instantly."

"Nasty Accident Near Knotting", ran another headline today, leading into the story that a gypsy had been knocked down and killed by a motor car driven by Lieutenant **Albert Masters (77)**, of Raunds and the Royal Flying Corps. The subsequent inquest found the airman, who at the time was home on leave, to be totally free of blame for the unfortunate man's death. Ironically, the young flyer would himself be the victim of a fatal accident less than six months later!

The quarterly meeting of the Raunds Wesleyan Methodist Circuit resolved on Saturday, **15 December**, that an "After War Committee" be formed, the object being that the committee would help Wesleyan soldiers, sailors and airmen, or those who had been engaged in War work, and also dependants of the fallen.

At the Urban Council monthly meeting on Monday, **17 December**, Dr McInnes reported five births and one death during November; no cases of infectious disease had been reported and the health of the district continued to be good. The clerk read a letter from Sgt L G H Lee, in which he wished the members of the council the season's compliments. On the motion of the chairman, it was decided to return the sentiment.

Wednesday, **19 December**, "Wanted – A Competent Man to work a Blake Sewer and Stitcher; good wages and war bonus – Unity Productive Society, Army and Navy Contractors, Ringstead."

On Thursday, **20 December**, the general shortage of food in the country was again illustrated when the Food Controller, Lord Rhondda, announced that with effect from 1 January, there would be one day per week upon which no meat, either cooked or uncooked, would be sold, including rabbits, fowls or game. Following up this announcement, Sir Arthur Yapp hinted that the Government would soon also have to take a strong line regarding the feeding of cats and dogs!

The next day the local Food Control Committees warned that persons found buying margarine etc in excess of current requirements risked a heavy fine. Soon afterwards in the county, a local ex-Army officer was fined £90 for hoarding large quantities of sugar, tea and coffee.

Friday, **21 December**, "Royal Theatre, Rushden, 26 December to 29 December, Three times daily at 2, 6 and 9, At Enormous Cost We Have Secured Exclusive Rights For This District of D W Griffith's Gigantic Spectacle – 'The Birth of a Nation' – 5,000 Distinct Scenes, 3,000 Horses, 18,000 People, Cost of Production £150,000. The Most Stupendous and Fascinating Motion Picture Ever Created!"

All creeds were represented on Sunday afternoon, **23 December**, at the annual musical service held in a crowded Wesleyan Church. Carols were sung, Miss Evelyn Sayer, from the London School of Music, sang the solo "O brightest day" and Mr W F Corby read the letter which had been sent with a gift of a postal order for 5s-0d to each Raunds serviceman, and also read from letters of thanks received. An instrumental quartette was given by Messrs O Pentelow, W Bugby, E Vickers, and W Groome. A collection for the Northampton Hospital realised £8-12s-6d.

Monday, 24 December, George Henry Hall MSM (59), died of injuries.

In another tragic accident today, Robert Munro, a 51 year old farm labourer employed by the Co-operative Society, died after falling from a float loaded with straw bales in the yard. An inquest verdict of "Accidental Death" was returned.

A very pretty wedding was solemnised at the Wesleyan Church today, the contracting parties being Miss May Hasseldine, the youngest daughter of Mr and Mrs J Hasseldine, of "The Lodge", Brooks Road, and Mr Sydney Groom, the third son of Mrs Groom and the late Mr Charles Groom, of Lawson Street.

A dance arranged by the employees of Messrs R Coggins and Sons in aid of a fund for providing fellow employees serving with the Forces with comforts was held in the Temperance Hall this evening, and was largely attended.

The Temperance Band, as was their usual custom on **Christmas Day,** played carols at various places in the town; a collection was made in aid of Band Funds.

In the morning, a charity football match was staged between Raunds United and Wellingborough Corinthians in which the visitors triumphed by 7 goals to 2.

On **Boxing Day**, a social was held in the Wesleyan Schoolroom, and was well attended. Games etc. were provided, and a sketch given by a number of young members of the Guild was much appreciated.

Another attractive wedding took place today at the Parish Church, as Miss Elsie May Chambers, eldest daughter of Mr and Mrs James Chambers, Park Road, married Mr Percy James Martin, the son of Mr and Mrs E Martin, of Ringstead.

The funeral of Lieutenant **George Henry Hall MSM (59)**, Royal Flying Corps, took place at the Wesleyan Church on Friday, **28 December**. He had met with a flying accident near St Neots on Thursday, 20 December, and had died in Cambridge Hospital on Christmas Eve. His body was brought from Cambridge by train, and was met at Raunds Station by a military escort from Wyton Camp, where he had been stationed, and conveyed to his grandfather's house in Harcourt Street, from whence the funeral procession started. The service was conducted by the Rev E P Blackburn; the remains being laid to rest in the graveyard at the back of the Church. As the mourners left the soldiers fired three volleys over the grave.

Appearing on the casualty lists as "wounded" today were town men Ptes H Jones, Essex Regt, J Hasseldine, Machine Gun Corps, and H Hasseldine, Leicester Regt.

A Fancy Dress Ball was held in the National Infants School this evening in aid of the Church Lad's Brigade Fund, raising £18. The music was provided by Miss Clarke (piano) and Mr Bert Clarke (violin), with Mr D Bamford acting as MC. The prizes to: *Group* – Miss Hornsby's "Group of Gypsies"; *Lady* – Miss T Brown, "Wood Nymph"; and *Gentleman* – Mr F Bugby, "Indian Prince".

Sunday, 30 December, Charles Mills (78), died at sea.

Monday, 31 December, John William Clark (36), died.

The last Raunds wedding of 1917 took place today at the Wesleyan Church, the contracting parties being Miss Rose Harris, the eldest daughter of Mr and Mrs Ralph Harris, of Primrose Hill, and Mr T W Gardiner of Ringstead.

Also today, the Midland Railway announced that there would be "important timetable alterations in January on the Main Line to St Pancras"; however, there was to be no change to the already meagre service provided on the Raunds line.

And the Food Controller announced that "No person after tomorrow (1 January) may make for sale or sell or offer or expose for sale, or buy or offer to buy, any ice pudding, ice cream, or water ice, or any article in the making of which any ice cream, or water ice, or ice pudding has been used."

Thus ended the third full year of the war; a bloody year in which 48 town men had fallen, compared to "just" 36 lost between October 1914 and December 1916. However, the misery was far from over, for although there were now less than 11 months of hostilities left to be fought; another 47 men of Raunds would be taken, including 5 after the signing of the Armistice!

5 – January to March 1918

Youthful desperadoes and the deaths resume.

JANUARY – The vicar, writing his first Parish magazine notes of the New Year, observed that "we have to mourn many during the past year who have made the greatest sacrifice, and while we mourn we also pay homage to them for their sacrifice and we will not forget."

He then paid particular tribute to **Arthur March (75)**, a keen church worker with an interest in the Institute, Church Scouts, and previous summer pageants; and **Leslie Nunley (83)**, the news of whose death in the Holy Land in April 1917 had only just reached church circles.

The Reverend described the recent sale of the Glebe as "making a big difference to the income of this living and taking a load off my mind", adding that "the sum raised for the endowment will in time also make matters a little more easy."

The Church Lad's Brigade was said to have made a good start, greatly helped financially by friends arranging entertainments during the past few weeks. Nearly £34 had already been raised against the £40 needed and thanks were made to Mrs A Camozzi for the two dances arranged by her on 20 and 28 December.

Reflecting on the Bishop's pleasurable visit on 12 December, the Vicar noted that the collection for the County Prisoners of War Fund had amounted to £9, and in addition to this, £3-14s-0d had been given by the Day School children, whilst the Christmas Day collections had yielded £6-5s-6d.

Wednesday, **2 January**, and in an announcement that would have struck terror in the hearts of Rance's connoisseurs of fine ale, the first newspapers of 1918 noted that there was a severe shortage of beer in the district after the Christmas holidays!

On Thursday evening, **3 January**, a social was held in the Wesleyan Schoolrooms in aid of the funds of the National Children's Home and Orphanage. Games, amusements etc were provided, and a programme of vocal and instrumental music dialogues, recitations and sketches was given. The proceeds amounted to £5-6s-0d.

The first of a series of lantern lectures, arranged by the Local War Savings Association, was held in the Temperance Hall on Friday evening, **4 January**. Entitled "The War on Land", and illustrated with the latest pictures from all the battle fronts, the readings were given by Mr A D Rawlings, and the lantern manipulated by Mr C W Vorley.

On view today at Northampton were the 39 samples of the new varieties of standard war time boot shortly to be introduced by the War Office.

And in London, the Office of Works announced that the National History Museum at South Kensington was "required immediately to house the registry of National Friendly Societies"; this provoked vigorous protests against the Government by many natural history societies across the country.

Saturday, **5 January** - "Accomodation Land to Let: The fields near to Raunds, the property of Mrs A M Sharp, will be let to an approved tenant subject to two of the enclosures being brought into tillage. Apply to Arthur G Brown, Auctioneer, Thrapston."

Monday, **7 January**, was "Plough Monday" and in accordance with custom, the authorities in London held a "grand court of wardmote" – the only business being the swearing-in of special constables.

At the County Appeals Tribunal today, the board heard that an 18 year old Raunds machinist, single, formerly an assistant to his father repairing boot and shoe machinery, whose original appeal had been adjourned for two months pending a medical examination, had since been removed by the Labour Exchange to take up munitions work at Motherwell, Scotland. The appeal was duly dismissed and the man was informed that he must apply for re-examination at Motherwell.

The local branch of the Boot and Shoe Union met this evening and heard that they had now lost nearly 200 members on active service, the second highest of any branch in the union. The speaker observed that "War is a stupid and futile game – international disputes ought to be settled by arbitration!"

The assembly also decided to give another concert under the auspices of the branch at the VAD Hospital, Higham Ferrers, and granted the sum of £1 towards cigarettes.

Tuesday, 8 January, President Wilson delivers his "Fourteen Points for Peace".

On the day that the U.S. President made his position clear to the Kaiser, the Raunds Distributive Co-operative Society Ltd appeared before Thrapston Petty Sessions, charged with "being the owners of certain meat, and exposing the same for sale for the food of man, the said meat then being diseased and unfit for the food of man; also having deposited on their premises the said meat for the purpose of sale etc; further, having deposited on their premises for the purpose of sale etc, two other portions of beef." In addition, the Society's manager/secretary and shopman/slaughterman were summoned for aiding and abetting.

The Rushden Inspector of Nuisances, acting as temporary inspector for Raunds, gave lengthy evidence on behalf of the prosecution; Dr McInnes, also confirmed that, when he had examined the suspect meat, he had found clear evidence of tuberculosis being present. After the summoned officers of the Society had presented their defence, the Bench retired to consider their verdict.

The first summons, exposing for sale, was dismissed. The chairman then said that although there was nothing against the general conduct of the Society, it was their duty to inflict severe penalties when meat unfit for human food was concerned. The Society was fined £20, and the shopman/slaughterman £5; however, the charge against the manager/secretary was dismissed. The prosecuting barrister was also awarded costs and the Society was ordered to contribute £10.

"Raunds Soldier Missing" was a headline in Wednesday, **9 January's** local newspapers. Mr A Hazeldine, of Midland Road, had just received the news that his nephew, Private **A Hazeldine (61)**, of the South Wales Borderers, had been wounded in action between 23 and 25 November, 1917, but after passing through the regimental advance post, had disappeared without trace!

Thursday, 10 January, the United States Senate approves giving women the vote.

The Local Appeals Tribunal met again this evening and in a busy session reviewed no less than 28 separate cases, with surprisingly only eight of them coming from the boot and shoe trade; other trades making an appearance included a watchmaker, three butchers, three bakers, and a railway clerk. The majority of the successful applicants were granted exemption until 31 March or 30 April.

Today, the Ministry of Food clarified the fact that it would be an offence not only to sell meat but also to eat it on meatless days, and persons breaking the law would be liable to penalties, just as food hoarders were.

On Friday, **11 January**, it was reported that local men, taken as prisoners of war at the Battle of the Dunes, were now receiving Red Cross parcels regularly; and relatives could be reassured that the Steelback boys were now all smiling again!

Appearing on today's casualty lists, thankfully only as "wounded", was the town's R Mayes, M/225694, of the Army Service Corps. There was also some good news for Mr and Mrs W Agutter, who had just received the tidings that their son, Company Runner George Agutter, MM, of the Middlesex Regiment, previously reported as missing, was now confirmed as a prisoner of war in Germany. Encouragingly, he was said to have a bed and some blankets and to have received a Red Cross parcel.

The second of four lectures arranged by the Local War Savings Association was held in the Temperance Hall this evening, the subject being "What is the Navy doing?"; connective readings were given by the Rev E P Blackburn and once again Mr C W Vorley manipulated the lantern. Before the lecture, an address was given to the children when the hall was crowded.

The Raunds Food Control Committee met at the Council School on the evening of Tuesday, **15 January**, to deal with agenda items that clearly illustrated the continuing decline in the country's food stocks. The Executive Officer reported that certificates had been issued to all local butchers in accordance with their applications, based upon a 50% reduction of their October sales.

Another letter was then read, this time from the Divisional Food Commissioner in reply to their application for urgent supplies of margarine to be sent to the town. The Commissioner regretfully advised them that there was currently an unusually small supply of the product in the country, and to divert any appreciable amount to one area would cause a shortage elsewhere.

More than ten inches of snow fell across the county during Tuesday night and Wednesday morning of 15 and 16 January.

A public meeting, arranged by the Education Committee of the Raunds Distributive Co-operative Society, was held in the Temperance Hall on Wednesday, **16 January**, when, considering the unsatisfactory weather conditions, there was a good attendance. Councillor W R Smith, JP, of Norwich, Co-operative and Labour candidate for East Northants, addressed the meeting at some length on the subject of Parliamentary representation and the entrance of Co-operators in the political arena. His address was freely applauded and questions were invited, but none were forthcoming.

Two cases were presented at today's County Appeals Tribunal. A 38 year old, married, boot and shoe repairer made a personal appeal for renewed exemption and was granted an additional three months, on the condition that he helped others if required. The appeal by the employer of a 38 year old, married, glazier and hot water fitter was also successful, three months final exemption being given.

Also today, there were lively scenes at Kettering where not even the snow could deter hundreds of folk from gathering outside the provision shops believing that margarine would be on sale. Sadly, there were no supplies to be had and shop managers had to call in the constables to disperse the agitated crowd.

A juvenile missionary meeting was held in the Wesleyan Schoolrooms on Thursday evening, **17 January**, with Mr A Pendered in the chair. The meeting opened with hymns and a prayer, followed by a violin solo by Miss Louie Pettit, Master A Clark accompanying at the piano. Mr Willis Rands gave a report on the juvenile missionary work for the year, which showed the income to be more than last year by several pounds. A large number of Sunday School scholars, dressed in costume, then took part in a novel missionary sketch entitled "The Magic Cloak".

Meanwhile at Higham Ferrers, it was revealed that the local VAD Hospital had suffered its first death, after over 1,000 "boys" had passed through its wards. The soldier, a 20 year old Glaswegian private, had been a patient there for ten months.

The Kettering Leader of Friday, **18 January**, carried two contrasting stories on Raunds men: the first told how Private **John William "Willie" Clark (36)**, of Francis Terrace and the Middlesex Regiment's Trench Mortar Battery, had been accidentally killed three weeks earlier when some ammunition had unexpectedly exploded. The second related how Sgt J W Plant, of Spencer Street and the Egyptian Expeditionary Force, had been awarded the Military Medal for devotion to duty after being wounded, describing him as "a modest hero". ***(Plate 25)***

And another town man appeared in this week's casualty lists, Private G Brawn, 18459, of the Northamptons, having been wounded the previous Monday.

The third of the war lantern lectures was held in the Temperance Hall this evening, when Mr J Shelmerdine JP, presided over a good attendance. The subject was "The War in the Air", and presented by the team of Messrs Rawlings and Vorley.

Private George Henry Richardson, of the Canadian Expeditionary Force, and a native of Raunds, was married to Miss Florence Gertrude Buckle, of Rushden, on Saturday, **19 January**. Pte Richardson, an older brother of town casualty **Herbert Richardson (99)**, had been in Canada when war broke out and had immediately enlisted in the Canadian contingent. He had been in France for over two years until being wounded and returning to England.

This evening, the members of the Temperance Band arranged a dance, in aid of band funds, in the Temperance Hall, the music being supplied by members of the band; Mr Joseph Vorley acted as MC.

At the Urban Council's monthly meeting on Monday, **21 January**, a letter was read from the local branch of the Boot and Shoe Operatives Union in which they advocated that all coal coming into the district should be commandeered. The Coal and Coke Supplies Committee promised that supplies should be dispatched immediately. The acting sanitary inspector reported on the prosecution of the town's Co-operative Society with regards to diseased meat; the members expressed their appreciation of the actions and attentions given by the Inspector.

Another letter from the same Union was then read in which they requested the Council to prepare a scheme for the erection of houses for the working class. The matter was referred to a sub-committee comsisting of Messrs Smith, Batchelor, Gates, Shelmerdine and Asbery.

"The Palace Theatre, Rushden, Monday, for three days: The Big, Merry and Bright Pantomime – 'Dick Whittington and his Cat' – in Eight Magnificent Scenes – Matinee Wednesday at 2.30."

New boot and shoe trade war bonuses were agreed by a meeting at Leicester on Tuesday, **22 January**. To be added to each full week's earnings from 1 February, females of 20 and over would receive 8s-0d; 18 and 19 year olds, 6s-6d; and youths from 18 to 20, 6s-6d. For males earning up to 35s-0d, the bonus would be 16s-0d; whereas those earning more than 45s-0d would only receive 10s-0d.

This evening, at a meeting of the Local Food Control Committee, letters were read from the Thrapston Committee and the Raunds butchers, both regarding the proposed increases of meat prices, the butchers particularly requesting a greater increase. It was decided to recommend to the Joint Food Control Committees that larger increases should be permitted on the better joints of both beef and mutton.

The Executive Officer then reported that he had received complaints of the price charged for sugar by one of the town's retailers, and that upon investigation he had obtained evidence that the allegations were well founded. It was therefore decided to call the attention of the retailers to the same and to issue a warning.

Further afield, it was reported that while 17 year old Miss Gladys Blatherwick was watching the operation of a tank in Nottingham, a gang of thieves cut off the long tresses of her beautiful auburn hair. So skilful were the perpetrators that she did not realise her loss until a friend called attention to it!

At the meeting of the Church School managers on Thursday, **23 January**, a most serious item was on the agenda; the cost of the amount of water used during the last quarter, £4-6s-9d, as compared to less than £2 per quarter for the three preceeding years. The Local Education Authority had upheld that the managers had to bear the cost of the carelessness of their caretaker as they (the LEA) would only pay the average of the corresponding 1915 and 1916 quarters.

It was therefore decided that the chairman would put before the caretaker, the gravity of his neglect, both in leaving the water running and not having been to clean the Infants' lavatory during the whole of the Christmas holiday until the wastage was discovered by the headmaster. The man would also have to pay the difference between the amount contributed by the LEA, the managers' share, and the total; a balance of £3-2s-0d.

In another economy measure announced today, owing to the shortage of petrol, the motor 'bus service to Raunds from Wellingborough was to be curtailed.

Thursday, **24 January**, "Wanted – A strong, intelligent Girl to help in picture framing and photographic work; good wages and permanent job to a suitable person – C W Vorley, Photographer, Raunds."

In connection with the local Savings Association, the last of a series of lantern lectures was held in the Temperance Hall on Friday, **25 January**. Mr W F Corby presided over a good attendance. The subject of the lecture was "The money behind the guns", the readings being given by Mr O Woodman, the lantern being again manipulated by Mr C W Vorley.

"Thanks – Mr and Mrs W Clark and Miss E Hall, of "Westfields", Raunds, wish to thank all kind friends for the sympathy shown to them in their great loss:

In remembrance of our dear son;
We often sit and think of him, And wonder how he died.
To think we could not say goodbye, Before he closed his eyes.

From his loving mother, dad, brother and Edith."

On Sunday afternoon, **27 January**, an organ recital was given in Chelveston Parish Church in aid of a War Shrine for "Chelveston's soldiers who are so nobly serving King and Country". Fifteen shillings and sixpence was raised.

The newly-formed Raunds branch of the Kettering and District Foremen's Society met at the Coffee Tavern on Monday, **28 January**, with Mr James Coles presiding. Following the ordinary business a general discussion took place respecting the introduction of piece work in various departments of boot factories.

Tuesday, 29 January, the Prohibition law is ratified in the United States to begin in 1920.

In response to the recently announced limits in the length of ladies boots, necessitated by the countrywide shortage of leather, the following amusing little ditty appeared in today's Evening Telegraph:

"Nellie has a little foot, in fact she has a couple,
The boots she likes to put them in, are high topped, smart and supple,
But since their height has been curtailed, she's learning where the pinch is,
Her latest war economy is, Boots of seven inches!"

"Stanwick Hospital Committee – Result of the Grand Prize Distribution in aid of the Funds of the Northampton Hospital: 1st – 7492, 2nd – 10040, 3rd – 7677 ....

We, the undersigned, certify that this draw has been duly carried out, and the above are the correct winning numbers; W J Blackwell, W R Lovell.

Prizes may be had on application to the Secretary, F Partrick, and must be claimed within seven days or forfeited. 29 January 1918."

The annual meeting of the Hospital Week Committee was held on Wednesday evening, **30 January**, and the accounts for the year showed receipts to have been £352-16s-9d, £230 of which had already been forwarded to the county treasurer. It was therefore decided to send forward a further cheque for £120, making a total of £350 for the year, thus creating a record and exceeding the previous best by £75.

The Council School managers also met this evening and were told that children under five had been excluded from the Infant's Department for three weeks on account of the prevalence of whooping cough. A letter was read from the Education Committee stating that they had agreed to an increase in the caretaker's wages of £5 per annum. The attendance report showed a decrease of 17 on the register as compared with the previous period. Mr Shelmerdine pointed out that the decrease was not peculiar to the school, but general throughout the country.

The Northamptonshire District Committee of the Agricultural Wages Board met on Thursday, **31 January**, and George E Jarvis, 41 Grove Street, was appointed as representative of the local workmen.

In the evening, the half-yearly meeting of the Distributive Co-operative Society took place, Mr T Pentelow presiding. There was some discussion with respect to the distribution of butter, margarine, and lard, and it was decided to write to the local Food Control Committee asking that the supply of fats coming into the town might be pooled so that there would be a more equal distribution.

"Increase in Price – Notice to our Readers and Newsagents – Owing to the increasing price of paper (which has now reached five times its pre-war figure), and the further Government restrictions of supplies, it has become necessary for us to follow the example of 750 other newspapers throughout the country by increasing the price of the 'Evening Telegraph' from ½d to 1d from 1 February."

FEBRUARY – In his Parish Notes, the Reverend Aldred announced the commencement of Lantern Services in the Church beginning on Ash Wednesday, then continuing on Friday evenings at 7.30pm. The work of the Missionary Society would be the subject for the first few weeks covering their activities in Japan, North West Canada, South Africa and the Holy Land.

The Vestry Class had, at their annual meeting, elected their committee as follows: secretary, V Sykes; members, W Gibbs, J Pound, F C Coles, H Putt, H Harrison and W Ellingham. They also disclosed that their social held on 24 January, had raised £4-10s-0d for the Northamptonshire Prisoner of War Fund.

The 1917 Church Accounts were published and showed that expenditure included £19-0s-0d for the hire of the Picture Palace, £4-0s-6d for Aircraft Insurance, and £1-0s-0d for "Sweeping the Walls". Parish Magazine receipts included £5-0s-0d for advertisements and £19-3s-2d for magazines sold.

Rev Aldred rejoiced in the news that at last the uniforms for the Church Lad's Brigade had arrived, noting that in future the lads would drill in khaki and attend their first Church Parade on Sunday morning, 3 February. He also announced the promotion to Lance-Corporal: Privates E Eaton, H Freeman, E Taylor, E March, K Hodson, A Lawrence and L Heath.

The results of the recent Scripture Examinations held at the Day School by the Diocesan Inspector for religious knowledge revealed that: "The Standard I children showed plenty of keenness and interest, with a good proportion in the top group of scholars showing a sound and intelligent knowledge of the syllabus; the large group examined (67) in the Infants' Department displayed an admirable knowledge of their lessons; and the babies were being very suitably taught."

Finally, added to the "Died in the Service of their Country" lists were **John William Clark (36)** and **Leonard Walter Minkley (79)**, who had both given their lives during the closing months of 1917.

Raunds men listed in the "Victims of the War" column in the Rushden Echo on Friday, **1 February**, were: Killed, **Nunley, L (83)**, 200689, Northants Regiment; and Wounded: Manning, S, 27178, Northamptons, and Brown, J G, 27588, Ox and Bucks Light Infantry.

A public meeting arranged by the Independent Labour Party was held in the Temperance Hall this evening when Mr F W Miller presided over a fair gathering. The speaker was ex-Private C J Simmons (late Worcester Regiment) who gave a very outspoken address entitled "A Message from the Trenches". On the subject of the possible resumption of peace negotiations, he declared that if the Government troubled to take a vote of the men in the trenches they would find an overwhelming majority in favour of negotiations. He claimed that the Independent Labour Party had been misrepresented as it demanded a democratic peace which would leave the world free from the menace of militarism, what was needed was a real lasting peace, instead of a patched up peace as in years gone by.

"Arthur G Brown & Sons - Notice of Sale at Raunds on Thursday, 21 February: Five Cart Horses – 'Duke', 'Kitty' (believed to be in foal), and three fillies; 14 head of Cattle – seven in-calf cows, one in-calf heifer, five yearling heifers, and one yearling bull; Five lambs; Ten Pigs – one yelt, eight young pigs, and one in-pig yelt; Poultry; and a good assortment of Farm Implements, upon the premises at Brooks Road, by instructions from Mr Wm Pettitt; sale at 11 o'clock."

At the Wesleyan Church on Sunday, **3 February**, special Home Missions services were held, and in the afternoon, solos were rendered by Mrs J W Hall, Mr J W Hall was the accompanist and the collection, in aid of the Northants Prisoner of War Fund, amounted to £20.

For stealing a cycle, the property of Mr Walter Dix, a farm labourer from Friendly Lodge Farm was fined £2 or a month in prison at Thrapston Police Court on Tuesday, **5 February**.

The town's Food Control Committee met for the last time on Wednesday evening, **6 February**, when a letter was read from the Distributive Co-operative Society expressing regret that the maximum retail price of sugar had been inadvertently exceeded, and stated that the violation of the Order would not be repeated. The Society also wrote suggesting the pooling of the supply of fats coming into the town. After discussion, it was agreed to leave the matter in the hands of the soon-to-be-appointed District Committee. Two applications from consumers asking to be allowed to change their registered sugar retailers were received, but in neither case did the committee consider the reasons sufficient to justify a change.

There then followed a special meeting of the Urban Council to receive the resignation of the local Food Control Committee in order that the course might be clear for the appointing of the proposed Joint Area Committee. The resignation was accepted and Messrs E Batchelor and W F Corby (executive officer) were elected as representatives of the town's council on the new joint committee.

The Temperance Society held their annual meeting in the Temperance Hall on Thursday evening, **7 February**. The secretary said that the society had made steady progress during the year, and he thought it was a fact to be proud of that they were able to hold their annual meeting this year in the new committee room which was free from debt.

All of the local newspapers on Friday, **8 February**, reported the appearance in the "London Gazette" of 8 January, 1918, of the award of the Meritorious Medal (sic) by His Majesty the King on 38885, Sgt-Major Medlock, G A, RAMC, "for conspicuous and distinguished service during the recent operations".

Two town men made personal appeals to the County Tribunal at Northampton today: Walter H Millard, 18, single, B2, a motor engineer, was given three months exemption subject to him being employed by the Food Production Committee as a motor tractor driver. However, Walter Davis, 35, married, the manager of the town's Co-operative Society bakery, had his exemption curtailed to 15 March despite claims by Mr W W James that the society "did 25 sacks a week".

The Food Control Joint-Committee for the Wellingborough District made up of the local committees was appointed at a meeting held at Higham Ferrers town hall this evening. Miss A Beeby represented Raunds at the meeting.

At Wellingborough Police Court, a Raunds lad, summoned for working a horse whilst in an unfit state (the horse not the lad!), had his case dismissed. However, three Stanwick men were heavily fined for allowing the incident to occur.

And the Northamptonshire Union Bank Ltd, Raunds branch open daily, in its 81st annual report of the directors, announced a net profit of £73,937-9s-8d for 1917.

Raunds delegates attended a meeting held at Wellingborough Working Men's Club on Saturday, **9 February**, organised by the Northants Branch of the Working Men's Club and Institute Union to discuss the parliamentary bill to improve children's care and education under local authorities.

The meeting resolved to ask for the establishment of a complete school medical service for the treatment of ailing children; the reduction in size of all classes in elementary schools to 40, and ultimately 30 pupils; the abolition of all exemptions from school attendance under 14, rising to 15 within 5 years; the development of a system of free secondary education for all; and for the qualification for entrance to universities to be on merit not on money!

On Tuesday evening, **12 February**, at the Church of England Infants' School, a "Cinderella" dance was held, and was well attended, the arrangements for which were admirably carried out by Mrs A Camozzi. For dancing the music was supplied by Mr Bert Clark (violin) and Miss Clark (piano). Mr D Bamford ably carried out the duties of MC. The proceeds were in aid of the Church Lads' Brigade Equipment Fund and amounted to upwards of £6.

In connection with the branch of the Young Helpers' League, the annual box opening took place on Wednesday evening, **13 February**, at the Manor House, in the presence of the treasurer (Mrs A Camozzi) and the secretary (Miss Kirk). The boxes, when opened, were found to contain the gratifying sum of £4-2s-6d.

At the latest Local Appeals Tribunal, a dozen or so appeals were presented and exemptions until 31 March or 30 April were granted in most cases, however, four lucky applicants received conditional exemptions subject to them remaining in their existing employment. At the close of the meeting the chairman, Mr A Camozzi, JP, called attention to the recent issue of the Co-operative Society magazine "The Wheatsheaf", in which, under Raunds notes, it was alleged that local Tribunals were run in the interests of private traders and their friends. As he was the only private trader on the Tribunal he considered it was intended as a personal reflection upon him, which he considered to be hardly fair. Several of the members pointed out that the decisions given by that Tribunal in the case of Co-operative employees and which the military authorities had appealed against, proved conclusively that the Society's repeated applications had not been unfairly dealt with.

"Be Patriotic – Meat is Scarce, Try Government Scotch Herrings, 4d per lb, Sold at the 'Star Supply Stores', High Street, Raunds."

The Food Distribution Committee met on Thursday evening, **14 February**, and a letter from the Divisional Food Commissioner was read with respect of the shortage of margarine in the district and giving information that the Ministry of Food had been asked to send a consignment to Raunds as an emergency measure.

Mr Batchelor then raised the question of meat distribution and remarked that a good deal of dissatisfaction was in existence amongst the workers, who complained that if the butchers' shops were only to be opened one day a week they preferred them to be opened so that they could get meat when they were at work, and not for the weekend. Mr Bellamy responded saying that it was useless to open the shop if they had no meat to sell, and with the limited quantity allowed them, one day was quite sufficient to distribute it. It was ultimately decided to ask the butchers to meet and to agree upon which customers each would supply to lead to an equal distribution.

This evening, a public meeting, arranged by the Education Committee of the Distributive Co-operative Society, was held in the Temperance Hall, Mr T Pentelow presiding over a fair attendance. The speaker was Mr Will Rogers, of Northampton, who gave an address on "Sham and Real Democracy". During the meeting two solos were rendered by Miss Louie Smith, Mrs H Ruff accompanying at the piano.

"To Let – House and Shop, 2 High Street, Raunds, where the principal hairdressing and tobacconist business in the town has been carried on for years – Apply to W F Corby."

The award of the Military Medal to Lance-Corporal W Bettles, of Midland Road and the Northamptonshire Regiment, was celebrated in the local journals on Friday, **15 February**. The since-promoted Sergeant Bettles was a member of the Territorial Force and had been serving abroad since the start of the war. The 26 year old had gone out to Egypt in June 1917 and up to the present time had got through without a scratch. ***(Plate 26)***

A public meeting was held in the Temperance Hall this evening to consider the formation of an Allotment Association for Raunds. Mr W F Corby presided, supported by Mr A D Ground, F.R.H.S., and Mr J Shelmerdine, JP, horticultural representative. Mr Ground gave a very interesting address on the "Aims and usefulness of the Allotments Association, and the benefits of forming a local branch." After a number of questions had been asked and answered, it was unanimously decided to form an association for the town, the following officers being appointed pro tem: president, Rev E P Blackburn; secretary, Mr A D Rawlings; committee, Messrs W Lack, J Allen, G Phillips, F Bass, and F Wilmott.

Also revealed today was that the cost of maintaining Northamptonshire lunatics had nearly doubled since the war began!

In the afternoon, Mr George Lee attended planting of an oak tree in the "Mayor's Avenue", Wellingborough, by their current council chairman, Mr W Saddington, JP; Mr Lee had been the councillor's first headmaster and made "a few pleasing remarks" at the close of the ceremony.

And also at Wellingborough today, a "gang of youthful desperadoes" were found guilty at the Police Court of breaking into Irchester Railway Station and of attempting to escape while in custody by forcing the bar of the trap door. A 13 year old lad was ordered to receive six strokes of the birch, whilst his three older accomplices were committed to trial at the Quarter Sessions.

In connection with the Wesleyan Church, the annual Guild Festival was held on Sunday, **17** and Monday, **18 February**. Special services were preached on Sunday morning and evening by the Rev E A Parkes, of Bedford, at both there were good congregations. On Monday evening, Mr Parkes gave a very interesting lecture in the schoolroom on "Thoreau, the Teacher of the Simple Life". The Rev E P Blackburn preached and collections were taken at each service in aid of the Wesley Guild Funds.

The Urban Council met in the evening on the Monday and was informed that the Central Food Production Committee required them to ensure that the Hospital Field was placed under arable cultivation. As the council was without team labour and implements, it was suggested that the land be sub-let for the purpose.

The medical officer, Dr McInnes, reported 6 deaths and 4 births registered in the district during January. There were also 13 notifications of infectious diseases: six of both measles and tuberculosis, and one of erysipelas; whooping cough was also still present, necessitating in the closure of the two schools' Infants' Departments.

On Tuesday, **19 February**, four Raunds citizens appeared before the Thrapston Police Court charged with lighting offences and all received 10s-0d fines.

A very interesting and pretty wedding took place today at Lyme Regis, Dorset. The bridegroom was Mr J W Jones, Royal Engineers, and his bride was Miss Amy C Harris, of Lyme Regis. Before going to France, Mr Jones was engineer and surveyor to the Raunds Urban Council and had recently been in charge of a gang of German POWs road making behind the lines.

"Everyone knows that in Spring, when insects are plentiful, eggs are plentiful. To get eggs in Winter, give birds 'Karswood's (Harmless) Poultry Spice', containing ground insects; Packets: 2d, 6d, & 1/- from Gant, 6, High Street, Raunds."

Thursday, 21 February, Allied forces take Jericho.

A Raunds soldier stood before a special sitting of Thrapston Police Court today, charged with being a deserter from the Depot at Northampton since 27 January. Evidence of arrest was given by PC Newberry who stated that in answer to the charge, the prisoner said he did not intend to go back. The magistrate remanded the prisoner to await an escort.

"For Sale – Quantity of outside and inside good Panel Doors and Sash Windows, already glazed. Apply: Asbery & Sons, Raunds."

Special services relating to the Local Preachers' Mutual Aid Association were held in the 12 chapels of the Raunds Wesleyan Circuit on Sunday, **24 February**. The guest preacher at Brook Street was Mr Douthwaite from London and such were the power and eloquence of his addresses that collections raised over £10 and six promises were made of an annual subscription of £1-1s-0d each.

It was reported on Monday, **25 February**, that among the clergy of the Peterborough Diocese serving as chaplains to the Forces was W S Bethway, curate of Raunds.

"This week is Tank Week in Northamptonshire, and tanks will be visiting all parts of the county raising money for the War Effort!"

A curt advertisement in the Evening Telegraph on Tuesday, **26 February**, placed by the Raunds Boot Manufacturers' Association, threatened the boys and girls currently out on "illegal" strike with criminal proceedings unless they immediately returned to work. However, in their defence, the Boot and Shoe Operatives Union promised to support all those summoned. ***(Plate 9)***

On the same day, the above association held a meeting at the Coffee Tavern chaired by Mr John Adams, JP CC, who introduced the guest speaker, Mr Swaysland, as "the greatest authority on boot manufacturing in the world". The speaker was reciprocally complimentary during his lengthy address on boot manufacturing throughout the world, describing Raunds as "the most important place for making Army boots in the country!"

On Wednesday, **27 February**, the "New Inn", Ringstead, was the scene of the official inquiry into the sad case of the deaths of a father and his two young sons, whose bodies had been discovered in the village, early the previous day. After hearing evidence from several witnesses, including the parish constable and Dr Bird of Thrapston, the coroner summed up and then instructed the jury to consider their verdict; they promptly returned this as murder of the two boys by the father, followed by suicide by the latter while of unsound mind.

"Wanted – Experienced Pressman, Constant Employment, Best Wages, Apply: Neal and Gates, Raunds."

At the meeting of the new Joint Food Control Committee held at Higham Ferrers on Thursday, **28 February**, there was much discussion of the Food Controller's orders to ration meat to 20 ounces of butcher's meat per week per adult and children over 10, and half that for children up to 9 years old. And on the subject of margarine, Mr W F Corby controversially claimed that Raunds and Stanwick had not had their 1½ ounces per head since Christmas as the Wellingborough and Rushden committees had largely commandeered the wholesale supplies!

When tempers cooled it was resolved that a letter be written to the Divisional Commissioner at Nottingham protesting that supplies to Raunds and Finedon (who had also raised a similar complaint) had not been delivered.

A meeting of the Trades Union Labour Council was held in the Temperance Hall in the evening, the following associations being represented: the Boot and Shoe Operatives' Union, the Distributive Co-operative Society, General Committee and Educational Committee, the Independent Labour Party, the Amalgamated Union of Co-operative Employees, the Agricultural Labourers' Union, and the National Union of Railwaymen.

Also that evening, the Raunds Gas Company held their annual meeting at the Coffee Tavern, with Mr G E Smith in the chair. The directors' report stated that an increase of a quarter of a million cubic feet of gas had been sold as compared with the previous year. Notwithstanding the increase in the price of coal and all other materials, the profits of the company had been well maintained, without having recourse to increasing the price of gas.

And the Raunds Fire Brigade was among those represented at the North East Association of Fire Brigades' annual meeting held at Spalding today; the town's brigade boasting 13 members.

* *

W H Spicer
Plumber, Glazier, Gas-Fitter and General House Decorator
Thorpe Street, Raunds

M C Bellamy
Family Butcher
Raunds
Good Quality Sausages and Pure Lard
Quality Good, Prices Moderate

Mrs Lyne
Practical Milliner
"The London House", Raunds
Hats and Bonnets etc renovated and re-trimmed
A choice assortment of BLOUSES always in stock

* *

MARCH – The vicar opened his parish notes this month saying how glad all were to see Mr Bethway at the recent Sunday service, adding how well he thought he looked, in spite of all he had been through at the Front since last October. There was news from an old choir boy and his brother; Ernest and Charles Purser had written from somewhere in the States telling how they were both now in the Aviation Signal Corps and had recently passed their examinations in photography.

Grand Evening Concerts were to be given by the children of the Day School Upper Department on Wednesday, Thursday, and Friday of Easter week. They would consist of songs, dances, and a charming play entitled "ToMorrow". The whole of the proceeds would be devoted to the Day Schools Funds.

Finally, there was Church Lad's Brigade news; an excellent dance, arranged by Mrs Camozzi, had been held on Shrove Tuesday, in aid of the Equipment Fund. So far part of the necessary equipment had been bought, but still the band instruments and rifles remained to be purchased. Uniforms, costing £37-4s-9d, had been paid for from receipts of the dance, the "Watch Draw", and donations.

The Casualty Lists issued on Friday, **1 March**, included the name of Pte **Charles Mills (78)**, Middlesex Regiment, "missing believed drowned" in December 1917.

At lunchtime today, the employees of Messrs John Horrell and Son left off work a few minutes early to make a presentation to Mr R Jacobs, a foreman of the firm, who was leaving Raunds to take up a boot repairing business at Kettering. The presentation of a beautiful timepiece was made by Mr J C Horrell who expressed the regret of the firm that Mr Jacobs was leaving them after many faithful years' service, but wished him well in his new venture.

A major feature of today's "Cousin Claude" children's page in the Kettering Leader was a letter from Marguerite Garner, of Marshall's Road, who told of how she and her brothers liked to spend their freetime reading, especially her father's "big war books with pictures of the Boer War". She added that her father was now serving in Salonika and had asked for a local paper to be sent out to him, and she had duly obliged with the latest edition of the Leader.

For her contribution, Marguerite was "highly commended", as were the town's H W Lawrence, Evelyn P Sharman, and Eric W Turner for their efforts. Edith Coles, of Marshall's Road, went one better being awarded a "Goodwill Pencil" in the latest "Popular Penmanship" competition, whilst John Richardson also received a commendation.

The annual meeting of the Northamptonshire District Rechabites took place at Rushden on Saturday, **2 March**. Raunds representatives were Brothers H W Lawrence, G T Brown, J Harrison, and J P Hull. Among the resolutions passed were a proposed levy of 1s-6d per annum on all members not on active service to cover the contributions of members who were on active service, and a protest against the use of food stuffs for the making of alcoholic drinks during the war.

The first meeting of the newly constituted Co-operative Council for East Northants took place at Wellingborough's Garden Street Rooms and of the officials elected, Mr J Coles was chosen to represent Raunds.

In the evening, a well attended whist drive and dance were held in the Temperance Hall arranged by the employees of the St Crispin Productive Society, in aid of a fund to provide their fellow employees who were on service with comforts. In the whist drive, Mrs R Abbott took first prize for ladies, Mrs H Clark being second; Mr John Allen won the first gentlemen's prize, the second being won by Mr V Vorley. Dancing was then indulged in, the music being supplied by Messrs J H Stubbs (piano) and Bert Clarke (violin); Mr E Batchelor was the MC.

On Monday morning, **4 March**, the death occurred of Mrs Ellen Rooksby, Red Row; widow of the late Mr Owen Rooksby. The seventy-five year old had been ill for a considerable time. She left two sons to mourn their loss.

A newspaper snippet today stated that since the outbreak of war, over 1,250,000 servicemen had been fed at the buffet at Waterloo Station!

The Confirmation service was held on Thursday evening, **7 March**, in the Parish Church when the Bishop of Leicester inducted 46 candidates.

The result of "Tank Week" in the county was announced on Friday, **8 March**. An impressive total of £1,609,951 was subscribed, with Rushden, over £90,000, and Irthlingborough, £52,000, at the head of the list. Somewhat pointedly, the town of Raunds was highlighted as having decided to take no official part in the effort, although no reason was given!

At Thrapston Police Court today, the local constabulary objected to the renewal of the cinematograph licence of the Raunds Picture Palace on account of the law proceedings in 1917. Despite representation by the applicant's solicitor that the offences referred to related to the previous licensee, and producing many favourable testimonials from the residents of Raunds as to the conduct of the establishment and of the good quality pictures shown, the Bench, after much deliberation in private, would only grant a final extension until 6 April, to enable the tenancy notice of one month to be served.

In the evening, the newly-formed town Allotment Association met with the Rev E P Blackburn in the chair and over 60 members attending. The officers and committee members were formally elected following on from the meeting of Friday, 15 February. It was decided that the name be "The Raunds Allotments' and Smallholders' Association".

The preacher at the Wesleyan Church on Sunday, **10 March**, was the Rev J Shrimpton, of Bedford. In the afternoon he spoke on "Our Mercies", solos were rendered by Mrs W T L Flood, of Rushden, with Mr J W Hall accompanying at the organ. Collections were taken for the Palestine Famine Fund.

At the fortnightly meeting of the Raunds branch of the Kettering and District Shoe Trade Foremen's Association on Monday, **11 March**, Mr W Childs, of Rushden, gave an interesting paper on "Forme cutting and marking up of lasts". He illustrated his talk with examples of lasts and patterns.

"Raunds people can assist to avert the paper famine by sending their waste paper to 'Journal' Dept, Thrapston, 'Argus' Dept, Rushden, or 'News' Dept, Wellingborough."

The Thrapston Board of Guardians met at the Poor Law Institution on Tuesday morning, **12 March**. The annual return of the vaccination officer (for 1916): in Raunds of 149 births, only 9 were successfully vaccinated, with 132 statutory declarations being made, caused much discussion culminating in the chairman concluding that "we might as well abolish the whole thing and save money!"

A recital was given in the Baptist Chapel on Wednesday, **13 March**, by Dr C H Merrill (Mus D Dunelm FRCO) who was a native of Raunds, and whose visit was greatly appreciated. The occasion was the reopening of the organ which had been practically remade, only a few pipes and the case being used. The work was carried out by Mr J Tanner. Mr W H Lovell presided at the opening, and Miss Louie Smith was the vocalist, the whole of the proceedings being of a most satisfactory character, both musically and financially.

A Food Control meeting took place in the Council School on Thursday evening, **14 March**, when among the topics discussed were new meat and food application card forms, the postponement by the Ministry of Food of the scheme for controlled distribution of margarine, a question from the Distributive Co-operative Society as to who they should approach with respect to fixing the wholesale price of fish, the inclusion of boot factory hands in the district list for additional rations, the question of sugar for jam-making, and the inclusion of dairy butter in the general scheme of food distribution.

"Wanted – good Pressman for Army and Navy work, good wages, constant employment; Apply: Tebbutt and Hall Bros Ltd, Raunds."

The result of the election for the new assistant secretary of the local branch of the Boot and Shoe Operatives Union was announced on Friday, **15 March**, with Raunds' Mr E Batchelor taking the honours. A resident of the town for 22 years and a member of several civic committees, he polled 520 of the 847 votes cast.

On Saturday, **16 March**, the marriage of Pte Leonard Hodson, Army Service Corps, the eldest son of Councillor and Mrs James Hodson, to Miss Dora Bawcutt, of Kingsthorpe, took place at the Parish Church. The bridegroom was attended by Mr Owen Pentelow, bandmaster of the Temperance Band, and Misses Minnie Hodson and Winnie Bawcutt were the bridesmaids. The bridegroom was a member of the band before joining the Colours, and members of the band met the newlyweds at the bottom of Church Hill and played in front of the carriage to the residence of the bridegroom's parents, where the reception was held.

The quarterly meeting of the Raunds Circuit of the Wesleyan Methodist Church was held this afternoon. The meeting heard that membership had grown by 11 on the quarter and 25 on the year, the current membership being 520. General receipts had exceeded expenditure by £7-2s-4d, and the increase in the stipends of both ministers was unanimously approved. The Preachers' Conveyance Fund had a balance in hand of £8-12s-6d, Mr W F Corby being heartily thanked for his work in this area, and the Circuit Magazine account showed a balance in hand for the year of £2-18s-5d, which, in view of the extra cost of printing, was considered to be most gratifying. Hearty invitations were given to the Revs E P Blackburn and J L Gillians to remain another year in the Circuit, which was accepted in both cases. The members of the meeting and other friends were then entertained to a war-time tea by Mr A Hazeldine.

In the evening a public dance was held in the Temperance Hall arranged by the Temperance Band, in aid of the Temperance Society funds. There was a good company present and the music was supplied by members of the band.

Mrs Augusta Willmott, wife of Mr Arthur Willmott, Hill Street, died suddenly on Sunday morning, **17 March**, although she had been out and about and apparently in good health the previous day.

The Urban Council held its monthly meeting on Monday, **18 March**, and before the commencement of business, the chairman congratulated Mr Batchelor on his election to the office of assistant secretary to the local branch of the Union of Boot and Shoe Operatives. The medical officer, Dr McInnes, reported seven deaths and four births registered in February (all four births were girls!), four of the deaths were of persons over 65, the other three children under 5, from whooping cough and its complications.

A plan showing the proposed alterations to the "Wellington Works" for Messrs Lane and Hulett was approved. Correspondence was read with respect to putting under arable cultivation the Hospital Field, and it was decided to get in a crop of mustard, if approval was obtained. Messrs James Adams, James Hodson, J Shelmerdine, and G E Smith were then reappointed overseers for the year.

Finally, the annual report of the Fire Brigade was submitted, and it was decided to convey the thanks of the council to Captain Adams and his men, and offer the congratulations of the council on the efficiency of the brigade.

At Thrapston Petty Sessions on Tuesday, **19 March**, two Raunds married women cross-summoned one another for assault. The Bench, however, considered this to be a family feud, dismissing both cases; each party having to pay their own costs.

Also appearing in the dock was a Raunds farmer, summoned for attempting to have barley, which was fit for human food, ground for pig food. At the hearing he withdrew his original plea of not guilty and changed it to guilty explaining that he had only taken this action to try to save his pigs, which he now had to sell at a loss. He was fined £3 plus £1-2s-6d costs, the chairman adding that future cases would not be treated so leniently.

Wednesday, **20 March**, "Notice to Boot Repairers – a meeting will be held in the Ambulance Rooms, Station Road, Rushden, on Thursday 21 March, at 5.45pm for the purpose of forming a Rushden and District Boot Repairers' Association. Traders from Raunds, Irthlingborough, Finedon, Irchester, and Higham Ferrers are invited to attend. Particulars of the Rationing Scheme will be given and arrangements made for registration."

Thursday, 21 March, the Germans launch their first spring offensive, "Operation Michael". Arthur Abbott (8a), killed in action, John Archer (14), died.

After not suffering a war casualty for nearly three months, the town was about to be rocked by the loss of ten men in as many days as the Germans made their final bid for victory before the arrival at the front of many thousands of United States servicemen tipped the balance overwhelmingly in favour of the Allies.

Friday, 22 March, Frederick Norris (81) & Frank Herbert Shrives (103), both killed in action.

Saturday, 23 March, "Big Bertha" begins shelling Paris from 74 miles.

"Wanted – Hairdresser's Assistant (junior or discharged soldier would do); good chance and wages; Apply: W Dodson, Hairdresser, Ringstead."

Sunday, 24 March, George Webb (122), died of wounds & George James Whitmore (131), killed in action.

In the middle of a grim few days for the town, Lt **A C Masters (77)**, RFC, paid a flying visit to Raunds today and gave a daring aerial display which was watched by local folk with intense interest. He then landed at Irthlingborough, where his machine was put under guard, before resuming his journey the next morning.

Daylight Saving began today for the next 27 weeks, and with the dates adopted this year, 24 March to 29 September, summertime was extended by five weeks. The measure was expected to produce increased food production from allotments and greater economy in fuel and light.

Monday, 25 March, 2nd Lieutenant Walter Tull is killed in action.

Mr Mason gave an address on "Boot Closing" at the Shoe Trade Managers' and Foremens' Association meeting held at the Coffee Tavern this evening. A discussion subsequently arose regarding the crimping machines in Army uppers.

A Raunds man, Mr Owen Bugby, 73, of High Street, died in the Thrapston Workhouse Infirmary today from injuries sustained on 5 January. The deceased had been walking in the roadway in Hill Street when he was knocked down by a 4-wheel trolley owned by Palmers Stores. He was taken to his home by PC Newbury and Dr McInnes was called, and found to have fractured his collar bone and a rib. He had been transferred to the Infirmary a few days later where he was attended by the medical officer to the workhouse. He subsequently became ill with jaundice and died today. The coroner did not consider an inquest necessary.

Thursday, 28 March, the German advance is halted. This is the final turning point of the war. William Henry Groom (56), killed in action.

"Wanted – Labourers and Painters for Kettering and Raunds; Top wages and out-of-town expenses paid. Apply to: O P Driver and Sons, Contractors, Kettering."

Friday, 29 March, Jack Chapman Coles (40), killed in action.

Today was Good Friday and in the Wesleyan Church, the Rev E P Blackburn conducted a service in the vestry which was well attended. Meanwhile, at the Parish Church, the usual three hour service was held from 12 noon until 3pm when the preacher was the Rev P Robson of Rushden. In the evening a good congregation gathered for a lantern service.

Meanwhile at Higham Ferrers, a cow with suspected anthrax was cremated under the supervision of local police officers.

And as a reminder to those at home that the war was not only just being fought on the Western Front, the Kettering Leader published a photograph of "Northants Men in India" showing men of the Middlesex Regiment on the North West Frontier at Solan; one of the men pictured being Pte H Burton of Raunds.

On Saturday, **30 March**, it was revealed that the recent wholesale rejection of Army boots by the War Office had caused great dissatisfaction among manufacturers, especially as no indication had been given as to the alleged defects.

Also today, it was stated that in 1917 the county had produced 16,000 tons of potatoes, but consumed 27,300 tons, a deficit of 11,300 tons, prompting Lord Rhondda to appeal to every man who had a farm, garden or allotment to plant more of the crop and make the county self supporting!

Sunday, 31 March, Horace Bugby (29) & Jack Pentelow (89), both killed in action.

* *

CW VORLEY
Photographer & Picture Framer
Brook Street, Raunds
A fine selection of Ready-Made Frames and Mouldings
Satisfaction guaranteed in any kind of
Photographic Work
Photographs copied for Lockets and Enlargements

* *

6 – April to June 1918

Conscription for women and 401 jam makers.

APRIL – The Rev C C Aldred began his April Parish Notes with the news that he would be leaving Raunds for Abington, Northampton in June. He said that it was always hard to leave people who are kind and sympathetic, especially at a time like the present, but all should pray for him who will come to the town and give him the same generous welcome that he, himself, had received.

As a closing gift to the town, he proposed the creation of a "War Shrine" in the Church and asked for relatives of men who had fallen to send to him a photograph of their loved one. These would be placed on display in a frame "as some slight token of our respect for the sacrifice they have made for us".

The results of two fund raising events closed the month's notes: Mrs Camozzi's Easter Tuesday dance in aid of the School Funds had realised £7; and the school concerts held that week had raised over £21 clear of expenses. Special thanks were expressed to Mr Rawlings, his teachers, the children, and several willing helpers, who had put in an immense amount of work on the production.

Monday, 1 April, the Royal Air Force and Women's Royal Air Force are formed.

As the shortage of coal in the country bit deeper, a new gas and electricity rationing scheme began on Tuesday, **2 April**, whereby the consumption in any quarter, for any purpose whatsoever, had to be reduced by one sixth. There were some exemptions: hospitals, nursing homes, the railways, and Ministry of Munitions' establishments; but the restrictions would affect everyday life, for example: no hot meal could be cooked or served in a restaurant, boarding-house or club between 9.30pm and 5am, no lights could be used in theatres, music-halls, kinemagraph halls or other places of entertainment between 10.30pm and 1pm, and no lights could be used at any time in shop fronts.

A very pretty wedding was solemnised at the Parish Church this afternoon when Mr F W Evans, of Rotherham, late of Raunds, married Miss E B C Kirk, only daughter of the late Mr F Kirk, and granddaughter of Mrs Amos, of Thorpe Street.

"In Memoriam – In ever loving memory of our dear son and brother, **John William Elliot (48)**, Pte, Royal Enniskilling Fusiliers, who was killed in action in France, 1 April, 1917:

One year has passed, our hearts still sore, As time goes on, we miss him more;
No morning dawns, no night returns, But what we think of him,
How hard it is to part with those, We hold on earth so dear;
The heart no greater trial knows, No sorrow more severe.
We know, dear one, you did your best, May God grant you eternal rest.

From his loving mother and father, sisters and brothers, Raunds, 1 April, 1918.

"Raunds Footballer Killed by Gas"; on Wednesday, **3 April**, news reached the wife of Pte **George Webb (122)**, Machine Gun Corps, that her husband had died in France from the effects of gas. "Pudden" was well known in local football circles having once been both captain and centre forward for Raunds Town.

Locally, the death was recorded of old Rance inhabitant Mr Alfred Nunley, of Hill Street. The 79 year old had been confined to his bed for about 18 months.

On Thursday, **4 April**, it was reported that Pte Ralph Cox, of Hill Street and the Northamptons, had been admitted to the 12th (St Louis, USA) General Hospital, Rouen, with shrapnel wounds in the neck.

In the afternoon and evening the annual meeting of the Rushden, Thrapston and District Sunday School Union was held at the Ringstead Baptist Chapel. Miss A Beeby, of Raunds, was re-elected hon sec of the International Bible Reading Society and was also re-appointed as one of the district's Scripture examiners.

The Raunds District Old Age Pension Sub-Committee met in the evening and considered seven new claims. Three were allowed at full rate of 5s-0d and one at 3s-0d per week; the other three were disallowed, one on grounds of excessive means and two as the applicants would not attain the statutory age until 1920.

Friday, 5 April, the Germans call off "Operation Michael". Richard Smith (106) & Ernest White (126), both killed in action.

Monday, **8 April**, "Victoria Theatre, Kettering – Tu/We/Th: The Sensation of London – The Great Bairnsfather Musical Play: 'The Better 'Ole" as played at the Oxford Theatre, London.

Prices: 6d to 3/- (tax extra), 'The Better 'Ole" is the Greatest Draw in London!"

Tuesday, 9 April, the Germans begin their second spring offensive around Armentieres.

News of three more Raunds men appeared in the local press today. The first, and most alarming, concerned the disappearance of Pte **John Archer (14)**, of Thorpe Street and the Norfolks, during a German attack on 21 March. He was subsequently listed as "missing presumed killed" by the Army Council. The next related to Pte Albert Webb, of Chelveston Road and the Machine Gun Corps, brother of **George Webb (122)**, who, like his brother, had been a victim of gas and was now recovering in a Casualty Clearing Station. Finally, it was reported that Pte Peter York, of Newtown Road and the Yorkshires, was recovering in hospital in Cardiff from wounds to the mouth.

The Thrapston Guardians met this morning and accepted the following tenders: Funerals, Mr James Lawrence, Raunds, £3-13s-6d (coffin @ £3, hire of hearse @ 13s-6d), an increase of 5s-0d on the previous year; coke for the Children's Home Raunds Gas Co, 27s-0d per ton, provided there is coke at the works when required.

Nationally, it was announced in Parliament today that every man who was 50 and under would now be liable to military service under the new Man Power Bill.

The Church School managers met this evening to interview the two job applicants they had discussed the previous Friday. The outcome, however, was disappointing in both cases. At the weekend, Miss Oakley had visited the Rev Aldred and told him she had now taken another post; whereas Miss Childs stated that she would not consider accepting the position for less than £100 pa (the post was advertised at £90 pa plus £5 for every two years certificated). The managers decided that, from what they saw of the applicant, she did not meet their requirements.

"Raunds Bandsman Killed" referred to the news received on Wednesday **10 April**, by Mr and Mrs Walter Bugby, of Grove Street, that there only son, Pte **Horace Bugby (29)**, of the Northamptons, had been killed in action. Horace was a well known musician and member of the Raunds Temperance Band.

Another town man met his end today, this time much closer to home. James Moules was working on the roof of the new works of the Northampton Electric Light Co Ltd at Hardingstone, when he fell 45 feet and was badly injured. He was picked up in an unconscious condition and conveyed to hospital, where he died.

Over 800 boot trade cases were presented at the County Tribunal today including the following from Raunds and district: Adams Bros, 15; R Coggins and Sons, 11; John Horrell and Son, 3; Walter Lawrence, 5; Neal and Gates, 2; C E Nichols, 4; Regulation Boot Co, 7; St Crispin Productive Society, 7; Owen Smith, 5; Tebbutt and Hall Bros, 4; Unity Co-operative Society (Ringstead), 5; John J Peck (Stanwick), 2. All cases were granted open exemption until 31 July.

"Wanted – General: Cycle for girl aged 10, must be in good condition: Fred Corby, Raunds."

Thursday, 11 April, George William Thurlow (115), killed in action.

At the Local Appeals Tribunal this evening, there were ten applications for exemption, most of which were adjourned to allow the members to understand the conditions of the new Bill going through Parliament; to this one member remarked that "soon we might be appealing for ourselves!"

However, one case that they did rule on was of our old friend, farmer Strangward, who held a certificate from the County Food Control Committee; the members agreeing that exemption could continue as long as the certificate remained valid.

Also today, it was reported that two children had appeared at their local Food Control office with seven rat's tails for which they asked 7d, and were very disappointed to be told that there was "nothing doing".

Friday, 12 April, Ralph Pentelow (91), killed in action.

At the County Tribunal held today, the manager of the Co-operative Society bakery department made a personal appeal for exemption. It was said that the Society had been unable to obtain a substitute for him and they baked 25 sacks of flour weekly. Countering this Captain Cook suggested that a woman might be found to do the work. A final two months was granted subject to substitution.

"In Memoriam – In ever loving memory of Lance Corporal **John Henry Bamford (19)**, killed in action, 11 April, 1911:

No one knows how much we miss him, Some may think the wound has healed,
But they cannot see the sorrow, Deep within our heart concealed.

From his loving wife, mother and father.

Saturday, **13 April**, "Raunds Food Control Committee – Wanted: Competent Person to take charge of the Office (male or female), previous office experience essential, typewriting and shorthand desirable. Applications, stating age and qualifications, and salary required, to be sent to the undersigned not later than Tuesday, 16 April. W F Corby, Executive Officer, Local Food Office, Raunds."

"Thanks – Mr and Mrs J P Archer, 12 Park Road, Raunds, desire to thank their many friends for their expressions of sympathy shown to them in their great sorrow."

Sunday, 14 April, Marshall Foch is appointed Colonel-in-Chief of the Allied forces on the Western Front.

One wonders if Rance boot manufacturers and workers would have felt any sympathy when they read on Monday, **15 April**, that in Germany, 28,000 out of 31,000 boot and shoe factories had closed and dismissed their employees; and the remaining 3,000 businesses were having to pay a monthly subvention to the closed establishments, hence the high price of German boots and shoes.

The Urban Council met this evening and Mr E Batchelor was elected chairman for the coming year, with Mr J Shelmerdine as vice-chair after Mr W Gates declined the offer. After it was resolved to write to Mr L G H Lee and Mr Jones, the surveyor, both of whom were in France, the members turned to the day's business.

A letter was read from the London and North-Western Railway Co with respect to the train service on the Northampton to Peterborough branch, regretting that no departure from the current timetable could be made. The medical officer, Dr McInnes, reported two cases of measles and three of tuberculosis during March; and five deaths and four births (all male) had been registered.

His annual report showed: the estimated population of the town in 1917, 4009; total number of births, 62, 23 males and 39 females, below the national average; total number of illegitimate births, 5; total number of deaths, 41, below the national average; number of deaths from tuberculosis, 9, including 6 of pulmonary tuberculosis (1 male and 5 female), 1 of tuberculosis meningitis, and 2 of other related diseases; total number of infectious diseases notified, 28, of which 16 were of tuberculosis (including 10 of the lungs), 6 of German measles, 4 of erysipelas, and 1 each of diphtheria and cerebro-spinal fever. At the end of 1917 an epidemic of whooping cough was just developing, and was to see its height in early 1918. The veterinary inspector had carried out 494 inspections of cows and heifers, and found 11 secreting milk unfit for human consumption; these were kept under observation until sold or slaughtered.

The monthly meeting of the Factory Foremen, held in the Temperance Hall, heard an address from Mr E Catlin, leather factor, on "The prospects for Raunds after the war". His main thrust was that Army contracts would be distributed over a much larger area and that the town would be wise to try to create a civilian trade.

An old and highly respected inhabitant of the town died this evening in the person of 89 year old Mrs Augusta (Gusta) Bailey, widow of the late Mr John Bailey. For a great number of years she had carried out the duties of nurse and midwife.

At the Thrapston Petty Sessions on Tuesday, **16 April**, the Raunds Distributive Co-operative Society were fined £30, including costs, for selling fish at a price exceeding the maximum price provided by the Fish Prices Order, 1918.

On the same "bill", a Raunds farmer was summoned for selling certain hay to a Sudborough man, contrary to the Defence of the Realm Regulations. The case against the defendant was that he had sold 15cwt of sainfoin, which had been "reserved" by an Army buyer, to his farmer colleague. Pleading not guilty, the accused explained that the load was his settlement of a debt for using a mower. The Bench accepted this explanation and dismissed the case with just a caution.

On Wednesday, **17 April**, heavy rains caused large areas of the Nene Valley to become flooded with many allotments on low-lying land being under water.

"We Are Seven!" headlined an illustrated story in the Kettering Leader of Friday, **19 April**, and told of the seven Smith soldier brothers of "A Patriotic Raunds Family": Albert, Alfred, Arthur, Ernest, Richard, Sydney, and Walter. Sadly the publishing of the story coincided with the unofficial news being received that Pte **Richard Smith (106)**, Essex Regiment, one of the Raunds Boot Marchers of 1905, had been killed in action the previous week.

Two other Raunds men were also reported as wounded today; Pte H Agutter, Sussex Regiment, and Pte Herbert Arnold, Northumberland Fusiliers, both former Grove Street residents.

On a more cheery note, young Wesley Lawrence, of Lawson Street, raised a few smiles when his limerick was published today in a local journal:

There was a young ruffian called Fred, Who received a hard crack on his head,
He went in home crying, But he didn't mind lying, An hour or two extra in bed!

Saturday, 20 April, Charles Hall (58), killed in action.

Today it was announced that the Duston War Hospital was being reserved for neurasthenics or shellshock cases only.

Sunday, 21 April, the "Red Baron" is shot down.

Monday / Tuesday, 22 & 23 April, Zeebrugge and Ostend are raided by the Allies.

"Monday, **22 April**, – Food Rationing News: Lard, which has been on the 'free' list, when obtainable, will be rationed from 13 July."

News of the deaths of two more town men appeared in the journals of Thursday, **25 April**. Mrs Thomas Hall, of Harcourt Street, had received a letter informing her that her eldest son, 18 year old Pte **George Thurlow (115)**, London Regiment, had been killed in action on 11 April, just eight days after arriving in France! And down by "The Globe", Mrs J Pentelow, of Beech Hill, had also received a letter with the sad news that her second son, Pte **Jack Pentelow (89)**, East Surreys, had been lost sometime between 31 March and 4 April.

It was announced today that a "Conscription for Women Bill" was soon to be brought before Parliament. The proposer, Sir William Bull, was suggesting that all women between ages of 19 and 31 be conscripted, adding that he had received much correspondence from women over 31 supporting the idea!

"A Hero's Death – Raunds Man Slain Whilst Rescuing Wounded", was the stirring headline that appeared on Friday, **26 April**. Mr and Mrs G Norris, of Marshall's Road, had received the sad news that their eldest son, L-Cpl **Frederick Norris (81)**, Northants Regiment, had been killed in action on 22 March.

Another tale of an apparent town "casualty" was also published today. "The Pity of it! – Fatherless Bairns of a Raunds Hero" was the caption above the photograph of Pte Ernest Richardson, Surrey Regiment, his wife and six "now fatherless" children. Pte Richardson, an elder brother of **Herbert Richardson (99)**, had been listed as "killed in action between 21 and 27 March". But for once, the story had a happy ending as Ernest was not dead but had been taken prisoner. ***(Plate 7)***

A dance was held in the Temperance Hall on Saturday evening, **27 April**, arranged by the Misses Pollard and Lawrence, for the benefit of Mrs T Tansley, Rotton Row, who had been ill and confined to bed for some months past. There was a large company present, the music being supplied by Messrs W Knighton (piano) and W Burton (violin). Mr D Bamford carried out the duties of MC.

On Monday, **29 April**, a meeting of the local War Savings Committee and representatives of affiliated associations was held in the Council School. The secretary told the gathering that the County Committee desired that local branches should take control of the neighbouring village associations and asked that Raunds look after those of Ringstead, Stanwick, and Hargrave. On the subject of the sale of National War Bonds, it was suggested that, with the co-operation of the Council and Manufacturer's Association, a special week be designated.

"Raunds Church Institute – Corresponding Number Competition for the Benefit of Mr S Busby; Winning Numbers: 1st, 3049, 2nd, 2784, 3rd, 620; Prizes to be claimed within 7 days from J Pound, Secretary, 14 Sackville Street."

On Tuesday, **30 April**, Mrs H Stubbs, of Beech Hill, received a postcard from her husband, Pte Harry Stubbs, Royal Sussex Regiment, dated 29 March, saying that he was a prisoner of war in Germany, and that he was quite well.

* *

MAY – The vicar's notes this month were brief, the only topic being the good start made towards reducing the £282 debt of the School Building Fund. Several promises had been made although there were still some "promise cards" free should anyone else have been willing to help. He stressed that no amount was too small and thanked the following contributions already received: Mr and Mrs H Bamford, £1; Vestry Class 1917, £1-8s-0d; Mother's Union, £3; Mrs Nunley, £1; Mr W Gibbs, 5s-0d; and William Nunley, 10s-6d.

Six more names were added to the "Died in the Service of Their Country" list: **Horace Bugby (29)**, **Charles Mills (78)**, **Fred Norris (81)**, **Richard Smith (106)**, **George Webb (122)**, and William Ernest Richardson, who would later "return from the dead!"

Wednesday, 1 May, American troops join the front line at Amiens; Gavrilo Princip, assassin of Archduke Franz Ferdinand, dies of consumption in prison. Albert Charles Masters (77), died of injuries.

The Evening Telegraph of Thursday, **2 May**, published an interview with a Raunds marine, Pte S A Bamford, RMLI, son of Mr and Mrs J Bamford, Grove Street, home on seven days leave after taking part in the raid on Zeebrugge last week. Pte Bamford, who was on the "Vindictive", said that the survivors were well satisfied that they had attained their objective. Two of his brothers, Ptes **John Henry (19)** and **Thomas William (20)**, had been killed in the war in 1917.

This evening, an open air meeting arranged by the Educational Committee of the Distributive Co-operative Society was held on The Square when Mr William Rogers, of Northampton, gave an address on "More Money; God save the people".

The Old Age Pensions Sub-Committee also met this evening and a pensioner raised the question as to whether she was entitled to a pension at a higher rate owing to the death of her husband. Her pension was increased from 1s-0d to 5s-0d per week. The pension officer also raised the question with respect to a pensioner who had become an inmate of the Union, and the pension was discontinued.

For Rance folk, the Friday, **3 May's** headline that caught the attention was "Aviator Accidently Killed". The story being that Lt **A C Masters (77)**, RAF, only son of Mr Charles Masters, motor and cycle agent, had, two days previously, collided with another aeroplane, when a strap of his machine broke, and fallen a distance of 2,000 feet to his death. The twenty year old had been in training in Lincolnshire and was expected to go to France very shortly.

Another town man posted as missing this week was Pte James Moules, Cambridgeshire Regiment, son of Mrs J Moules, High Street.

An illustrated story "Northants Men in India" was published today, and showed the town's Ptes Ezra Collins and Albert Barritt, Norfolk Regiment, in front of the Bangalore Barracks.

At the Church of England School manager's meeting this evening, Miss Macleod sent in her resignation as Uncertifed Assistant in the Upper Department, and Miss Darby also resigned, on account of her money. In response to this the managers decided to ask the Local Education Authority to raise her salary by £18 to bring her into line with Miss Lodder, in the hope of persuading her to stay. Mr Rawlings' salary was next considered, and it was unanimously resolved to ask the LEA to raise his annual remuneration by £24 to £164 per annum.

The "In Days Gone By" column in the Kettering Leader recalled how, on this day in 1868, the four cornerstones were laid for the Finedon Temperance Hall and the Raunds Temperance Band "enlivened the proceedings".

The funeral of the late Lt **A C Masters (77)**, took place at the Wesleyan Church on Sunday afternoon, **5 May**. The courtege proceeded slowly from the residence of his parents headed by a number of Rushden Volunteers with reversed arms, followed by the Raunds Temperance Silver Band and representatives of many of the town's organisations and associations. The coffin was covered with the Union Jack, on which was placed the late Lieutenant's cap and belt, and carried high by six brother officers of the 61st Squadron, RAF. After the service in the Church, conducted by the Rev E P Blackburn, the procession wended its way to the graveside at the back of the Church where the burial took place. The Volunteers fired three volleys over the grave, and the buglers sounded the "Last Post" amongst the many handsome floral tributes.

On Tuesday, **7 May**, a Midland Railway labourer from Wellingborough was fined £1 with 10s-6d costs or one month in prison at Thrapston Police Court, having been found guilty of stealing two pairs of boots, the property of Edith May Black, Brook Street, Raunds.

"Thanks – Mr and Mrs C Masters wish to thank their many friends for the expression of sympathy shown to them on the death of their son, Lt **Albert C Masters (77)**, also for the floral tributes sent; Raunds, 7 May 1917."

The Local Tribunal met at the Council School on Thursday evening, **9 May**, and nine boot and shoe appeals were granted exemption until 31 July to bring them into line with other boot factory cases. The Distributive Co-operative Society appealed for three of their men and was granted similar exemptions. Thirteen other appeals were presented from various other occupations, twelve received exemptions; however, unlucky number thirteen's appeal was dismissed!

A public meeting in connection with the Allotment Association was also held this evening, in the Temperance Hall, when the address was given by Mr C F Lawrence, FRHS, Horticultural Supervisor to the County Council. The subject of the address was "Gardening in War Time" and dealt with potatoes and beans, their diseases, and remedies for them. The Rev E P Blackburn presided over a good audience, the association now numbered over 90 members.

"In Memoriam – In ever loving memory of dear **Will(iam Webb Chambers (33))**, only son of Mr and Mrs W W Chambers, 18 Beech Hill, Raunds, killed in action, 9 May, 1915 (Battle of Aubers Ridge):

Days of sadness oft come o'er us, Tears in silence often flow,
Thinking of the day we lost you, Just three years ago.

From his sorrowing father, mother, sisters and fiancée, Winifred Linnitt.

The trend of sad news continued on Friday, **10 May**, with the report of Pte **W H Groom (56)**, Northumberland Fusiliers, being wounded (this was later upgraded to "missing presumed killed"); Pte A W Hazeldine, Machine Gun Corps, being in hospital suffering from a sprained ankle; and Pte A H Clark, Northamptons, twice wounded previously, now a prisoner of war in Germany.

Two Raunds men employed by J J Peck Ltd, Stanwick, appealed to the County Tribunal today and received exemptions until 31 July in line with other shoe cases.

On the food front, it was reported today that 401 fruit growers at Raunds had applied for sugar for jam making.

And two more town youngsters collected Cousin Claude prizes this week; Sidney G Denton, of Rotton Row, winning a "Goodwill Pencil" in the "Bonnie Buttonholes" painting competition, and Edith Jessica Underwood, of Newtown Road, amusing readers with this entry in the "Are You Tickled?" competition: Teacher, "Tommy, how many is the half of 8?", Tommy, "On top or sideways?", Teacher, "What do you mean by 'on top or sidways?'", Tommy, "Why sir, half from the top of 8 is 0, and half from the side is 3!"

At the meeting of the local Co-operative Societies on Saturday, **11 May**, delegates voted overwhelmingly in protest against the fine of £30 inflicted on the Raunds Society for selling fish above the maximum price.

The funeral took place this afternoon of Salvationist Miss Doris Norris, who had passed away the previous Tuesday after a long illness. A full Salvation Army funeral was conducted in the Citadel by Captain Cecil Chapman; a band attended made up of Wellingborough, Rushden, and Raunds bandsmen, also a number of small girls, dressed in white and each carrying a bunch of white flowers, represented the Sunday School. The procession marched to the cemetery, where Captain Chapman oversaw the interment watched by a gathering of nearly 200, many from the Regulation Boot Company and Messrs Adams Bros as well as family and other friends.

This evening, the members of the Raunds Temperance Band paraded the town, when a house to house collection was taken for the benefit of Mrs T Tansley and Mrs A Richardson, of Rotton Row, both of whom had been ill for some months past. A corresponding number competition also took place for the same persons.

The Urban Council met on Monday, **13 May**, and heard in a letter from the Wellingborough Motor Omnibus Company that they were unable to give Raunds a better service, and warned that before long, owing to the shortage of drivers and petrol, would have to discontinue some routes altogether. Letters were also read from Councillor L G H Lee and Cpl J W Jones (surveyor), both who were on active service in France, thanking the members for the good wishes sent to them from the annual meeting.

The medical officer, Dr McInnes, reported five deaths and seven births registered during April, with three cases of infectious diseases being notified. The Surveyor and Inspector presented his report upon which the following propositions arose: That the bridge on the Station road be repaired, and the watercourse from that point down Vicarage road be cleaned out; and that a house in Marshall's Road be disinfected and the bedding destroyed, following a case of acute tuberculosis.

Finally, the members considered a letter from the Registrar General and subsequent recommendation of the Thrapston Guardians, that, following the death of the Registrar for the Thrapston Sub-District, the Thrapston and Raunds districts be amalgamated for the purpose of the registration of births and deaths. The council agreed to this as a temporary measure for the duration of the war.

"Thanks – Mrs T Hall and Family, 3 Harcourt Street, Raunds, wish to thank their many friends for their kind sympathy in the sad loss of their dear son and brother, Pte **George Thurlow (115)**, killed in action in France on 11 April."

"Luxury Tax – From the appointed date there shall be charged: On all payments made in respect of goods sold or supplied, accommodation supplied, or service rendered, at any place of luxury in Great Britain or Ireland, an Excise duty of an amount equal to one-sixth part of the payment. Luxury articles of less than one shilling in value are exempt. The duty is recoverable from the seller and is to be denoted by and collected by stamps."

The annual meeting of the Raunds and District Nursing Association was held in the Temperance Hall on the evening of Tuesday, **14 May**. In her report, the secretary, Mrs J V Spicer, stated that membership currently numbered 548; the balance sheet showed receipts of £132-15s-3d, and expenditure of £89-17s-5½d. On a more disappointing note, a letter was read from Nurse Pym resigning her position as she was taking up an appointment in Warwick. Her resignation was accepted with regret; several members remarking on the excellent manner in which she had discharged her duties during the short time she had been at Raunds.

Percy F Rushton, bank clerk, 37, married, Grade 2, of Thrapston, appeared before the County Tribunal today. He was said to be "practically the manager of the Raunds branch, and the only skilled man left at the bank apart from the manager at Thrapston". He received a further three month's open exemption.

"Wanted, for shoe room, a good Man for treeing machine; also a first class Operator on forepart parer (finishing dept); R Coggins and Sons Ltd, Raunds."

The C of E School managers met again on Wednesday, **15 May**, and decided to ask the Local Education Authority to advertise the position of Headmistress of the Infants' School. An application was received from J H Stubbs for the post of certified assistant in the Upper Schoool and the managers decided to ascertain from the secretary of the LEA the position of Mr Rawlings as regards military service if Mr Stubbs should be appointed.

The identity of the new vicar was revealed on Thursday, **16 May**, when the Bishop of Peterborough confirmed the benefice of Raunds upon the Rev Cecil Curtis, curate of St Mark's, Peterborough, in succession to the Rev C C Aldred.

"Wanted – Two Rooms in Raunds for the District Nurse; Apply, stating terms, to Mrs J V Spicer, 29 Park Road, Raunds."

"Thanks – Mr and Mrs Norris, of Raunds, desire to offer thanks to all who have shown such kindness and sympathy in the time of their bereavement."

On Friday, **17 May**, another Raunds man, Pte **G Whitmore (131)**, Northants Regiment, was reported as missing; again this would later be amended to "missing presumed killed". His wife had contacted the commanding officer of his unit regarding his welfare and received the regretful news in reply.

The Food Controller today announced the abolishing in Great Britain of the compulsory meatless day in eating places; the change being made in view of the new meat rationing measures.

"To Be Sold by Auction by Messrs Pendered and Son Ltd, at the 'Hind Hotel', Wellingborough, on Wednesday, 29 May, at 4 for 5 o'clock: Raunds Meadow, for a considerable distance adjoining the L & N W Railway and recently purchased by the late Mr Walters with a view of acquiring sidings for working the valuable beds of iron ore and limestone under the land."

Sunday / Monday, 19 & 20 May, the last and largest German air raid on Britain leaves 49 civilians dead.

The Temperance Band, conducted by Mr Owen Pentelow, gave a concert on The Square after divine services on Whitsunday evening, **19 May**, in aid of band funds.

The anniversary of the Baptist Sunday School was celebrated today when the services were conducted by Pastor Goodenough, of Chatteris.

An aeroplane crash landed in a field off the Raunds to Stanwick road on Monday, **20 May**. The aircraft had circled over the district for some time, clearly experiencing engine trouble, the pilot looking for a suitable landing place. As the machine crossed the road it hit the telephone wires and smashed one of the poles; one of the wings was broken off and it came down nose first in the field. The propeller was smashed and the engine partly buried in the ground. Fortunately, the airman, Lt Calverly, from Wyton Camp, escaped unhurt.

Away from the aviatory tribulations, at the Parish Church, the Central Northants Association of Church Bellringers held their annual meeting. Ringing commenced at 11am, but owing to food restrictions, the usual luncheon was omitted.

At the County Appeals Tribunal at Northampton on Wednesday, **22 May**, Ernest A Warth, a Raunds agricultural case, was granted a three month (open) exemption.

"Catarrhal May is a byword. Prevent and cure Nasal Catarrh, Head Colds, Hay Fever, and nose and throat infections by using 'Nostraline' Nasal Specific. Instant Relief or money back; 1s-3d bottles from Alice M Gant, High Street, Raunds."

On Thursday, **23 May**, it was reported that Denford had been the rendezvous of Whitsun holidaymakers from all round the district, especially from Kettering, on Monday and Tuesday. The two boathouses were full of people and it was almost impossible to obtain a boat without waiting a considerable time. Bathing in the River Nene was also very much enjoyed by the young people.

The casualty lists continued to bring grief for the town on Friday, **24 May**, with the death finally being presumed of Pte **J Spicer (110)**, Machine Gun Corps, some eight months after he had been listed as missing. Added to the "Wounded" list were Pte A Allen, Middlesex Regt, and Ptes J Burgin and **F H Shrives (103)**, both of the Northamptons; and once more, the latter would later be presumed "killed in action".

The extraordinary story of a Wellingborough Salvationist soldier's bogus Victoria Cross claim also appeared today. The private, stationed at Chatham with the Salvation Army Band attached to the Northants Regiment, had previously submitted the story of his daring deeds and investiture to the local newspapers, but on investigation these had been proved to be totally false!

Saturday, **25 May**, "Wanted – Queen Mary's Army Auxiliary Corps: the War Office requires at once 5,000 Cooks and 2,000 Waitresses for service with the Army at Home. Men are urgently needed in France, and every woman will release a soldier. Forewoman Cooks: £45 pa, Forewoman Waitresses: £40 pa, Assistant Cooks and Waitresses: £25; Board, Lodging, and Uniform provided."

Monday, 27 May, the third German spring offensive, codename "Blucher", is launched starting the Third Battle of the Aisne. Herbert Bates (22), killed in action & Sydney Smith (108), died of wounds.

Mr A G Brown today offered for sale by auction, by instruction of Messrs P Phipps and Co, the property in West Street, until recently licensed premises, known as the "Barber's Arms Inn", and paddock, stablings etc. The lot was started at £200, but at £340 it was withdrawn.

"Wanted – Strong Youth for farm and dairy work; good wages; can live in if desired: Amos Lawrence, "The Hall", Raunds."

Tuesday, 28 May, the Battle of Cantigny, the United States 1st Division wins its first independent action.

The Ministry of Food today again urged people patriotically to eat frozen meat, of which there was a large supply. Meanwhile in Rushden, the news that a shopkeeper was selling two boxes of matches per person resulted in a big rush and the rapid sale of the whole stock.

Friday, **31 May**, and the month closed with five more Raunds men, all of the Northamptons, appearing on the Casualty lists: Pte **Ernest White (126)**, son of Mrs E White, 80c High Street, and Pte E J Elliott, being reported missing; Ptes R W Cox and F S Tidbury, listed as wounded; and Pte L Arnold, a father of eight, wounded and a prisoner of war.

Two Raunds men appealed to the County Tribunal today, James P Bates, boot maker, 36, married, Class A, employed on Admiralty boots, was granted one final month's exemption; Walter H Millard, tractor driver, 18, single, Grade 3, received a six month extension, conditional on him remaining in agricultural work.

The dangerous corner near Stanwick Parish Church was accountable for what might have been a very serious accident today. Miss Florrie Dickenson, of Higham Ferrers, lost control of her machine and had a nasty spill, breaking one tooth and loosening two others, and she had a very severe shaking. Mrs A Firkins took her in and attended to her until she was able to proceed home.

There were fears today of a forthcoming rationing of tea and it was predicted that the likely allowance would be 2 oz per head per week, excluding children under 6.

Ernest Clarke, of Park Road, collected a "Goodwill Pencil" from Cousin Claude for his winning "Palestine" map drawing competition entry; Kathleen Eady was highly commended.

"Notice – On and after Monday, 24 June, no newsagent will be permitted to return unsold newspapers to the publishers. The order will make it generally necessary for newsagents to stock only newspapers that are actually on order from their customers. The 'Kettering Leader' strongly advises readers who have not already booked to do so at once to avoid disappointment."

* *

A fact worth knowing
Is that the Renowned "Nil Simile"
Brand of Ladies' and Children's
BOOTS and SHOES
Can be obtained from
F A ABBOTT, High Street, Raunds

* *

JUNE – It was very much a case of "it's goodbye from me and it's hello from him" in this month's Parish Magazine as vicars old and new said their pieces. The Rev C C Aldred wrote "My Dear Friends, you will all be glad to read the letter Mr Curtis has sent us. I feel sure you will give them the same kind welcome and generous support you have always shown us. As we shall be leaving you after 9 June, Miss Aldred and I thank you for all your kindness and friendship during the past few years, and in a very real way we wish you all – God be with you."

The Rev Cecil Curtis wrote "My Dear Friends, it is now common knowledge that the Bishop has appointed me to be the successor of your good vicar at Raunds. I fully realise the difficulty of following so good and able a man, and one who so deservedly has the confidence and friendship of his parishioners. I am at present unable to give an approximate date of my induction, but I hope the period of sequestration will not be unduly prolonged."

All who had given flowers for the War Shrine in the Church were thanked, the good reverend observing that "it is a little we can do in memory of those we love." Finally, four more names were added to the list of those who had "Died in the Service of Their Country": **Albert Masters (77)**, **Jack Pentelow (89)**, **Ralph Pentelow (91)**, and **George Thurlow (115)**.

Saturday, **1 June**, saw the annual treat for the children of members belonging to the Distributive Co-operative Society. The host assembled in glorious weather on The Square at 2 o'clock, and, headed by the Temperance Silver Band, marched to the field on the Society's farm where sports etc were held. In the evening a public meeting was held at which Mr R C Wallhead, parliamentary candidate for Coventry, addressed the gathering on "The Future of Democracy". The band then played for dancing until dark.

The Sunday School Anniversary services in connection with the Primitive Methodist Church took place on Sunday, **2 June**, when Mr Jesse Brown, of Wellingborough, addressed the scholars.

On Monday, **3 June**, it was reported that several boys were charged at Thames Police Court with playing leap frog in the street – ah bring back the good old days!

Two public meetings were held on Wednesday, **5 June**, in the Co-operative Society large room under the auspices of the Wellingborough District Labour Party. The first was at 6pm, for all women interested in Labour representation, when Mrs Wilson, of Rushden, president of the Women's Section of the Labour Party, gave a very interesting paper on "Women's Franchise". The second meeting was held at 8pm for both sexes. The chairman stated that the object of both meetings was to establish a strong local Labour Party for all election purposes and a number of names were enrolled to act as an Election Committee.

Thursday, **6 June**, "Notice – All Leather Workers (Male and Female) seeking employment are advised to Keep Clear of Higham Ferrers pending a settlement of current dispute! – Association of Shoe Leather Workers."

On Saturday, **8 June**, in response to the call from the military for more men, it was announced that, under a new National Service Order, many exemptions, especially of Grade 1 men of various ages, would be withdrawn from 22 June. Significantly included in the trades listed were bootmakers!

"Wanted – Pressman for Army and Navy work: Tebbutt and Hall Bros, Raunds."

Sunday, 9 June, the fourth German spring offensive on the Western Front is launched.

This afternoon, as the enemy once again advanced on our lads in France, all denominations of Rance-folk gathered at the Parish Church for a united service. The Temperance Silver Band marched to the church and also played selections during the service which was conducted by the Rev C C Aldred, supported by the Rev E P Blackburn. A collection was taken at the close in aid of the Northants Prisoner of War Fund and realised £13.

Could things get any worse? – Wartime shortages were apparently hitting all corners of civilian life as today it was announced that the lack of tennis balls, which had been noticeable all season, was developing into a famine!

Several town folk made appearances at the Thrapston Police Court on Tuesday, **11 June**. A carrier was fined 2s-6d for failing to subdue the lights of his house; a clicker was charged yet again of disobeying a maintenance order for his son on a reformatory ship, and given seven days to pay the arrears plus costs; and a wounded soldier from Derby was summoned by a local single woman on affiliation and ordered to pay 4s-0d per week until the child was 14, plus £2-3s-0d costs. The accused told the court that although they had walked out three or four times, he could not marry her as he had an invalid father!

That evening, a large and representative gathering of the town's parishioners assembled in the Central Hall of the C of E School, when a presentation and farewell gathering to the vicar (Rev C C Aldred) and Miss Aldred, who were shortly leaving Raunds for Abington, Northampton, took place. Mr J Shelmerdine, JP, people's warden, presided, observing that although they regretted his going away, they congratulated him on his new appointment as "by his kindness he had won the hearts of the young people and the parishioners generally".

Mrs T Wingell presented Miss Aldred with a beautiful weekend dressing-case on behalf of the women of the Church and parish "as a token of their love and regard for her during the six years she had so lovingly and ably assisted the vicar in his duties". Mr A Camozzi, vicar's warden, presented Mr Aldred with a splendid pocket-case, containing £50 in notes, with the following inscription on a silver plate: "Presented to the Rev C C Aldred, MA, Vicar of Raunds, 1912-1918, by his parishioners, in grateful appreciation of faithful and devoted service, June, 1918."

"Wanted – A good Hot Wax Machinist on Army and Navy work; Best Wages paid to a competent hand: Unity Productive Society, Ringstead."

Results of the Raunds Evening School examinations were announced on Thursday, **13 June**. *Home Nursing (St John Ambulance Association), Passed and gained certificate:* Nellie Ireland, Rose A Bailey, Sarah E Sykes, Sarah Lyne, Annie Eady, Mabel Peacock, Dorothy L Tether, and Elsie M Ash; *Shorthand (Pitman's examination), Passed and gained certificate, Elementary A:* Dora Pendered, Gladys Essex, Mildred Phillips, Marie Adams, Edna Corby, Winifred Lansom, Kathleen Brown, Edith Burton, Horace Matthews, and Arthur Corby; *Elementary B:* Edith Lawrence, Bernard Mayes, Walter Coles, Edna Willmott, and Violet Bailey; *Theory:* Winifred Betts; *Speed:* Lottie Hall.

The Local Appeals Tribunal met this evening at the Council School. Owing to the chairman being again absent, and to his not having attended a meeting of the Tribunal since the raising of the military age to 51, the clerk was instructed to write and ask his intentions, the members considering it to be hardly fair when some of their own members' appeals were being heard that the Tribunal should be without his guidance. Sixteen separate appeals were then considered and exemptions until 31 July and 30 September were granted. A seventeenth appeal was dismissed when it was learned that the man had since joined up. The appeals of two Tribunal members were adjourned.

"National Union of Boot and Shoe Operatives, Rushden and District Branch – a Special Meeting of all Operatives working in the Welted Departments, will be held at the Trade Union Club, Higham Road, Rushden, on Monday, 17 June, at 8pm; Business: the Piecework Statement."

"The Thrapston and Raunds Journal will be enlarged with tomorrow's issue by a magnificent 'Pictorial War Supplement', full of splendid pictures and interesting war items; the very thing for that boy of yours at the Front! No extra postage required for the 'Journal'."

Friday, 14 June, the fourth German spring offensive is halted.

Two more town men's names appeared on the casualty lists today: Pte **E White (126)**, Northamptons, being listed as "missing", and Pte R Titchmarsh, Northumberland Fusiliers, classed as "wounded".

On the day that the Germans were again thwarted it was announced by the National Service Ministry that men of 49, 50, and 51 years would shortly be called up for medical examinations by the Army Medical Board.

"Auction Sales – Henry H Bletsoe, favoured with the instructions from Mr T C Jeeves, will offer for Sale by Auction, at the Temperance Hall, Raunds, on Thursday, 27 June, at 6 o'clock in the evening: A Highly Fertile Arable and Grazing Farm (it is believed valuable beds of ironstone and limestone underlie on considerable portions of the Estate). Known as "Grove Farm" with a Pretty Residence situated in the town of Raunds, and very suitable for a gentleman requiring a Country House; Set of Farm Buildings, and 3 Cottages, and about 120 acres of Arable, Pasture, and Rich Meadow Land, now in the occupation of Mr T C Jeeves, and possession can be arranged for entry at Michaelmas, 1918."

Saturday, **15 June**, saw another "Brilliantly Successful Hospital Week Display at Raunds". With the exception of one or two showers early in the afternoon, the weather was very favourable. The place of assemblage for the procession was in the grounds of "The Maples", in Wellington Road, the residence of Mr John Horrell, where the judging of the fancy dress competitions took place.

Among those taking part in the procession were: Mounted marshals (in the Fitzwilliam Hunt garb); Raunds Temperance Silver Prize Band; Higham Ferrers Volunteers; members of the Raunds and visiting Fire Brigades in uniform; members of the Raunds Urban District Council and representatives of other public bodies; representatives of neighbouring Hosiptal Week Fund Committees; tradesmen of the town; members of the local Friendly Societies; Raunds C E School Upper Department tableaux "Flora", and Infant Department tableaux "Cinderella's Wedding" (very effective, but not for competition); Irthlingborough Drum and Fife Band; Raunds St Mary's, Higham Ferrers and Rushden Church Lads' Brigades; the children, adults and factory fancy dress competitors; and the Higham Ferrers and Rushden Wesleyan Boys' and Girls' Brigade.

The parade made a halt in The Square, where a selection was played by the band, and then proceeded to the grounds of "The Hall", kindly lent by Mrs Coggins. Guests on the platform included the Right Rev Dr Woods, the Lord Bishop of Peterborough, Major L C H Brassey, MP, and Mr Milner Gray, CC, prospective Liberal candidate for East Northants. Mr W F Corby announced letters of apology, including those from Lord Lilford (who had, with his usual generosity, enclosed a cheque for £10), and Mr J Bruce of Leeds, (who had sent ten guineas).

Winners in the fancy dress were: *Children's Individual Get-up*, Mary Mitchell (Orange and Lemon); *Children's Best Group*, The Juvenile Rechabites (The Flower Queen and her attendants); *Factory Challenge Shield*, Messrs Coggins and Sons (Messenger of Peace); *Adult's Individual Get-up*, Mr R Ward, Stanwick (John Bull, with bulldog); *Walking Group*, Miss Ida March's party (Welsh Girls), who gave the 20s-0d prize back to the fund; *Comic Group*, Thrapston Bright and Breezy Band.

Winners of the sporting events, held in the Greenhouse Field, were: *100 Yards Handicap, Boys under 14*, Herbert Abbott; *Boys 14 to 18*, Bernard Groom; *Girl's 80 Yards Handicap*, Edith Coles; *Men's 60 Yards Dash Handicap*, J Pound; *Veterans' 80 Yards Flat Handicap*, W Wheleran; *Tug-of-War*, Sgt Ellingham's team; *Skittles Competition*, Mr Bernard Hazeldine.

The Temperance Band played for dancing in the evening in the Greenhouse Field, and in the grounds of the Hall, "Will Eagle's Jolly Boys" gave an alfresco concert.

Included in today's Kettering Leader "Kitchen Recipes in War Time" supplement were Lettuce Soup, Jellied Meat Fingers, Pastry without Fat, White Stew (Bacon in diluted Milk), and Puree of Pea Pods – Yum Yum!

The Urban Council met on Monday evening, **17 June**, at the Council School when the medical officer, Dr McInnes, reported that six births and one death were registered during May, and three cases of notifiable infectious diseases had been reported. A letter was read from the County Council with respect to the notification of births, and the need for securing the more efficient notification of the same. It was decided to reply that they believed the act to be carried out very satisfactorily in the district.

The Surveyor reported that the water supply had been well maintained (no pun intended), and a recent analysis of water was submitted, and was considered very satisfactory. A letter was received from the agent for Mr A W Hollis submitting an estimate for the repair of the fence in Manor Street, which had been damaged by the council's horse, and asking the council to pay half the cost of the same. The clerk was instructed to reply that the council adhered to their previous proposition, namely £2 towards the repair.

Looking back in time to fifty years ago today (1868), it was reported that a three year old cat belonging to Mr James Pulpher, of Raunds, had given birth to over 50 kittens in two years; whilst today in 1893, it was reported that the attention of the Thrapston Board of Magistrates was required for four hours in investigating the circumstances connected with the brutal assault upon the police at Denford Feast, by four Raunds men, two of whom were sent to prison for six months, one for three months, and the other fined.

Tuesday, **18 June**, "Wanted – Good Sole Cutter; Constant Employment; Best Wages: Neal and Gates, Raunds."

"Raunds Hospital Fete 'Corresponding Number Competition', Winning Number: 3397; Prize to be claimed within 7 days from Mr W Agutter, 19 Harcourt Street."

At a meeting held on Wednesday evening, **19 June**, the townsfolk of Raunds pledged to raise £500 for the Lilford Fete, soon to be held at Lilford Hall in aid of the Northants Prisoner of War Fund. More than £225 had already been promised and it was hoped that the visit of the Royal Marine Band on Feast Monday would considerably augment that amount. ***(Plate 12)***

The monthly meeting of the town's Hospital Week Fund committee was held on Thursday, **20 June**, and the treasurer, Mr H W Lawrence, presented the balance sheet of the previous Saturday's demonstration and parade. Total receipts were £203-6s-1½d, and expenses were £35-5s-6d, leaving a balance of £168-0s-7½d, beating the previous best of last year, by £17.

It was announced on Friday, **21 June**, that, under an Order made by the Director General of National Service, all Shoe Trade occupational exemptions from military service to Grade 1 or Category A men born in or after the years stated below, were being withdrawn: Firemen and head warehousemen, 1885; sole cutters and rough rounders, 1883; clickers, pullers-over, lasting machine operators, Blake sewers, heel and edge trimmers, and edgecutters, 1880; carters or lorrymen (horse or power), 1885; all other classes of workmen in the boot trade, 1875.

News of the latest town casualty was published today when it became known that Pte **Arthur Knighton (68)**, Royal Inniskilling Fusiliers, the son of Mr and Mrs C W Knighton, of Bridge Street, had been confirmed as "killed in action" on 3 December, 1917. The 20 year old previously worked for Messrs Coggins and Co.

Also today it was reported that a Raunds soldier previously listed as "missing" had now been found to be a prisoner of war in Germany. The parents of Pte A H Clark, 14 Park Road and the Northamptons, had just received a postcard from their son.

On Saturday, **22 June**, Raunds Conservatives visited Rushden Vics for a friendly game of bowls, the "Vics", however, were not so amicable, winning 71–46.

Early signs of what was to prove to be a global catastrophe manifested itself in the district on Monday, **24 June**, with the news that work at many local factories had been seriously affected by "influenza colds" striking down hundreds of workers.

Tuesday, 25 June, the Battle of Belleau Wood, the United States 2nd Division Marines are victorious.

At the Petty Sessions this afternoon, a Raunds labourer was summoned under the Poor Law Act, 1899, for taking a child out of the control of the Guardians, at Woodford, on 24 April. It was stated that all of the man's children were admitted to the Workhouse on 9 January, 1911. They had been adopted by the Guardians on account of the mode of life of the father, who himself had been in the Workhouse several times. The man had been called upon to pay 6d a week for each child, but refused to sign the agreement, and had not paid anything. The child in question, now 16, had been placed in service at Woodford Mill, but on 24 April she was fetched away by a brother. The father was fined £5 or a month, to be remitted if the girl was returned to the Workhouse by Saturday.

On Wednesday evening, **26 June**, a most successful whist drive and dance took place in the grounds of "The Hall", by kind permission of Mrs Coggins, jointly arranged by Mrs Warth, "Raunds Grange", and Mrs Amos Lawrence, who generously provided the refreshments. The winners of the drive were: 1st, Mr A Bugby; 2nd, Mr James Adams. Mr A Camozzi was the MC. During the evening several fancy articles were offered for sale, given by the ladies mentioned above, and the excellent total sum of £35 was raised for the County Prisoner of War Fund. The Raunds Temperance Band kindly gave their services.

"Wanted, Immediately, Competent Clerk, male or female (if male, ineligible), to take charge of accounts and general office routine of company; Apply, stating qualifications and age, with salary required, to Secretary, Gas Co, Raunds."

The previously advertised auction sale of "Grove Farm" took place in the Temperance Hall on Thursday evening, **27 June**. Bidding started at £6,000 and advanced by £100 bids to £7,400 at which figure it was withdrawn. The farm not being sold, the three cottages adjoining were not offered.

"Merry and Bright, Local Lads who are Seeing it Through" headlined a story on Friday, **28 June**, about county men serving in Royal Naval Division, "Hawke" Battalion, "somewhere in France", including Rance's Able Seaman George Stock.

But there was also grimmer news that Pte **W H Groom (56)**, Brooks Road and the Northumberland Fusiliers, had been listed as "missing since 28 March". From the Northamptons, also listed as "missing", was Pte **F H Shrives (103)**, as was Pte T Lack, Scottish Rifles, whilst Pte C Matson, Cheshires, was reported "wounded".

There was, however, happier news for housewives with the announcement that new potatoes would be reduced to 2½d per pound from Monday, 1 July.

"Wanted – a Room, in business part of Raunds, for Dental Surgery, one day a week; State full particulars to Surgery, 39 Abington Avenue, Northampton."

The anniversary services at the Wesleyan Church on Feast Sunday, **30 June**, were conducted by the Rev J H Sanders, of Ramsbottom, formerly of Thrapston. Both morning and evening services were well attended and collections were taken in aid of Trust Funds of the church.

The Temperance Band gave a couple of concerts today. The first was held on "The Hill" near the residence of Mrs R Coggins, at 4.30pm, and the second on The Square at 7.30pm. Mr O Pentelow, bandmaster, conducted, and there were good numbers present, especially at the evening concert. The collections, which were taken in aid of the Band Funds, showed considerable increase on last year.

* *

MOTOR BUS GUIDE
and
RAILWAY TIME TABLE
One Penny Each
F W MARCH, 17 High Street, Raunds

F HALL
24 High Street, Raunds
Practical Boot & Shoe Maker & Repairer
Ladies' and Gent's Boots Made to Order
Hand Sewn a Speciality
The Best of Materials only used
All kinds of Uppers obtained to order

* *

PROMINENT CITIZENS

1) Mr John Adams,
Urban Councillor, Justice of the Peace
and boot factory joint-owner.

2) Dr Archibald McInnes,
who took over Dr Mackenzie's
practice in the town in July 1917.

3) Mr E Batchelor,
Urban Councillor and
Boot and Shoe Operatives' Union
representative.

4) Miss Pulpher,
a staunch temperance worker
for over 60 years!

(All Kettering Leader)

5) The Raunds Fire Brigade stand in the ruins
of E W Stanley's "Wellington Works", February 1917.
(Kettering Leader)

6) The wedding party of Raunds Belgian refugee Mlle Mitge Vliegan and
M Jean Joseph H Desherhaut, of the Belgian Army, April 1917.
(Kettering Leader)

7) Private Ernest Richardson and family; Pte Richardson was reported killed in action in March 1918, but had, in fact, been taken prisoner. (Kettering Leader)

8) Miss Florence Vorley married Pte A N Edwards in November 1917 (Kettering Leader)

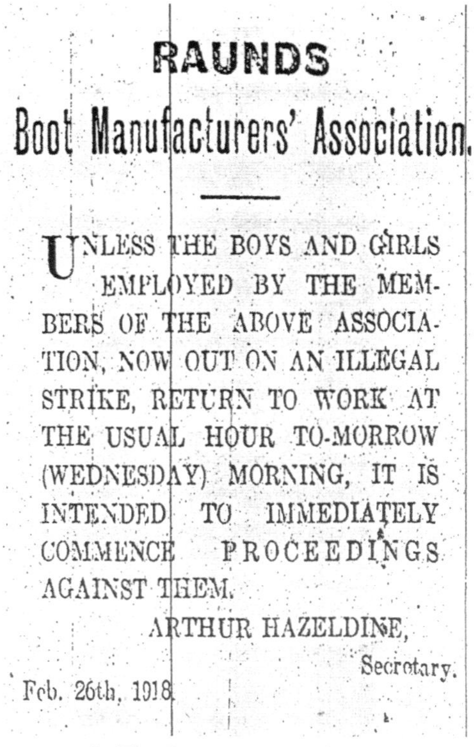

RAUNDS

Boot Manufacturers' Association.

UNLESS THE BOYS AND GIRLS EMPLOYED BY THE MEMBERS OF THE ABOVE ASSOCIATION, NOW OUT ON AN ILLEGAL STRIKE, RETURN TO WORK AT THE USUAL HOUR TO-MORROW (WEDNESDAY) MORNING, IT IS INTENDED TO IMMEDIATELY COMMENCE PROCEEDINGS AGAINST THEM.

ARTHUR HAZELDINE,
Secretary.

Feb. 26th, 1918

9) The Boot Factory Owners get tough with striking youngsters, February 1918. (Northants Evening Telegraph)

10) Messrs Coggins and Sons' workers present "A Coster's Wedding" at the 1919 Hospital Week Demonstration.
(Kettering Leader)

PALACE, RAUNDS,

MONDAY, MARCH 18th, AND DURING THE WEEK.
The Mystic Lady, the Great

AAZELIA,

THE SECOND-SIGHT WONDER,
The Lady with the 10,000 Dollar Brain.
Must be seen to be believed.
Bring Photos of those you wish to inquire about.

THURSDAY NIGHT ONLY at 7.30,
AAZELIA will give a

Special Performance for Ladies Only.

AAZELIA tells you anything you want to know about absent friends or relations, or those in hospital. Write down any sensible question you like, and AAZELIA will answer it without seeing the message. Also have you lost anything? If so, see AAZELIA.

11) A interesting evening for the ladies at the Palace Theatre, March 1918.

RAUNDS FEAST.

MONDAY NEXT, JULY 1st,

Special Engagement of the

Band of the Royal Marines

55 PERFORMERS.

TWO OPEN-AIR CONCERTS
in the

Greenhouse Field,

AFTERNOON 2.30 EVENING at 7.
Admission 6d. Seats extra.

Proceeds for the Northamptonshire Prisoners' of War Fund.

INDOOR PERFORMANCE IF WEATHER UNFAVOURABLE.

12) The Marines come to town to help celebrate Raunds Feast, July 1918.

(Northants Evening Telegraph)

13) The Distributive Co-operative Society buildings and neighbouring cottages decorated for the "Peace Day" celebrations in July 1919. (Vorley/SJB)

14) Children of the town dress up to celebrate "Peace Day", July 1919. (Vorley/SJB)

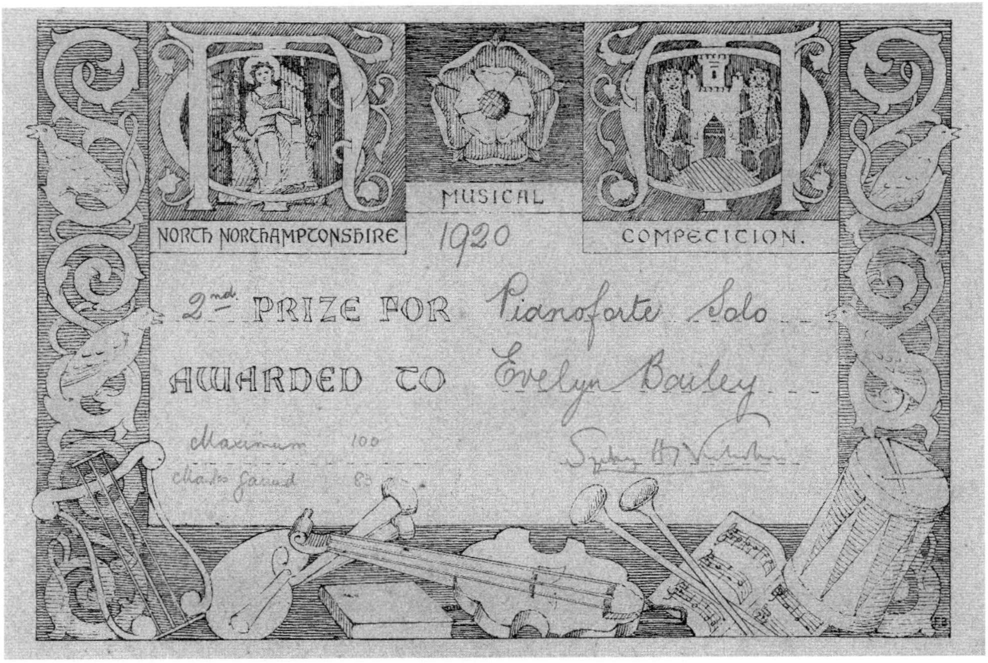

15) Evelyn Bailey's 2nd Place Certificate from the
1920 North Northants Music Competition.
(SJB)

16) Raunds Town FC's captain, G W Chambers, is presented with the
"Scott Gatty Trophy" by Mrs Scott Gatty after their 4-2 triumph
over Stotfold in May 1920.
(Kettering Leader)

17) The War Memorial unveiled in the Parish Church by the Archdeacon of Oakham in May 1920.

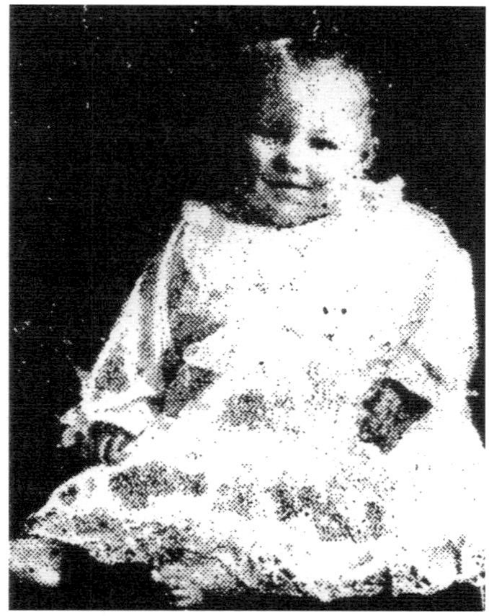

18) Baby Ina Lucas, taken to Australia by her widowed soldier father in 1920.

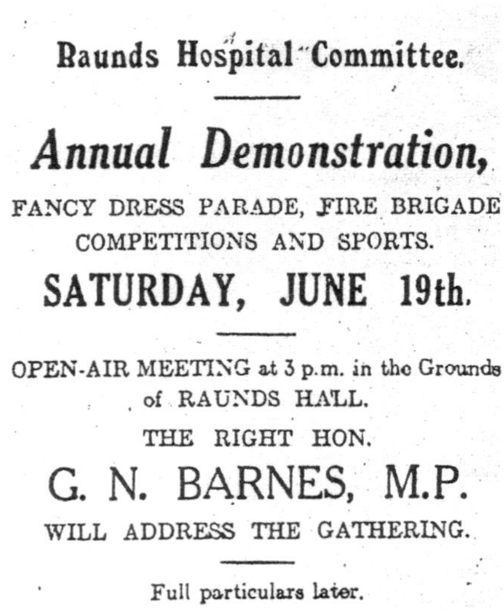

Raunds Hospital Committee.

Annual Demonstration,

FANCY DRESS PARADE, FIRE BRIGADE COMPETITIONS AND SPORTS.

SATURDAY, JUNE 19th.

OPEN-AIR MEETING at 3 p.m. in the Grounds of RAUNDS HALL.

THE RIGHT HON.

G. N. BARNES, M.P.

WILL ADDRESS THE GATHERING.

Full particulars later.

19) Another Hospital Week Demonstration approaches! June 1920.

(left: Vorley/SJB; top right: Kettering Leader; bottom right: Evening Telegraph)

20) Raunds Coffee Tavern Football Club, 1920-21,
"A Promising Team".
(Vorley/SJB)

21) Townsfolk pose by the wrecked pumping equipment "down the meadows",
but how many of these innocent bystanders also took part in the raids in July 1921?
(Kettering Leader)

22) Crowds gather around the newly unveiled Town War Memorial on The Square in October 1921.
(SJB)

SOME RANCE MILITARY MEDAL WINNERS

23) Private George W Agutter,
Middlesex Regiment.

24) Sergeant H Pell,
Sussex Regiment.

25) Sergeant J W Plant,
Egyptian Expeditionary Force.

26) Corporal W Bettles,
Northamptonshire Regiment.

(All Kettering Leader)

7 – July to September 1918

Postal dissatisfaction and the town's blackest day.

JULY – In his final parish notes before leaving Raunds, the Rev C C Aldred wrote "I take this opportunity of thanking all who so very kindly gave Miss Aldred and myself such handsome gifts. We shall always remember our time with you with gratitude. I know you will all give Mr and Mrs Curtis the same warm welcome and loyal support you gave us."

He also wrote of an old Raunds resident, Mary Groome, who had recently died in Canada, "For 14 years she was a nurse at St Olave's Infirmary, Bermondsey; in 1913, she proceeded to Canada, where for five years she was associated with Montreal Cathedral, as nurse and deaconess."

Finally, the name of **Arthur Knighton (68)** was added to those who had "Died in the Service of Their Country".

Monday, 1 July, William Andrews (11), killed in action.

Feast Monday, 1918, was a red-letter day in the history of the town, as it was favoured for the first time with a visit of a military band, the proceeds being in aid of the Northants Prisoner of War Fund. The event was a great success as large numbers of residents from the town and surrounding district were entertained to a musical treat by the Band of His Majesty's Royal Marines. ***(Plate 12)***

Tuesday, 2 July, the millionth American soldier arrives in France.

As the numerical advantage of the Allies continued to increase, it was reported to the Thrapston Board of Guardians, at their monthly meeting today, that the Raunds girl who had been removed from her place of service by her father had not been returned, in spite of the severe penalty hanging over the father. The Board duly decided to ascertain what further legal steps they could take in the matter and also resolved to inform all local boot and shoe factories (in one of which the girl had started work) that if they employed her they would be liable to proceedings.

The meeting also heard from their medical officer, Dr McInnes, that he had the prospect of joining the RAMC in July, and that his substitute at Raunds would be Dr F A Maynard, MB, CM (Edin). The Contracts Committee then confirmed acceptance of the bread tender from Mr Beeby for the Raunds Children's Home.

The long-awaited Lilford Fete in aid of the Northants Regimental Prisoner of War Fund and the County Nursing Association took place on Wednesday, **3 July**, in glorious weather. Raunds' T H Warth and Amos Lawrence presented Lord Lilford with a cheque for £600 as the town's contribution; the Lord responded "We thank you from the bottom of our hearts", and went on to commend the Hospital Week effort, and alluded to cricket and other happy associations with the town during the past 25 years. In the auction of farmer's gifts, a cheese given by Mr Billington, of Raunds, was cut into three pieces and made £2-14s-0d.

Appearing on the Casualty Lists released on Friday, **5 July**, was Gnr F Reynolds, Royal Garrison Artillery, reported as "wounded".

And also today it was confirmed that from 14 July, lard would be rationed and retailers would only be permitted to sell the delicacy to their registered customers and only at the rate of 2 ounces per head per week.

The annual treat of the scholars attending the Church of England Sunday School was held on Saturday, **6 July**. Owing to food restrictions the usual tea had to be dispensed with. The children assembled at the Schools at 4.15pm and marched to the Vicarage, where sports competitions etc were held in the paddock. The Marathon race for the members of the Vestry Class also took place, the winner being H Freeman, the Temperance Band then played for dancing until dusk.

At the monthly meeting of the local Boot and Shoe Operatives' Union branch on Monday, **8 July**, it was decided to transfer the branch funds from the Northants Union Bank to the Co-operative Wholesale Society Bank. The members next agreed to send £5 to the Maybole Strike Fund. Finally, the meeting strongly protested against exempted men being forced to join the Volunteer Training Corps and being made to drill after doing a hard day's work in the factories.

The schools of the town were closed today and tomorrow owing to the teachers being engaged on writing out the new ration books, the distribution of which was completed by the postal authorities the following day.

The sudden death occurred on Tuesday morning, **9 July**, of Mr George Chapman, of Lawson Street. The 49 year old was at work at the St Crispin boot factory when he complained of feeling unwell, and said that he would have to go home; soon after reaching home he expired. He had been married for less than a year.

At the Thrapston Petty Sessions today, a chartered surveyor, of Stevenage, applied for a licence for the Palace Cinema, Raunds. On the last occasion the licence was applied for the Bench were not quite satisfied with the then licensee and refused a licence for more than a month. It was explained that the whole of the business had now been taken over by different people and the whole tone would be raised. The application was acceded to.

A 15 year old Woodford lad was charged with stealing a bicycle, value £1, the property of Ebenezer Hazeldine, from an out-house in Rotton Row, Raunds on 26 June. Pleading guilty, the lad said that he took the machine "for devilment" and when he knew the police were after him he had returned the bike to the shed. He was fined £2, and bound over in £10 for 12 months.

This evening, the Urban Council met for a special meeting at the Council School to consider the appointment of a committee and Local Fuel Overseer under the recently issued Household Fuel and Lighting Order. Also considered was an application from council employees to work half an hour less per day to bring their hours in line with the agricultural workers. The members acceded to the request, and in future the workers would commence work at 6.30am!

It was reported on Wednesday, **10 July**, that the parents of Sgt Harold Betts, Leicester Regiment, had received a postcard from the British Red Cross Society saying that the name of their son had come through on a list of Prisoners of War being held "somewhere in Germany".

A Food Control meeting was held this evening and heard that the issue of ration books in the parishes of Raunds and Stanwick had now been completed. Two applications for additional rations on medical grounds were received; one being a case of tuberculosis was approved, and in the other case, a favourable recommendation was made to the Ministry of Food.

Also this evening, a demonstration on "Potato Spraying" had been arranged to take place on the new allotment near the Council School and although there was a good number present, owing to the unsuitable weather, the demonstration had to be postponed. A talk on the benefits of spraying took its place.

The Local Appeals Tribunal met on Thursday evening, **11 July**, the first piece of business being to unanimously pass a resolution protesting against the retention of younger men in protected occupations whilst men up to 50 years of age were being passed into the Army. As had been similarly done by the Kettering and Finedon Tribunals, copies of the resolution were then sent to the Prime Minister and the Minister of National Service.

A letter was then read from the Assistant Director of National Service asking the Tribunal to impose the "Volunteer" condition where exemption was granted if there was a Volunteer Corps within a reasonable distance. A large number of appeals were then considered from men who had been decertified by the recent Order raising the military age including eight from men, all married aged between 46 and 50, called up under the new Military Service Act, for these, open exemption to 30 October was granted in each case.

It was reported today that townsfolk were expressing considerable dissatisfaction on the recent reduction of postal facilities. Previous to the war the town enjoyed three deliveries and three despatches daily, which, however, had been reduced some time ago to two of each. Now, under the latest alteration, the only delivery daily was commencing at 9am, and the only despatch was at 3.15pm. The inhabitants quite reasonably resented the fact that they could go to adjoining villages and post letters at least two hours later than could be done in the town!

It was also announced today that the recent local effort on behalf of the County Prisoner of War Fund had raised £639-4s-5½d, this was made up of: Subscriptions, £562-19s-6d; whist drive at "The Hall", £35; net amount from the concert by the Band of HM Royal Marines, £41-4s-11½d.

"Wanted at Once – good Operator on Stitching Machine, Army and Navy work, constant employment and best wages; Apply: St Crispin's Ltd, Raunds."

The Church School managers met on Friday, **12 July** and reviewed an application from Mr Rawlings for permission to apply for the post of Local Fuel Overseer; to this they agreed unanimously.

Another Raunds parent, Mrs E E Fairy, of Thorpe Street, was the recipient today of a postcard from the British Red Cross Society advising her that the name of her son, Pte Harry D F Fairy, Queen Royal West Surreys, appeared on the list of Prisoners of War being held in Germany. Mrs Fairy was delighted to receive this news as her other son, **Arthur (49)**, had been killed in action the previous October.

"In Memoriam – In loving memory of Dr William Mackenzie, of "Aberlour House", Raunds, who died on 12 July, 1917; So sadly missed by his sister Elsie, Beloved by all."

"Notice of Sale by Arthur G Brown: Raunds, Saturday, 27 July, 100 head of Poultry and numerous appliances, by instructions from Mr George White; Sale at 3pm, Full particulars from auctioneer."

A garden fete in connection with the Wesleyan Church's Foreign Missions was held at "The Maples" on Saturday, **13 July**. There was a missionary tableaux and other attractions, in which the scholars and other young people took part. During the evening an address was given by the Rev Franklyn G Smith, who had spent 30 years in Spain. The Rev Smith also occupied the pulpit at the Wesleyan Church the following day.

Monday, 15 July, the final German spring offensive, "Friedensturm", begins.

The Urban Council met again this evening and decided to pay the sum of £3 to Mr George Norris in lieu of the replacement for bedding destroyed, following a case of a notifiable infectious disease. A letter was read from the postmaster at Wellingborough stating that it was hoped shortly to accelerate the morning delivery, and to close the box for despatch an hour later than at present. This was not considered to be satisfactory and it was decided to contact the Councils at Irthlingborough and Finedon with a view to joint action for an improvement.

The medical officer, Dr McInnes, reported three births and one death registered in June and two notifications of infectious disease. The Finance Committee recommended the tender of Mr W Peck be accepted for carting at 2s-9d per ton, and 12s-0d per day for day work. The clerk reported that there were four applications for the post of Local Fuel Overseer, viz Messrs G L Miller, L Sharp, H A Sanders, and A D Rawlings, the last named being unanimously appointed.

"Rushden Palace, Mon, Tue and Wed; Exclusive to this Theatre, The Great Scottish Photo-Play: 'On the Banks of Loch Lomond', a Lassie's Love Story taken in the Highlands and Fragrant with Heather; also 'A Milk-Fed Vamp'."

Tuesday, 16 July, Tsar Nicholas II and his family are executed by the Bolshevics.

Thursday, 18 July, a massive Allied counter attack starts on the Western Front.

On Friday, **19 July**, the wife of Pte W E Richardson, who was being held a prisoner of war at Bayreath, received a letter from the hospital chaplain saying that her husband was suffering from wounds to the face and hand, and feared that he would lose the sight of his left eye.

Today it was announced that Newfoundland, our oldest colony, had contributed proportionately more sailors and seamen to the war effort than any other country in the world – "It is 'Jack Tar's Cradle'" said Sir Hamar Greenwood, MP.

In connection with the Raunds Nursing Association "Need for Nurses" week a baby show and jumble sale were held in the Vicarage grounds on Saturday afternoon, **20 July**, when there was a large gathering. For the baby show there were 30 entries and the judges awarded the following 1st prizes to: *Group 1, babies under 6 months,* Baby Dickerson; *Group 2, 6 months and under one year,* Baby Webb; *Group 3, one year and under two years,* Baby Ruff. Encouragement prizes for the babies that had improved most from birth: *Group 1,* Baby York; *Group 2,* Baby Arnold; *Group 3,* Baby Robinson; *Group 4, twins under two years,* Babies George and Mary Cox (Hargrave). The special prize given by Mr T Broker for the "Best Baby in Raunds" was won by Baby Webb.

A whist drive was also held, Mr A D Rawlings acting as MC. The winners were: *Ladies,* Mrs R Abbot; *Gentlemen,* Mr L Kirk; *Hidden Number, Ladies,* Miss L Lawrence; *Gentlemen,* Mr T Gates. The Temperance Silver Band played selections and for dancing till 10. The net result of the effort was about £25.

"Notice – Raunds Gas Light and Coke Co Ltd hereby give notice that owing to the increase in the price of Coal, the Price of Gas will be increased by 2d per 1,000 cubic feet as from the date of the last meter reading." Also today, Desborough's Gas Co increased their equivalent price by 9d!

Monday, **22 July**, "Wanted – Young Lady to take charge of bookkeeping – Apply giving references and wages required, to Palmer's Store, Raunds."

Tuesday, 23 July, Frederick Bowman Angood (12), killed in action.

On another day that the town's casualty count increased by one the Hospital Week Fund Committee met at the Temperance Hall. The accounts showed a year to date balance in hand of £231-17s-7½d, of which £25 had been forwarded to the county treasurer. A further £200 was duly ordered to be sent forward.

"Tenders – Raunds Urban District Council invite Tenders for the following Crops, growing upon their Sewage Farm, namely: 3 acres 10 poles of White Scotch Oats, 34 poles of Early Eclipse Potatoes.

Both lots are an exceptionally good crop, and can be seen at any time. The purchaser will be expected to harvest the Crops and remove them at the earliest opportunity.

Tenders to be delivered at my office not later than noon on Monday, 29 July, W F Corby, Clerk to the above Council."

The District Education Sub-Committee met on Wednesday evening, **24 July**, and the attendance report for the quarter showed a decrease of the average number on the register of 51.8 against the previous year, the present number being 1,060. The percentage of attendance was about the same, being 89 as against 89.1 the previous year. It was decided to close the town's schools for the summer holiday at 4pm on Thursday, 1 August, and to reopen on Monday, 9 September.

"Wanted – A Good Operator on Consol Laster, Gimson Machine; Army and Navy Work; Good Wages; Constant Employment: St Crispin's Ltd, Raunds."

The Thrapston and District Shire Horse Society held their annual show on Thursday, **25 July**; the large number of entries and the outstanding quality of the exhibits all bearing eloquent testimony to the value and popularity of the society among local breeders. Mr Walter Denton, of Raunds, captured most of the honours of the day including the President's (Lord Lilford) prize and the Shire Horse Society's silver medal.

The Local Appeals Tribunal reconvened this evening at the Council School and the first ten cases reviewed were those requested by the military authorities to be re-examined. In every case the period of exemption previously granted was reduced or dismissed altogether. Twelve personal appeals then followed to which ten were granted exemptions of two or three months; the remaining two cases were adjourned pending medical examinations.

It was announced today that Vegetable shows would be exempt from the new entertainment tax.

On Friday, **26 July**, it was officially confirmed that Pte **Jack Haxley (60)**, of Gladstone Street and the Machine Gun Corps, had been "killed in action". The deceased soldier had at one time been captain and full back of Raunds Town FC.

An article "A Dip into "Northants History of 100 years ago" today observed that "one mile west from Stanwick is Raunds, a village pleasantly situated on an eminence. The church is a curious, ancient building, with a lofty steeple at the western end. There is a spring of petrifying quality in the neighbourhood, and the remains of a sculptured cross near the north side of the church.

About a mile and a quarter to the north of the village is a place called Mill Cotton. There are remains of a square entrenchment where various Roman coins have been turned up by the plough. At Mallows Cotton, not far distant, ruins of numerous buildings have been discovered."

"Offical Notice – Live Stock (Sales) Order, 1918 – Pursuant to Clause 71 of the above Order, I hereby give notice that on and after the 22nd day of July 1918, every owner of live stock fit for slaughter must send his stock to Thrapston Market (Raunds/Ringstead/Hargrave) or Wellingborough (Stanwick/Chelveston). It is an offence against the Defence of the Realm Regulations for owners to send their stock to market elsewhere; Live Stock Commissioner, Ministry of Food."

A meeting of the Northamptonshire Education Committee was held today and a letter from the Controller of Horticulture on the question of the collection of blackberries was discussed. The Board were being approached and asked to co-operate with the collection by securing the assistance of school teachers and children. As for last year, arrangements were being made to then convert the fruit into jam in the county or the immediate vicinity.

The Rev C Curtis, the new Vicar of Raunds, preached farewell sermons at Peterborough on Sunday, **28 July**, in the morning at St Mark's, and in the evening at St Barnabas's. The next day he was presented with a cheque for £100, subscribed to by over 620 parishioners and friends, an album containing the subscribers' names, and a beautifully executed framed testimonial.

The ongoing case of the Raunds girl removed from her placement in service at Woodford was again reviewed by the Thrapston Board of Guardians at their meeting on Tuesday, **30 July**. The girl had written saying that she had now got a place in service at Rushden, and that she hoped the Board would give her permission to go, as she wished to work and get an honest living. It was also stated that the father had not gone to gaol. The members decided that once the girl had returned to the Children's Home, they would be prepared to assist her going to the situation at Rushden; however, they also insisted that the magistrates warrant regarding the father should be enforced.

The Board also reported that they had made proposals by which 58 beds at the Workhouse could be offered for German Prisoners of War and their guards, providing that the master was not taken for military service.

The 53rd half-yearly meeting of the Raunds Distributive Co-operative Society was held at the Temperance Hall this evening. The secretary reported that sales for the half-year were £24,795-17s-6d, an increase of £1,323-11s-9d on 1917. The Disposable balance of £1,060-0s-2½d was set as a Dividend of 1s-3d in the £ general, and 1s-0d in the £ for coal. Prize winners for the allotments were also announced as follows: Stanwick Road, Mr W Harvey; Park Street, Mr W Agutter.

* *

A Large Stock of
Sweets, Flour, Fruit and Chip Bags
And all kinds of Wrapping Papers
In large or small quantities, at lowest prices
F W MARCH, 17 High Street, Raunds
And Bridge Street Printing Works
Telephone No.6

* *

AUGUST – ***The Spanish Flu pandemic begins; more than 25,000,000 die worldwide in the next 6 months.***

In his first Parish Notes, the Rev Cecil Curtis wrote from Peterborough: "To The Parishioners of Raunds, My Dear Friends, I hope shortly to be amongst you and am now in a position to tell you my future arrangements. I have now finished my work at St Mark's, Peterborough, and have arranged for the removal of my furniture on 14 August. On the following day, Thursday, 15 August, the Archdeacon of Oakham has kindly consented to Induct me to the living of Raunds at 7pm. I am therefore looking forward to 18 August, when I hope to spend my first Sunday amongst you; Your future friend and Vicar, Cecil Curtis."

He reported that the Church Lads' Brigade had journeyed to Northampton on 27 July, to take part in the Swimming Competitions; LCpls March, Lawrence, Freeman, Taylor and Pte Gates all qualifying for certificates from The Royal Life Saving Society. In connection with the hope of having a good band, the generous gifts of £1 each from Flt Lt G Hall and Cpl H Hall, former members of the St Mary's Boy Scouts, towards the purchase of instruments was acknowledged.

The accounts of the fete held at the recent Sunday School Treat were announced as: Total Receipts, £22-6s-4d, including *Sweet Stall*, Miss Black, £2-11s-11d; *Hoop-la*, Mr and Mrs J Pound, £2-3s-9d; *Skittles*, Messrs F C Coles and H Putt, £1-19s-0d; *Darts*, LCpl E March, £1-13s-0d; *Sugar Competition*, Mr J Stubbs, 19s-10d; *Doll*, Misses E Pettit and G Corby, 17s-9d; *Postcard*, Misses H Clayton and F Kirk, 12s-1d; *Flower Selling*, Misses F Bates and M Clayton, 8s-9d. Expenditure included: *Band*, £2-8s-0d; Rixon Bros, *Buns*, £1-15s-0d; Palmer's Stores, *Cigarettes*, 13s-0d; and Star Tea Co, *Biscuits*, £1-0s-10d.

Finally, more names were added to those who had "Died in the Service of Their Country": **William Andrews (11)**, **Fred Angood (12)**, and **Jack Haxley (60)**.

Friday, **2 August**, the local papers all carried the story that Pte **Fred Angood (12)**, of Park Road and the Middlesex Regiment, had been killed by a shell on 23 July. His wife and two young children had been living at her mother's home at Thrapston while he was away.

"In Memoriam – In loving memory of dear **Cyril (38)**, son of Mr and Mrs Clarke, 13 High Street, Raunds, who died of wounds in France on 3 August, 1917:

Could we have raised his dying head, or heard his last farewell?
The blow would not have been so hard, to us who loved him well.
He is gone but not forgotten, never will his memory fade,
Fondest thoughts will ever linger, in that land where he is laid.

From his loving mother, father, Ivy, sisters and brothers."

Raunds' Misses Astley and Wilkins charmed the crowd in the fancy dress competition as "Billiards" and "Folly" at the Thrapston Grand Parade and Garden Fete held on Bank Holiday Monday, **5 August**, in aid of their "Soldier's and Sailor's Comforts Fund".

The news that Mrs Wm Andrews had received confirmation of the death on 1 July of her husband, Pte **William Andrews (11)**, Northants Regiment, was reported on Tuesday, 6 August. The twenty-seven year old had three young children and formerly worked for Messrs J Horrell and Son, shoe manufacturers.

And at the Thrapston Police Court today, a fine of 5s-0d was inflicted on a town shoehand for riding a bicycle without a lighted lamp at 11.15pm on the highway at Raunds on 20 July.

Thursday, 8 August, the Second Battle of Amiens begins.

Today may have turned out to be "the blackest day in the German Army", but for Raunds, its darkest hour was still six weeks away!

At home, Woodford held a successful day for the county Prisoner of War Fund this afternoon and a party from Raunds won the "Comic Group" prize in the fancy dress competition. Whilst at the Earls Barton Hospital Fete, Raunds Fire Brigade joined those of the home town and Wolverton in the procession through the village. The Rance boys then took part in the Hose-Cart and Manual competitions but were unsuccessful in both.

The casualty lists of Friday, **9 August**, included the names of Pte **G W Thurlow (115)**, Middlesex Regiment, "killed in action", and Pte G Talbot, Northants Regiment, "wounded".

Today, Thrapston and Oundle district agricultural labourers were said to be asking for double pay and £2 beer money for the harvest month; and Lord Curzon stated that Northampton and Leicester areas had made 60,000,000 boots for the Allies.

It was announced on Saturday, **10 August**, that the blackberry crop would be good this year and children were to be paid 3d per pound for gathering them. The fruit would then be made into jam for the use of the Army.

At the end of his vacation today, a Northampton holidaymaker ruefully observed: "I was on the river all the week, and on the only fine day I fell out of the punt!"

The Temperance Band gave concerts in Raunds and Stanwick on Feast Sunday, **11 August**, Mr O Pentelow conducting. There were good attendances and collections were taken for the band funds.

Monday, 12 August, the end of the Second Battle of Amiens with the Germans in retreat.

"The Palace, Raunds – Mon to Fri, Continuous Performance, 6.30 to 10.20, Sat, Three Separate Performances, 2.30, 6, and 8.15.

M, T, W – 'Clancy's Millions', 'The Fatal Ray' (episode 2),

T, F, S – 'Durand of the Bad Lands', and Star Programme of Comedy, Scenic and Topical Films.

Prices (tip-up chairs throughout): 3d, 6d, 9d, and 1s-0d (tax extra), Booked seats 1s-0d (tax extra)."

Most local factories resumed work after the holidays on Tuesday, **13 August**, but many workers then left off at dinner time for the day.

"Coal Shortage – Everybody Asked to Burn Less", said the Government on Wednesday, **14 August**; "Although no one will have enough coal, we appeal to every man and woman in England to save coal even out of your allowed rations."

The new vicar (the Rev C Curtis), was welcomed on Thursday, **15 August**, by joyous peals of bells. The induction took place in the evening at the Parish Church, with the Revs F C Boultbee, Hargrave, and H A Curtis, Pytchley, contributing prayers and lessons; the Archdeacon of Oakham then preached a sermon before conducting the induction ceremony.

Today it was reported that Mr F A Corby, of Hollington Road, had some white Leghorn chicks hatched on 1 April, and the first one started to lay on Saturday last, and also on Sunday and Tuesday.

On Friday, **16 August**, Pte Ralph Cox, of the Northamptons, the son of Mr H Cox, 6 Hill Street, was listed as "missing since 22 July". The twenty year old had been in France for eighteen months.

The Raunds branch of the Agricultural Labourers' Union, having asked for £12 for harvest month wages, requested that Mr E Batchelor, assistant secretary to the local Boot Operatives Union, meet the committee of the Distributive Co-operative Society to discuss the matter. The victorious Mr Batchelor emerged with an agreement of the Society's committee to pay their agricultural workers £14 for the harvest month! And by now, the harvest was in full swing; there were some very fine crops, and, owing to the splendid weather, the work was going on well.

"In Memoriam – In loving memory of Pte **Thomas William Bamford (20)**, Northants Reg, killed in action, 16 August, 1917:

How we've missed thy loving presence, in our life as time goes by,
None but those who have lost their loved one, realise the bitterness of "Gone".

From his loving wife and children, Kettering."

The "Evening Telegraph" reported on Saturday, **17 August**, that "Opening their newly decorated and refurnished theatre with 'stars' of the first water like Bessie Barriscale and Mary Pickford, the new management of the Raunds Palace have struck the note of excellence in entertainment combined with restfulness and artistic comfort for their patrons. Such bold enterprise deserves great success, and we have no doubt that the good folk of the town and surrounding district will highly appreciate the efforts made of their behalf."

Monday, **19 August**, "Grindery Shortage – Fewer Nails for Boot Repairing" headlined the story that new permits granted for the purchase of grindery in the district would mean that quantities available would be less than those asked for, being equal to about 60% of the supposed actual requirements. Consequently, all boot repairers would have to put fewer nails in the boots and resort to sewing wherever possible.

And in an indication of how hard the Allies blockade of Germany and its neighbours was biting, Poland today announced that it was to have five meatless days a month, to be on the same footing with Germany.

At the Thrapston Petty Sessions on Tuesday, **20 August**, a Raunds butcher was fined 5s-0d for failing to subdue the lights of his house at midnight on 3 August. Supt Tebbey commented that "people are getting rather dilatory again and it's time they are given a fresh caution!"

The more serious case today, however, was the summons served on a Raunds youth by a Hargrave domestic servant for assault at Hargrave on 22 July. The complainant said that she was cycling from Raunds to Hargrave when, near to the Black Lodge, the defendant asked to borrow her pump. She got off and he pumped up his tyres but as she was getting on her cycle again, the defendant flung her to the ground, put his hand round her throat, and behaved indecently. She resisted and got up but he said that if she told anyone he would murder her! The youth pleaded guilty and the Bench sentenced him to two month's hard labour.

On a cheerier note, Sgt Harold Lee, the former Council School headmaster, arrived home on leave from France early today, having been conveyed from Wellingborough MR Station by a motor despatch rider.

Wednesday, 21 August, the Battle of Bapaume begins.

Mr Charles Bailey, of Marshall's Road, was reported on Friday, **23 August**, to have recently received "official intimation" that his third son, Pte **Fred Bailey (17)**, South Staffs Regiment, missing since last October, was now presumed dead. The deceased had formerly worked for Messrs Adams Bros and was a member of the Raunds Temperance Band. Mr and Mrs Frank Lawrence, of Grove Street, the parents of Pte **Herbert Lawrence (72)**, received a similar letter from the Army Record Office, the two nineteen year olds having disappeared on the same day.

A claim for £9-10s-0d for board and lodgings and trap hire was made by a Raunds woman at the Thrapston County Court today, against a Great Addington man. The complainant said that the man was managing director of a boot factory in the town and occasionally stayed overnight at her house and used the trap. The defendant said that he had no objection to paying his share but not the whole amount. The judge disallowed £4 of the claim, but allowed £5-10s-0d and costs. When the defendant stated that he would appeal, the judge retorted "You cannot appeal without leave, and this I refuse to give you!"

The 106th anniversary of the Wesleyan Sunday School was celebrated at the Wesleyan Church on Sunday, **25 August**. In the afternoon, at the annual flower service, the scholars presented the following gifts: 757 eggs, tomatoes, apricots, honey, stationery, cigarettes, and a large quantity of flowers. These were sent the next day to Duston War Hospital and the VAD Hospital at Higham Ferrers. Bibles and hymn books were presented to the scholars who had attained the age of 15 years, by Sgt Harold Lee, home from France on leave. The collections were for school funds and exceeded the annual expenditure of £30, by £4-13s-6d.

Monday, 26 August, Henry Allen (9), killed in action.

The lists of voters for Raunds and the adjoining parishes were reviewed by Mr H A Millington, registration officer, at a Court held at the Temperance Hall on Tuesday afternoon, **27 August**. Two town woman presented personal cases for being added to the voter's lists; a spinster from Francis Street was successful, but a married woman from Marshall's Road was not.

The Thrapston Board of Guardians also met today and, on hearing that no communication had been received from Raunds Urban District Council relating to a successor on the Board for the Rev C C Aldred, the chairman remarked "I understand they've not since had a meeting, probably gone out for a holiday!"

They then discussed the continuing case of the Raunds girl removed from her job in service at Woodford. As the girl had not returned to the Workhouse, the Board had instructed the police to execute the warrant against the father, and the man went to gaol. The girl had then returned but had absconded after just two days, going back to her home in Raunds. When it was suggested that a further summons be taken out against the father, the members were of the opinion that as he had not got hard labour, he probably wouldn't mind another month in gaol. It was then resolved to retrieve the girl and place her in service at Rushden as intended.

"Ministry of Food – The Shredded Suet (Minimum Prices) Order, 1918; Under the Order, on and after 1 September, 1918, Manufacturers, Wholesalers and Retailers may not sell Shredded Suet at a price exceeding the maximum price for the time being applicable under the Order. Manufacturer's price is 1s-3d per lb; Wholesaler's price is 1s-4d per lb; Retailer's price is 1s-6d per lb."

The Local Appeals Tribunal met on Thursday evening, **29 August**, and first reviewed the certificates of five men as requested by the military authorities. Personal appeals were then considered from eleven men. Six received exemptions ranging from two to six months; one case was adjourned pending a medical examination; one case was struck out as the applicant had since been rejected by the military; and the remaining three requests were dismissed.

Friday, 30 August, Charles William Layton (73), killed in action.

The rules for "pay, picking and packing" of the blackberry harvest were announced today. Everybody was invited to go blackberrying at a remuneration of 3d for each pound picked. There were, however, certain rules which had to be observed: immature berries were not to be picked; and over ripe berries were also to be left alone. The fruit was not to be picked immediately after rain, as it would become mouldy if packed when wet. Blackberries were not to be gathered except for food or jam making. The prices of sale had been fixed at 4d per pound to the public and private buyers, and 4½d per pound to jam manufacturers.

With the exception of the higher officers, practically the whole of the Metropolitan Police came out on strike today in demand for increased wages. The men returned to work after "gaining their end".

Saturday, 31 August, the end of the Battle of Bapaume, the German retreat continues.

Three more Raunds soldiers made the newspapers today: Mr and Mrs G Brown, Coleman Street, had received the surprising news that their eldest son, Pte G W Brown, Tank Corps, had been posted as "missing", just days after returning to France from home leave; Mr and Mrs Felce, Manor Street, had received news that their son, Pte W Felce, The Buffs, had been wounded in both shoulders and was now in hospital in France; and Mr and Mrs J Webster, "Providence House", had received notification that their eldest son, Pte George Webster, had been wounded and were anxiously waiting further news as to the nature of his injuries.

Several of the town's folk enjoyed success at the Tichmarsh Fete held today. In the fancy dress competition, groups representing "Welch Girls" and "The British Empire" came first and second and both handed back their prizes for the fund. In the sports, J Bettles won the "boys under 13, 100 yards" and H Ball came third in the "men over 40" race over the same distance; he also won the prize in the "Coal" competition. In the singing competition, Miss Winnie Pentelow and Mr H Bamford were victorious in the "Ladies" and "Gentlemen" classes respectively. The Raunds Temperance Band played in the Club Room for dancing and in all, over £200 was raised for the village's "Soldier's and Sailor's Comforts Fund".

"Wanted, At Once, Experienced Operator on B.U. Consul Lasting machine; Owen Smith, Raunds."

"Denford Soldier's Comforts Fund – Spoon Competition – Winning Number: 22, Won by Mr G W Groom, Denford."

* *

The Crown of the Rhubarb

A dish of stewed rhubarb is lacking
its crowning charm unless it is served with:

FREEMAN'S DEVONSHIRE CUSTARD

£1 War Certificates are given away every week
until the end of September 1918.

Send at once for details of the Great War Savings scheme.

A 2s-0d War Savings Voucher is sent free to every applicant.

* *

SEPTEMBER – *The Rev C Curtis' first month in office is marked by there being no surviving copy of the Parish Magazine in the archives!*

However, its rival publication, "The Raunds Circuit Wesleyan Methodist Church Record" commented: "We would like to take the opportunity of publicly welcoming to our midst, our new Vicar, the Rev Cecil Curtis, MA. We wish him every success in his work, and can assure him of the good wishes of the Non-Conformists and their willingness to co-operate with him in all efforts for the spiritual and moral welfare of the town. The Raunds people are noted for their heartiness and genuiness of their friendliness."

On Sunday, **1 September, Dennis Eaton (150)** was baptised at the Parish Church.

At the local branch meeting of the Boot and Shoe Operatives' Union on Monday, **2 September**, all reserved men who had recently altered occupations were reminded to notify the registration office at once, to avoid being called up although they were protected. The members also protested against the exceptional length of the August holidays! As many men with families had not been able to meet their expenses owing to no wages being paid.

"Official Notice – Ministry of Food – The Vegetable Marrow Order, 1918, comes into force on 4 September, 1918, and the following are extracts from same: Retail Price, maximum, 1d per lb or any part of, with a maximum price of 7d for any single Marrow. No charge for delivery is permitted. Licensed Jam Manufacturers are at liberty to purchase for jam manufacture in priority of other purchasers."

Tuesday, 3 September, the Germans' retreat reaches the Hindenburg Line. Evelyn Wood (135), killed in action.

A Raunds farmer appeared at the Thrapston Police Court today, summoned for allowing two sows to stray on the public highway at Ringstead on 15 August. Despite his protestations that they had not been "allowed" to stray and he did not see how they could have got on to the road, he was fined 5s-0d with 9s-0d costs.

"Notice – Will our numerous in and out-town customers kindly note that our Studio and Framing Works will be closed from Wednesday, 4 September to Wednesday, 11 September, after which date all orders will receive our immediate and careful attention; C W Vorley, Photographer, Brook Street, Raunds."

A nasty accident happened at Messrs Neal and Gates boot factory on Thursday afternoon, **5 September**, when a lad named Edward Smith, about 15 years of age, got his hand between the pulley and belting. He was immediately attended to by Dr McInnes, who bandaged up the hand and ordered his removal to Northampton Hospital, whither he was conveyed by motor.

"The Raunds Gas Light and Coke Co Ltd – Notice is hereby given that, commencing upon the first day of October, 1918, the Price of Gas will be as follows: By ordinary meter, 4s-9d net per 1,000 cubic feet; By prepayment meter, the discount previously allowed will be discontinued; P A Smith, Secretary."

A report on Friday, **6 September**, told how Mr Thomas Walker, Marshall's Road, had received news that his fourth son, Pte Frank Walker, Royal Fusiliers, was suffering from shrapnel wounds and was in Whipp's Cross War Hospital, Leytonstone. His third son, Pte Richard W, was a prisoner of war in Germany and also in hospital wounded.

Wellingborough had a plague of flying ants this afternoon, the roads being almost black with them.

Saturday, 7 September, George Henry Webb (123), died.

The unveiling of the memorial to the late Dr William Mackenzie, beloved physician to the district for 39 years, took place at Raunds cemetery this afternoon. Prior to the ceremony there was a procession from The Square headed by the Temperance Band, followed by town's Fire Brigade, the vicar, boy choristers, the Rev E P Blackburn, members of the Urban District Council, and tradesmen and parishioners. The ten foot high monument of red Aberdeen polished granite was erected over the good doctor's grave, costing £110-10s-0d. The sum was raised by the voluntary contributions of the residents of Raunds, Hargrave and Stanwick. The masonry work was carried out by Mr W Partrick.

Sunday, 8 September, Ernest Webb (121), died of wounds.

At this rate there soon wouldn't be more Webbs than spiders in Raunds!

The harvest festival services in connection with the Wesleyan Chapel were held today and Monday; the chapel being tastefully decorated by the lady members of the congregation. Considering the scarcity of fruit this season, there was an excellent show of a very fine quality; eggs and grapes also being very conspicuous amongst the gifts. Mr Milner Gray, of Luton, was the special preacher for the weekend and on Monday evening gave an address on the "League of Nations". The collections, on behalf of the Trust funds of the church, amounted to £107-0s-1d, and the proceeds of the sale of fruit etc amounted to £13-9s-0d.

On Monday, **9 September**, the parents of Sgt Harold Betts, of the Leicesters, received a postcard from France from their son describing how he had escaped from the captivity of the Germans after being taken prisoner on 27 May. Later in the day, Mr Betts senior was called to the telephone at Messrs Smith's factory, where he worked, and heard his son's voice. Sgt Betts informed his father that he was now in London and hoped to be home in the course of a few days.

Tuesday, **10 September**, "Raunds Section Blind and Crippled Children's Fund – Winning Numbers: 1st, 3690, 2nd, 4696, 3rd, 3101; W F Corby and Wm Agutter, Scrutineers. Prizes to be claimed within seven days from the Secretary, Mr J Hodson, 28 Marshall's Road, Raunds."

Today the War Office issued instructions that the supply of jam to German prisoners of war was to be discontinued; a case of conserving the conserves!

The Local Appeals Tribunal met on Thursday evening, **12 September**, and three men had their previously approved conditional exemptions reduced to three months (final) or dismissed altogether, after the military had requested a review of their cases. The next three applications were granted six month conditional exemptions. Of the final five cases reviewed, three were given three month exemptions and the other two adjournments pending medical examinations.

On Friday, **13 September**, the "Roll of Honour" published in the local newspapers included Pte J A Cuthbert, of Raunds and the Northamptons, who had been wounded no less than seven times!

It was also reported today that a hairdresser who appeared before the Camberwell Tribunal, said he thought he could get work at an aeroplane factory, to which the Town Clerk observed "So you want to get into another branch of hair craft".

"Wanted – Good Machinists and Finishers for Clothing; Best Prices and Bonus Paid; Applications to be made by letter to the Raunds Wholesale Clothing Co, by 27 September, or personally at the factory from 2 to 4; High Street, Raunds."

Wednesday, 18 September, Edgar Ellingham (47), Bernard Heath (62) & Walter Whiteman (129), all killed in action and Arthur James Wheatley (125), died of wounds.

The blackest day of the war for the town!

Thursday, 19 September, the Battle of Megiddo, Allenby's Allied forces crush the Ottoman army. Wilfred Dams (45), died of wounds.

Friday, 20 September, Norman Howard Mason (76), died.

On the day the town's only Merchant Navy casualty of the war died in far off South Africa, the local papers printed news that Pte **G Whitmore (131)**, of the Northamptons, had now been officially listed as "missing since March 1918"; and that Pte **Evelyn Wood (135)**, East Surreys, had been killed in action. The trio of bad news items was completed with the report that Pte A L Higby was being held a prisoner of war in Lechfeld, Bavaria, captured at the Battle of the Dunes.

But a happier revelation was the announcement of the award to Sgt H Betts, Leicestershire Regiment, of a Bar to his Military Medal.

Yet more casualties were reported on Saturday, **21 September**. Mr and Mrs William Allen, Grove Street, had received news that their son, Cpl **"Harry" Allen (9)**, Middlesex Regiment, had been killed in action sometime between 24 and 26 August; and news reached the town today that their Amateur Skating Champion and all-round sportsman, Pte F W Dix, Royal West Kents, had received wounds to both hands and was now in Bradford Hospital.

"Notice of Sales – Arthur G Brown – Raunds, Wednesday, 2 October – Plumber's and Painter's Tools and Requisites, Stock-in-Trade etc by instructions from Mr W B Sykes; Sale at 12.30."

The funeral of the late Miss Annie Harris, the 18 year old daughter of Mr and Mrs Ralph Harris, Primrose Hill, took place at the Wesleyan Burial Ground on Sunday afternoon, **22 September**. The teenager had suffered a long and painful illness.

On Tuesday, **24 September**, the Thrapston Guardians accepted the following tenders from Mr Beeby for their Raunds Children's Home: bread @ 8½d per 4lb loaf, flour @ 2s-7d per stone, seed cake @ 6d per lb, currant cake @ 8d per lb.

Looking back 50 years to 1868, the Kettering Leader recalled how, on the occasion of the village statute, the Raunds Temperance Society held teas for the Band of Hope members and adults, followed by a lecture by Mr J H Hollowell, of Northampton; and the powerful band of the Society paraded the town.

Wednesday, **25 September**, saw the report that Mr and Mrs C Williamson, High Street, had received news that their son, Pte F J Williamson, Royal West Surreys, had been wounded and admitted to the 11th Stationary Hospital, Rouen.

Thursday, 26 September, American forces launch a massive offensive in the Argonne, and although victorious, they suffer 120,000 casualties.

On the day that it was nearly too hot in the kitchen for the Doughboys, news arrived that Pte **W Dams (45)**, Primrose Hill and Essex Regiment, had died in France. The colourful former town butcher had been admitted to the 20th Casualty Clearing Station with gunshot wounds on the dreaded 18 September, and had died the following day. His wife had only received a letter from him on Monday of this week, so the sad news came as a great shock to her and their two sons.

Another town resident receiving worrying news today was Mrs Haynes, also of Primrose Hill, who was informed that her son, Pte Horace Hyde, Royal Fusiliers, had been severely wounded in both legs. He had lay for three days in a shell hole before being found. The former Temperance Bandsman and Regulation Boot Co worker was now at the South African Military Hospital, Richmond, Surrey.

Friday, 27 September, the Battles of (2nd) Cambrai and St Quentin, the Hindenburg Line is broken again.

As the positive news from the Western Front continued, it was announced at home that the rationing of jam would probably begin with the new ration books on 3 November; adults would get four ounces per week and children six ounces.

However, news also reached Raunds today that **Norman Mason (76)**, the 23 year old purser on the merchant vessel SS Yaraslavl, had died of pneumonia at Cape Town. The former Marshall's Road resident's funeral was attended by all of the officers from his ship. The casualty lists today also included the town's Pte **"Jack" Archer (14)**, of the Norfolks, listed as "missing since March 1918".

And things were really going from bad to worse for our Germanic cousins too, as it was reported today that the burgomaster of Tramm had recently received an express parcel which, when opened by the police, contained an "infernal machine"!

Saturday, 28 September, King Albert of the Belgians leads his troops at the Battle of Flanders.

A Raunds former prisoner of war arrived back from Germany today, as one of the exchanged prisoners who had landed at Boston; Gunner George Cunnington, Royal Garrison Artillery, the eldest son of Mr William Cunnington, of Hill Street, returning home minus a limb!

An interesting wedding took place today at Christ Church, Luton, when Pte C Matson, son of Mr H Matson, of Raunds, who had been in France for three years, was married to Miss A M Woodcroft, of Luton, a well known munition worker. After a reception at the bride's home, the happy couple left for Wellingborough. There were many valuable gifts, including a china tea service from the bride's fellow workers.

Sir Guy Calthrop, Coal Controller, issued a statement today that gas and electric light rations would commence from the meter readings to be taken from the period ending this month. Coal rations would start from the day the householder signed his requisition form, provided it was put in order prior to 31 October.

Sunday, 29 September, James George Cooper (42), killed in action.

Monday, 30 September, British and Arab troops capture Damascus.

The annual gathering of the Temperance Society was held in the Temperance Hall today (Statute Monday). The chairman, the Rev E P Blackburn, said that they had lost a great opportunity at the beginning of the war by not having total prohibition. The guest speaker, the Rev Canon Jephson, of Ecton, added that as a nation they must grip the temperance question more than ever before, as unless the country was prepared to deal with the liquor trade he would not "give a pin" for all the reconstruction schemes they could bring forward!

At the Higham Ferrers Police Court today, a Raunds man was summoned for driving a horse and cart without a rear lamp on 22 September. The defendant said his son was home from France and wanted to go to Rushden; he did not know the light was out or he would not have proceeded. He then went on to say that the summons was a silly one, and those who tried to enforce it would find themselves in the cart one day. This obviously did not endear him to the Bench who duly fined him 10s-0d!

*

*

8 – October to December 1918

Strangward's loss and the conflict is over!

OCTOBER – The Rev C Curtis began his Parish Notes with the news that the Harvest Festival Services would be held on Sunday, 6 October. The children were invited to bring offerings of eggs to their service at 2.15pm, the eggs to be sent to the wounded soldiers. On the following day, a public tea would be held in the school to be followed by the Annual Sale of produce in the Institute.

Notice was given of an "Hour of Sacred Music" on Sunday afternoon, 20 October. Mrs O'Connor, of Stanwick, and Mr B Sanders, of Rushden, having kindly consented to sing solos, and Mr Archer, "our worthy organist", giving the assembled a treat by playing selections on the organ. A silver collection would be taken in aid of the Prisoner of War Fund.

Thanks were given to Miss Jarvis, of Northampton, for cleaning and repadding the Chalice Corporals; and to Mr Fred Gilbert, father of **Jasper (54)**, an old parishioner and bell-ringer, in forwarding a dollar for flowers for the War Shrine.

The Church Lad's Brigade had spent a really enjoyable August Bank Holiday week "under canvas" in the Rectory grounds at Abington, by invitation of the Rev C C Aldred; and nine members of the company and the officer were also present at the 25th Anniversary celebration of the Kettering company in Wicksteed Park.

Finally, the following names were added to those who had "Died in the Service of Their Country": **Henry Allen (9)**, **Wilfred Dams (45)**, **Edgar Ellingham (47)**, **Norman Mason (76)**, **George Henry Webb (123)**, and **Evelyn Wood (135)**.

Tuesday, 1 October, von Ludendorff says that Germany must request a ceasefire.

The Raunds branch of the Shoe Trade Managers' and Foremen's Association met in the Co-operative Hall this evening. The speaker, Mr E J C Swaysland, of Northampton, said that Raunds for years had held the field for Government work against any competition, chiefly on account of its specially trained labour. He thought, however, that the future would be somewhat different and he advocated the town to develop a civilian trade. He also strongly advocated the intervention of the shop steward to talk over matters when disputes arose, and shorter hours, he thought, would also be beneficial and would not decrease output.

The distribution of prizes in connection with the Evening School took place in the Council School on Wednesday evening, **2 October**, when there was a fair gathering. Mr John Adams, JP CC, presided, supported by Mr J L Holland, secretary of the County Education Committee. It was reported that the session opened in October 1917 with 77 enrolled, against 74 the previous year. It was regretted that not enough students enrolled for the boot classes but it was hoped that more would join this year. Mr Adams commented that he was interested in evening schools; he had left school at eleven and had learnt more after than he did at school, as he attended evening school until after he was married.

Today it was announced that the butter output of all the creameries of Canada had been commandeered for Great Britain; and the maximum price had been fixed at 1s-11½d per pound. All stocks of tinned salmon had also been commandeered.

"Wanted – Yardman to live at lodge; good cottage and garden; Apply to A E Wingell, Raunds."

A mass meeting of workers employed in the boot and shoe trade was held in the Woodbine Club on Thursday evening, **3 October**. Mr E Batchelor, JP, a union official and member of the Arbitration Board, gave out the decisions agreed the previous day with respect to the revised scale of wages. The question of hand-sewn workers was also discussed.

The Old Age Pensions Sub-Committee also met this evening and considered three claims, two from Raunds and one from Ringstead. Two were allowed at the full rate of 5s-0d per week and the other disallowed owing to excessive means. There was also a question from the pension officer regarding the increase of a pensioner's means, and the pension was reduced from 5s-0d to 2s-0d per week.

Friday, 4 October, US President Wilson says that he wants an armistice based on his "14 Points". George Mundin Orton (85), died.

Today, came news of no less than six Raunds men! The deaths were reported of Pte **Edgar Ellingham (47)**, Royal Army Medical Corps, the son of the town's police sergeant; Pte **G H Webb (123)**, Northamptons, who had been taken ill and died in Palestine. Pte Webb had enlisted in 1913 and survived the Dardanelles campaign before serving in the Middle East for 3 years; and Pte **A J Wheatley (125)**, Royal Inniskilling Fusiliers, who had died of his wounds in France.

The remaining three men had fared slightly better: Mrs G Stock, Red Row, had received a letter from her husband that he was now a prisoner of war and well; Mrs F Reynolds, High Street, also received news that her husband, Gunner Fred Reynolds, Royal Garrison Artillery, had been slightly wounded by a gunshot in his back; and Mr and Mrs C Abbott, Kingswood Place, had learned that their son, LCpl Ralph Abbott, had been gassed in September and had spent time in three different hospitals in France before arriving at the Congleton Red Cross Hospital.

Also today, the boot manufacturers of Raunds decided to increase the wages of youths and females, the former by 5%, and the latter by 13 %, on top of their existing bonus.

Today, the Army Council issued the Wartime Boot (Manufacture and Sale) Order; this prohibited the manufacture or sale of war-time boots except under permit. A general permit was being issued to the wholesale and retail trade to deal in war-time boots. The purpose of the revised Order was to secure more uniform value in the war-time boots sold to the public, and to ensure that necessary supplies of boys and girls boots would be forthcoming. The Order fixed the rates of discounts that manufacturers could give to the distribution trade, and made the giving of these discounts compulsory.

Saturday, 5 October, the end of the Battles of (2nd) Cambrai and St Quentin, the Hindenburg Line falls.

The latest victory in Europe failed to enthuse the members of the Woodbine Working Men's Club today, as a flower show arranged for the benefit of members serving with the Colours received insufficient entries for the competition to take place. However, the exhibits received were sold, the proceeds being about £8.

In the evening, a meeting, arranged by the Friendly Society Council, was held in the Temperance Hall when an address on "Venereal Disease" was given by Brother W Smith, Grand Master of the National Order of Free Gardeners, to a limited attendance. A number of questions were asked and suitably answered.

Sunday, 6 October, the Second Battle of Le Cateau.

There was a crowded attendance on Monday, **7 October**, for the local branch meeting of the Boot and Shoe Operatives' Union, female members being well represented. Protest was made in regard to a few non-union men still refusing to fall into line in spite of the recent increases secured for them. As a result, the following resolution was passed unanimously: "That no new national terms of settlement be agreed to by the Union representatives that does not include all workmen in the trade (boys and girls under 18 inclusive)."

In the afternoon, the new Vicar and Mrs Curtis were welcomed at a tea held in the Church Schools. About 150 sat down to a meat tea arranged by Mrs A Camozzi and Mrs J V Spicer and before removing from tables a hearty welcome was accorded the newcomers by the churchwardens.

In the evening Mr T Richardson, MP for Whitehaven, addressed a meeting under the auspices of the Co-operative Society. The chairman, Mr James Coles, speaking of the local coal question, said that during the past few weeks 96 tons had been delivered in private trucks to a few houses, whereas at the same time their 800 registered members had only 80 tons amongst them!

"In Memoriam – In ever loving memory of **John Stanley Allen (10)**, private of the Royal Dublin Fusiliers, the only beloved son of Mr and Mrs F Allen; died of wounds received in action, 6 October, 1917, aged 19 years. Interred in Dozinghem British Cemetery, France (sic):

A loving son, a brother kind, a beautiful memory left behind;
We know, dear son, you did your best, and may God grant you eternal rest.
One year has passed, our hearts still sore, as time goes on, we miss him more,
His loving smile, his welcome face, No one can fill his vacant place.

From his ever-loving father, mother, and sisters and relatives, 2 Sackville Street."

Tuesday, 8 October, George Archer (13) & James Bond (23), both killed in action.

"For Sale – 10 £10 Shares with Dividends in the Raunds Gas, Light and Coke Co Ltd – Offers for one or any number up to ten shares to be forwarded to Mr T Stubbs, 39 Hill Street, Raunds, not later than Friday, 11 October."

Wednesday, 9 October, Cambrai is taken by the Allies, as are 110,000 German prisoners.

The Women's Co-operative Guild held a social and dance in the Temperance Hall this evening and Mr G W Coles, JP, of Rushden, gave an address on "Facts about Co-operation during and after the war". A musical programme was contributed to by the Misses York, Pentelow, and Dix, Mrs S Groom, and Messrs Coles and W Gibbs; Miss L Robinson accompanied the singing. After a short interval for refreshments, dancing proceeded, Mr Gibbs acting as MC, and music being supplied by Mrs Gibbs (piano) and Mr Burton (violin).

Sweet-toothed locals would have shuddered today to read that jam, marmalade, syrup, treacle and honey would be rationed as from 3 November.

"For Sale by Private Treaty – in the Parish of Raunds: Small Holding of 62 acres Arable and pasture Land, together with farmyard, stables, and open hovel thereas, conveniently situated in Brooks Road; Two Newly Built Dwelling Houses in Thorpe Street; Three Cottages with large gardens adjoining in Thorpe Street; and Three Cottages and useful orchard at rear in Midland Road. For full particulars, apply to W F Corby, "Hawarden House", Raunds."

Thursday, 10 October, Charles Henry Spriggs (111), killed in action.

A meeting of the Local Appeals Tribunal was held this evening and 25 separate cases were reviewed: one man (a butcher and slaughterer) was exempted for one month to allow the County Food Distribution Officer to consider the case; two men were granted two months exemption; three men three months; and nineteen, including the Tribunal's chairman and the clerk's brother, six months exemption.

The good news on Friday, **11 October**, was the award of the Military Medal to the town's Pte Ernest Harris, of the East Kents. However, things were not so rosy at home: the boot operatives of Raunds were threatening to strike if the town did not receive a sufficient supply of coal. It was said that in many houses there was no gas and that large families had been unable to cook food for four days together.

"In Memoriam – In loving memory of Pte **Arthur L Fairy (49)**, Norfolk Regiment, youngest son of Mrs E E Fairy, Thorpe Street, Raunds, killed in action in France, 9 October, 1917:

We cannot forget you, we loved you too dearly,
For your memory to fade from our lives like a dream,
Lips need not speak when the heart mourns sincerely,
And thoughts often dwell where they are seldom seen.
Days of sadness still come o'er us; tears of sorrow often flow,
Memory keeps our loved one near us, whom God claimed a year ago.

From his mother, brother, sister and Lillie."

"Thanks, Sgt and Mrs H Ellingham and family, Police Station, Raunds, beg to thank their many friends for their kind expressions of sympathy in the sad loss of their eldest son, Pte **E Ellingham (47)**, RAMC, killed in action, France, Sept 18."

Saturday, 12 October, the end of the Second Battle of Le Cateau.

"In Memoriam – In loving memory of **Dick Cobley (39)**, Norfolk Regiment, who died of wounds on 12 October, 1917, the son of Owen and Ellen Cobley, Raunds.

One year has passed our heart still sore; As time goes on we miss him more.
His loving smile, his welcome face; No one can fill his vacant place.
Could we have raised his dying head; Or said a last farewell,
'Twould not have been so hard to part; From him we loved so well.

From his loving father, mother, brother, sisters, and relatives, Marshall's Road."

"Official Notice – Curfew – Every night in October, the blinds must be drawn at 6pm; and every night in November, the blinds must be drawn at 5pm."

Monday, 14 October, the Allies drop the largest bomb of the war and retake Belgium.

Tuesday, 15 October, Thomas Ball (18), killed in action.

At the Thrapston Petty Sessions today, the Star Tea Company, Raunds, were summoned under the Sugar Order for knowingly delivering three-quarters of a cwt of sugar to a Raunds baker, for the purpose of his business, when no voucher had been issued by the Food Control Committee, between 13 July and 11 August, 1918. The baker was also summoned, for taking delivery of the said sugar. A Tea Company representative pleaded guilty to a "technical offence"; as did the baker. After the Bench had consulted in private, the chairman said there would be a fine of 40s-0d in each case. He added that they strongly hoped that no further cases of this kind would come to them as if they did, a heavier penalty would be imposed.

The wedding took place at the Parish Church on **Thursday, 17 October**, of Pte W Hall, RSBA, son of Mr and Mrs J Hall, of Higham Ferrers, and Miss Frances L Betts, daughter of Mr and Mrs H Betts, Thorpe Street. The bride was given away by her father, and the duties of best man were carried out by Sgt H Betts, brother of the bride, the recent heroic escapee from Germany.

"In Memoriam – In ever loving memory of our dear boy, Pte **G H Webb (123)**, the beloved son of Mr and Mrs S Webb, who died of sickness in Palestine on 7 September, 1918.

A loving son, a brother kind, a beautiful memory left behind.
We know, dear son, you did your best, and may God grant you eternal rest.

From his ever-loving father, mother, brothers and sisters, and Miss Rose Hammond, of London."

Friday, **18 October**, "Notice of Sales – Arthur G Brown – Raunds, Saturday next, 25 October: 130 head of Pure-bred Poultry, 2 Horses, 9 Pigs, Goat, 20 Doe Rabbits, Poultry appliances, Implements, Vehicles, Harness, and a few lots of Furniture, by instructions of Mr H O Hodson, who is giving up the poultry business; Sale at 12 o'clock; For full particulars apply to Arthur G Brown."

It was reported today that at the Poor Law Institution at Kettering, a woman who had taken up permanent lodgings for a month at the public expense, had given birth to a girl and called her "Cinderella"!

"In Memoriam – In loving memory of my beloved husband, William Sykes, who died 14 October, 1917, aged 79 years, Elizabeth Sykes, High Street, Raunds."

Saturday, 19 October, William John Chapman (34), died of wounds.

The Foreign Missions' Women's Auxiliary's annual meeting was held in the Wesleyan Schoolroom this evening, when there was a good company present. The speaker, Mrs Carr, from China, gave a very interesting address on "The Chinese Revolution and its effect on Missionary Work". There was also an exhibition of missionary curios and souvenirs sent by soldiers serving in India, Egypt, Mesopotamia, Palestine, and various other places, which aroused much interest.

Mrs A Camozzi and Miss F Kirk arranged a successful fund raising day today in aid of Dr Barnardo's Homes; in the afternoon the Temperance Band paraded the town, and a collection was taken and children sold flags. In the evening a dance was held in the Institute and was largely attended, the music being supplied by Mr J Stubbs (piano) with Mr D Bamford as MC. A corresponding number was also held; the total amount realised being over £20.

Sunday, 20 October, John Henry Laurance Robinson (102), died.

The "Hour of Sacred Music" was given in the Parish Church this afternoon in aid of the Prisoner of War Fund, when a collection realised between £5 and £6.

And down at the "Prims", the chapel anniversary was celebrated when the preacher for the day was the Rev W Bridge. In the afternoon, a people's service was held, when the address was given by Mr Bridge, Miss Butler was the soloist, and Mr J Tanner accompanied. A public meeting was held the following evening.

At the Council meeting on Monday evening, **21 October**, the clerk reported that he had not yet received a reply from the postal authorities with respect to improving the postal facilities. Mr Gates said that on most days a number of Raunds letters were posted at Higham Ferrers to catch their later postal collection. It was resolved to make further representations to the postal authorities.

The medical officer, Dr McInnes, reported three births and two deaths registered in September; there had also been one case of an infectious disease (enteric fever) during the period. The members then accepted the tender of Mr Ebenezer Lack, Wellingborough, to provide and plant trees and shrubs at the cemetery for £20.

On Tuesday, **22 October**, Mrs Robinson, 9 Hill Street, received a letter from the sister in charge of the No.2 General Hospital, Le Havre, France, advising her that her husband, LCpl **John Henry Robinson (102)**, was very ill with pneumonia. She also received two telegrammes from the Infantry Record Office: one refusing to grant her permission to visit him despite the severity of his case; the other one informing her of his death on 20 October!

Wednesday, 23 October, the battle of Vittoria Veneto begins, the Allies rout the Austrians.

The quarterly meeting of the Hospital Week Fund Committee was held at the Temperance Hall this evening. The treasurer reported year to date receipts of £266-8s-11½d, and expenditure of £227-7s-3d, £225 of which had been sent to the county treasurer. From the balance in hand of £39-1s-8½d, it was decided to send a further cheque for £35 forward.

Thursday, 24 October, Albert Summers (114), died.

"Shoe and Leather Trade – Foreman wanted, rough stuff department; experience of Army trade; Apply: Horrell and Son, Raunds."

Friday, 25 October, von Ludendorff resigns, Groner orders the immediate withdrawal of German forces in France.

By now it was clear that the end was drawing near for the Kaiser but for the town, the news being received continued to be grim. The demise of Pte **Bernard Heath (62)**, the son of Mr and Mrs J Heath, Marshall's Road, was reported today, a letter having been received from his platoon sergeant by Miss Betts of Marshall's Road; and Mrs S A Harrison, Thorpe Street, was advised that her son, Pte Arthur Harrison, of the Suffolks, had been wounded in the leg by a machine gun bullet.

The Liberal Literary Institute held their annual general meeting in the billiard room of the Coffee Tavern this evening, Mr A Hazeldine presiding. The treasurer's accounts for the year showed that general receipts were £42-11s-0½d, and expenditure £41-14s-4d, leaving a balance of 16s-8½d. The billiards account showed receipts of £21-17s-5d, and expenditure £13-7s-2d, a £8-10s-3d balance.

The death of Pte **W Chapman (34)**, of Westbourne Grove and the Royal Dublin Fusiliers, was reported on Saturday, **26 October**. He had been admitted to the 41st Casualty Clearing Station with severe head wounds on 18 October, and had died without regaining consciousness the next day.

Sunday, 27 October, Robert Arthur Frankham (52), died.

Mr George Nicholls, JP, Mayor of Peterborough, and ex-MP for North Northants, preached at the Wesleyan Church today. Solos and duets were performed at the afternoon and evening services by Mr and Mrs Robinson, of Thrapston, with Mr J W Hall accompanying at the organ. Collections in aid of the War Emergency Fund of the Wesleyan Church were taken at all the services.

Monday, **28 October**, "Thanks – Mr and Mrs H Robinson, 205 Regent Street, Kettering, desire to thank all kind friends for sympathy extended to them in the loss of their dear son Jack **(J H L Robinson (102))**, who died in the No.2 General Hospital, Le Havre, France, from influenza and pneumonia. 'His end was peace'."

Tuesday, 29 October, the German fleet at Jade refuse to engage the British fleet.

At this evening's meeting of the Church School managers, it was proposed and accepted that the Rev C Curtis be appointed as School Correspondent in place of the late Vicar, the Rev C C Aldred.

"Wanted, Man for Revolution Press; Apply: R Coggins and Sons Ltd, Raunds."

Wednesday, 30 October, the Turkish army surrender on the Tigris.

The Council School managers met this evening and the clerk reported that the County Committee had approved the increase of the caretaker's salary as recommended. At the meeting of the District Sub-Committee that followed, the attendance reports were reviewed and showed an average number on the register of 1,060, as against 1,116 the previous year; and the percentage of attendance 86.4 as against 87.4. Two parents appeared before the committee, and each promised to send their children to school regularly.

"Unduly Optimistic Department": Reports from all quarters in the London area today confirmed the belief that the influenza epidemic was now stationary; if not actually on the wane. – *How far from the truth was this!*

On Thursday, **31 October**, the Raunds Distributive Co-operative Society complained to the Food Control Committee that the Thrapston and District Meat Distributing Association had not allotted their weekly supplies in proper proportion to the Raunds butchers, and asked the committee to take up the matter with them. After discussion it was resolved to adjourn the matter until the later returns from the butchers would be available.

* *

Old Artificial Teeth Bought
Any condition, 6d per tooth pinned on Vulcanite,
2s-0d each on Silver, 3s-0d each on Gold, 8s-0d on Platinum.
Also Highest Value given for Old Gold & Silver Jewellery.
Cash Offer by Return; If offer not accepted parcel returned post free.
Satisfaction Guaranteed
S CANN & CO, 69a Market Street, Manchester

(and you thought that "Cash For Gold" was a new idea!)

* *

NOVEMBER – Writing his Parish Notes the Rev C Curtis thanked all who had kindly supported the Harvest Festival, either through the donation of gifts or those who had "so tastefully mantled the Church in harvest garb". Church collections totalled £16-18s-6d, profit from the tea was £3-15s-8d, and the sale of produce realised £15-10s-10d, which amassed, he believed a record total.

On Sunday, 3 November, a memorial Service would be held at 5.30pm, instead of the usual evensong, for all those who from the parish had given their lives in the cause of freedom and honour. There then followed a long list of those parishioners who had donated either money or flowers for the War Shrine; many of the names having lost loved ones during the past four years.

Finally, five more names were added to the list of those who had "Died in the Service of Their Country": **George Archer (13)**, **Thomas Ball (18)**, **James Cooper (42)**, **Bernard Heath (62)**, and **Arthur Wheatley (125)**.

The local headlines on Friday, **1 November**, were of the continuing spread of influenza throughout the county; all schools at Rushden and Wellingborough had been closed; and the local Boot and Shoe Union branch estimated that over 200 of their members were off work including 60 absentees from the Co-operative Wholesale Society factory at Rushden.

At the Wellingborough Petty Sessions today, a town shoehand was fined 10s-0d for trespassing after rabbits at Irchester on 19 October.

And George Denton, of Rotton Row, won a "Goodwill Pencil" from Cousin Claude for his story of the coming and going of a "very cross Aunt".

"Raunds Town War Charities Committee – Corresponding Number Competition, Winning Number: 3259; Scrutineers: Arthur Gates, L W Sheffield; Prize to be claimed within seven days from Mr J G Winsor, Lawson Street."

In aid of a fund for parcels to soldiers and sailors from St Crispin's boot factory, £14 was raised on Saturday, **2 November**, by a dance and social; Messrs J Stubbs (piano) and B Clarke (violin), supplied the music, with Mr S Groom acting as MC.

Also today, a Daisy Day in aid of the National Children's Home and Orphanage was held and a large body of young ladies went about the town selling flowers; a total of £11-14s-0d was contributed. Forty children from the county had been admitted into the Homes.

"Registration For Tea – Persons registered for tea must renew their registrations not later than 10 November by depositing with the retailer the 'spare counterfoil 2' on leaf 7 of their new ration books, properly filled in, otherwise they may be unable to obtain the necessary supplies of tea."

Sunday, 3 November, Austria / Hungary signs an armistice with the Allies and the German fleet mutinies at Kiel.

Monday, 4 November, the last major Allied attack on the Western Front takes place at Sambre.

Mrs Hannah Mitchell, of Marshall's Road, died today, at the ripe old age of 82.

Tuesday, **5 November**, was a sad day for our old farmer friend Strangward as his wife Sarah was buried at Bwlchygwynt Cemetery, Tregaron, Wales; the 36 year old mother of three had died of influenza with pneumoniac complications the previous Friday while visiting relatives.

"Thanks – Mr and Mrs Allen and Family, Primrose Hill, and Miss Pollard, desire to thank all kind friends for the sympathy extended to them in the loss of Cpl **H Allen (9)**, killed in action, 26 August 1918."

Thursday, **7 November**, "National Federation of Discharged and Demobilised Sailors and Soldiers, Rushden and District Branch; a meeting of Discharged and Demobilised Sailors and Soldiers will be held on Sunday, 10 November, at 10.30am, for Raunds and Stanwick men, at the 'Woodbine Club', Raunds."

Friday, 8 November, armistice negotiations begin at Compiegne.

As the peace talks in the woods began, news of two more Raunds casualties were reported in the local newspapers; Trooper **R A Frankham (52)**, of the Northamptonshire Yeomanry, having succumbed to pneumonia in Italy, and Mrs Archer, Workhouse Yard, having received official confirmation that her son, Pte **George Archer (13)**, was killed in action on 8 October.

"In Memoriam – In ever loving memory of Pte **Phillip Stubbs (113)**, Kings Royal Rifles, the dearly loved and only son of Joseph and Annie Stubbs, who died while in action, 3 November, 1916, aged 18 years:

Days of sadness still come o'er us; Hidden tears still often flow,
For memory keeps our loved one near us, Although he died two years ago.
It's hard to part with those we love, And hold on earth so dear,
The heart no greater trial knows, No sorrow so severe.

From his loving Mother, Dad and sisters, Raunds."

"In Memoriam – In ever loving memory of our dear mother, Sarah Nunley, of Raunds, who fell asleep on 6 November, 1911 – 'Until the day break'."

Saturday, 9 November, Kaiser Wilhelm abdicates. Wallace Payne (87), died.

On the day that old Bill scurried off to his bolt-hole in Holland, the Thrapston District Centre for the collection of blackberries announced its results for the season, and although the weather was as a rule unfavourable, the grand total showed an increase of nearly 200% on 1917. Included in the total gathered by schools of 20,071 lbs (just under 9 tons!), were 2,921 lbs by the Raunds Church of England Schools and 2,286 lbs by the Council Schools. Clopton Council School, with just 32 pupils, amassed an incredible 3,486 lbs!

The Rev R Little Rogers, of Bedford and formerly of Thrapston, who had been a missionary in South Africa, preached foreign missions sermons in the Wesleyan Church on Sunday, **10 November**, referring in the evening to the "Yellow peril!" In the afternoon Mr Rogers gave an address, and Miss M Sanders was the soloist.

Monday, 11 November, the British liberate Mons before dawn. The armistice is signed at 5am, to be effective at 11am.

The glad news the world had waited over four years for coincidentally reached Raunds at 11am! Mr W F Corby at once sent the tidings to the factories, which emptied immediately, and the whole town presented a lively appearance. The hooter was blown at the "Nene Works", the bells were ringing and flags flying; and the schools were closed for the day. One of the bellringers was 90 year old Mr William Nobles, of North Street, who, when he heard that the war was over, went to the church belfry and took part in ringing the bells.

The infamous Raunds clicker celebrated the world peace by making another appearance at Thrapston Police Court charged, once again, with disobeying a maintenance order made on 17 October, 1916. Supt Tebbey said that the defendant never paid unless brought to the court. The Bench duly made an order for payment forthwith, altogether £3-3s-0d with costs.

Also on the bill today was a town labourer, summoned for harbouring at Raunds on 6 November, a child placed under the control of the Guardians of the Thrapston Union. The defendant, a cripple, pleaded not guilty, and when told by the Bench he would have to return the girl or undergo imprisonment again, the man exclaimed "They can put a rope round my neck and hang me if they like!"

Today, Mr T C Jeeves presided at the annual Foreign Missions meeting and Mr Rogers gave an address on "The smoke of a thousand villages". The Rev E P Blackburn expressed thanksgiving for the cessation of hostilities, the choir singing the "Te Deum". The collection and subscriptions, about £70, far exceeded that total of previous years.

Also this evening, a "prayer and praise" meeting was held at the Baptist Chapel in celebration of peace; and a dance was staged in the Church Institute, the music being supplied by Mr J H Stubbs (piano), with Mr D Bamford acting as MC.

On Tuesday afternoon, **12 November**, the Temperance Band played for dancing on The Square when most of the parishioners turned out and old and young alike heartily took part. A dance was also held in the Church of England School on the same evening; the music being supplied by the ubiquitous Mr J H Stubbs on piano.

On Wednesday evening, **13 November**, a united service of prayer and praise was held in the Parish Church, when there was a large congregation, which included the members of the Urban Council and representatives of other public bodies. The Revs E P Blackburn and C Curtis conducted the service, a collection was taken in aid of the Red Cross Fund and the service was brought to a close with the "National Anthem".

A meeting was held on Thursday evening, **14 November**, of the Local Appeals Tribunal when a letter was read from the President of the Local Government Board saying that all cases pending before Tribunals should be suspended. Mr Shelmerdine, JP, the National Service representative, said that he had received similar instructions and thanked the members for the fair and considerate way in which the Tribunal had dealt with the cases. He added that it was unpopular work, but they had carried out their duties in a very fair and satisfactory manner.

The chairman, Mr A Camozzi, said that it was a happy ending, they had had a difficult and not pleasant duty to perform, but had tried to do their duty to the nation and to the applicants. After several more reciprocations of thanks amongst the members, the applicants entered the room together and were informed by the chairman that all cases were suspended indefinitely and that he felt relieved that they had got to the end of that work.

The Raunds Old Age Pensions Sub-Committee also met this evening when three claims from the town were considered and allowed at the full rate of 5s-0d per week. A question was raised by a pensioner whose pension was subsequently raised from 3s-0d to 5s-0d per week. A letter was read from Mr Walter Denton resigning his position on the committee owing to his removal from the district. This was accepted, the clerk being instructed to thank him for his services.

"Wanted – A Reliable Man as Gas Stoker; Apply: Manager, Gas Works, Raunds."

The local newspapers of Friday, **15 November**, featured photographs of the many area's men for whom "Peace Came Too Late"; included in the features were the town's **George Archer (13)**, **J G Cooper (42)**, and **C H Spriggs (111)**.

"Raunds – Arthur G Brown is selling by auction at the 'Cock Inn' on 21 November, 1918: a) 14 acres of freehold and copyhold arable and pasture land, situated close to the town of Raunds and suitable for a Small Holding; b) all that enclosure of pasture land situated adjoining Brooks Road containing 3 acres, 2 rods and now in occupation of Wm Pettitt together with the adjoining enclosure of arable land containing 10 acres, 1 rod, 21 poles now occupied by various allotment tenants; 'By instructions from the Raunds Tradesman's Sick Benefit Society, the owners.'"

Saturday, 16 November, Allied troops advance on Germany.

The War Charities Committee held a concert in the Wesleyan Schoolroom this evening in aid of the Christmas Parcel Fund for soldiers, the Red Cross, YMCA etc, the sum of £27 being raised.

At the Urban Council meeting on Monday evening, **18 November**, the chairman referred to the Armistice, observed that during the war they had to take up positions and do work that had been distasteful to them, but had done their best, and said that he hoped to see Councillor Lee and the surveyor back with them shortly.

The postmaster at Wellingborough wrote that a despatch from Raunds at 4.45pm had been arranged for, but he did not feel justified in recommending a second delivery. The members accepted this as satisfactory under the circumstances. The medical officer, Dr McInnes, was unable to attend owing to illness, and the usual monthly report was not forthcoming.

The Highway and Lighting Committee recommended that the County Council be informed that their proposal to discontinue the present annual grant of £300 and to pay one half of the actual cost of maintenance of the scheduled road was not considered acceptable. A circular letter was read from the Local Government Board with respect to the housing of the working classes. It was resolved that a special meeting of the council be held on Monday next to consider the matter.

Finally, a letter was read from the County Council requesting the council to send two delegates to a conference to be held at Northampton on Saturday, 30 November, to consider the question of a maternity and child welfare scheme; Messrs W Gates and J Hodson were appointed to attend.

"Official Notice – Ministry of Food – Notice is hereby given that the Maximum Retail price of Milk to be delivered in the Raunds District has been fixed by the Food Control Committee as: From 1 November, 1918 to 30 April, 1919: 2s-8d per gallon; John Bond, Food Distribution Officer for Northamptonshire."

On Tuesday, **19 November**, Mr J Hodson was elected a member of the Thrapston Board of Guardians in place of the now departed Rev C C Aldred.

A Women's Liberal meeting was held in the Temperance Hall on Wednesday afternoon, **20 November**, in support of the candidature of Mr Milner Gray. Miss Pulpher presided over a good attendance and congratulated women on having obtained the vote. Mrs Milner Gray said that though they were glad that women had won so much they looked forward to the time when other disabilities would be overcome, and when women under 30 years and not possessing the residential qualifications would have the vote as well as their sisters now on the register.

In the evening, Mr Milner Gray addressed a large gathering. He urged that after the war there must be a real democratic control of foreign policy, and the foreign policy must be democratic in reality. Justice, not vengeance, must be the object aimed at in the Peace Conference.

Thursday, 21 November, the German High Seas Fleet surrenders.

On Friday, **22 November**, news on the influenza epidemic showed hundreds of cases in Desborough and Rothwell, with all schools closed after at least 14 deaths!

A Flag Day was held on Saturday, **23 November**, arranged by Mrs A Camozzi, assisted by a large number of young ladies, in aid of the National Fire Brigade Union. In the evening a dance was held in the Church of England Schools on behalf of the same funds, when there was a good attendance. The music was unsurprisingly supplied by Mr J H Stubbs on the piano, and the MC duties were carried out by members of the Fire Brigade. The proceeds were nearly £19.

Monday, **25 November**, "In Memoriam – In ever loving memory of Pte **Edgar Jarvis (64a)**, 1st Northants, the dearly loved son of Mr and Mrs Jarvis, Stanwick, who was killed in action, 24 November, 1916:

It's only a mother who knows sorrow; It's only a mother who knows the pain,
Of losing her boy she loved so dear; Hoping in Heaven to meet him again.

From his ever sorrowing mother, father, brothers and sisters.

Tuesday, 26 November, the last German troops leave Belgium.

Two meetings were held on Wednesday, **27 November**, in the Temperance Hall in support of Mr W R Smith, JP, Labour candidate for the Wellingborough Division. Although important Union business prevented Mr Smith attending the women's meeting in the afternoon, he received a unanimous vote of confidence. In the evening he spoke forcibly on the reconstruction policy of the Labour Party. The State, he said, should bare the financial burden of providing a million homes as soon as possible after the war. The Treasury should also find the remaining money to provide a much better education system than that which existed today, based on the principle of equality of opportunity.

Mr and Mrs George Hunt, 16 Brooks Road, received the disturbing news on Friday, **29 November**, that their son, Pte L R Hunt, of the Northamptons, was admitted to the 5th General Hospital, Rouen, on 13 November, suffering from gunshot wounds in the left leg, which was shattered.

Two examples of the war hangover also appearing today were the restriction on the sale of high legged boots for women, so far as they were held in stock in this country, being removed, and the news that horses of the heavy type such as those used for drawing dust carts were now worth anything up to £150 each.

* *

F W MARCH
Has opened a SPECIAL SHOWROOM at
17 HIGH STREET, RAUNDS
With a full range of all the latest and most up to date
GRAMOPHONE RECORDS
Catalogues on application
Any Record not in stock obtained at the shortest notice

* *

DECEMBER – "The Great War – Thank God!" wrote the vicar in his first Parish Notes since the cessation of the hostilities. He went on to say that those two words were heard on the lips of all, for the horrors of war had been brought to a stay by what is called an armistice, which all hoped and prayed and believed meant nothing less than a just and abiding peace.

"When we think how we stood only a few months ago, how near the enemy was to Paris, and what danger threatened our own shores, it seems incredible. But victory is worthless unless it leads on in peace to something nobler than the past. We must endeavour to build up a new and better England, a new and better confederacy of British nations, a new and better world, wherein wars will be impossible!"

Of general church notes, the first Mother's Union meeting had successfully taken place on Wednesday, 13 November, with a service in the Church followed by an excellent war-tea in the Institute; and on a sadder note, the curate, the Rev W Bethway, had decided to resign on demobilisation, his reasons being that he thought it advisable to make a fresh start elsewhere.

Finally, two more casualties were added to the list of those who had "Died in the Service of Their Country": **Robert Frankham (52)** and **Wallace Payne (87)**.

The town's military deaths continued with the news that Mrs J Lawman, Beech Hill, had received a telegram on Sunday, **1 December**, from Catterick Camp, asking her to go at once, as her husband, Pte **Jesse Lawman (70)**, Norfolks, was very ill. Mrs Lawman and her mother-in-law went at once, but her husband died the following day from double pneumonia following influenza. He was buried in Raunds cemetery on Saturday, 7 December.

And there was grim news for Rushden farmers today with the news that three bullocks had been destroyed and cremated on account of suspected anthrax. German prisoners dug the cremation pits; the animals were valued at £85.

Monday, 2 December, Jesse Lawman (70), died.

Tuesday, **3 December**, "Wanted – Two Tons of Soot; Price to W Head, White House, Hargrave."

Wednesday, **4 December**, and a picture postcard posted in France in August 1914 by a Northants Regiment private was finally delivered to its Wellingborough destination this week. A local Frenchman had hidden the contents of the postbox for over four years before being able to hand it over to the British authorities.

On Friday, **6 December**, it was reported that Pte **George Orton (85)**, East Surreys, had died at Munster, Germany, as a prisoner of war. He had enlisted in August 1914 and had been taken prisoner at the Battle of Aubers Ridge on 9 May, 1915. He left a widow and two sons, one of whom, Arthur, was serving, and one daughter.

In a happier vein, the award of a Military Medal to LCpl Percy Rollings, Chelveston Road and Royal Scots, was announced today. The citation stated that the Raunds man, who also received a promotion, had been recognised for "bravery on the field during the big advance in Flanders".

"In Memoriam – In ever loving memory of Pte **Arthur James Knighton (68)**, 2nd Royal Inniskilling Fusiliers, who was killed at Passchendaele, 2 December 1917:

You are always in our thoughts, dear Arthur; It is sweet to breathe your name,
In life we loved you dearly; In death we do the same.

From his loving wife, mother, father, sisters and brothers, Bridge Street, Raunds."

Saturday, **7 December**, "Official Notice – Ministry of Food – Canned Tongue – the recent concessions by which Edible Offal, including Tongue, is made free of coupons does not include Canned Tongue or Tongue sold in glass containers. These must still be sold against coupons, and it is a contravention of existing orders to do otherwise; 6 December, 1918."

At Thrapston Petty Sessions on Tuesday, **10 December**, a Thorpe Street woman was charged with bigamy by marrying a Raunds man at Ringstead on 20 April, 1918, despite her husband, who she had married on 14 May, 1903, still being alive. The defendant pleaded guilty and was remanded in custody for a week.

Thursday, 12 December, British troops cross the River Rhine and occupy Cologne.

"For Sale – 6hp, 1913 Rex, 2 speed and free engine; cane sidecar and luggage carrier; overhauled and in perfect condition, £30. One shop-soiled Gent's Raleigh Cycle, £12; One Girl's Cycle, suit girl of 8 or 9 years, £5; One Ladies' Cycle, £6: H Gaunt, 21 High Street, Raunds."

"Sift Your Cinders", proclaimed a headline on Friday, **13 December**. It was said that the output of 10,000 miners was wasted yearly, for although coal was scarce, it was believed that many householders were losing the full value of their rations by failing to sift their cinders thoroughly. It was estimated that there was wasted annually cinders equal in heating value to 2,226,000 tons of coal!

Also today the "Kettering Leader" contained an abundance of General Election paraphernalia; however, folk anticipating a pleasant trip over Christmas were informed that there would be no excursion trains during the holiday period.

Saturday, 14 December, Britain goes to the polls in the General Election.

The medical officer, Dr McInnes, made a welcome return to the monthly meeting of the Urban Council on Monday, **16 December**, after his absence through illness. He reported six births and three deaths during October and three births and four deaths during November; two cases of infectious notifiable diseases were also reported in each month.

In view of the shortage of gas it was resolved that the street lamps be not lighted for ten nights during each moon. The application from the residents of Newtown, asking that the lamp on Newtown Green should be lighted in addition to those already decided upon was granted. Next, the members decided to plant three lime trees on a piece of ground at the bottom of Manor Hill.

A plan showing a small addition to the coach-house in High Street for Mr Horace Gaunt was approved; and a letter was read from the L and N W Railway Co. intimating that an additional train each way on the Northampton and Peterborough branch would commence on 1 January, 1919.

The clerk called attention to the order as to the hours of polling in Raunds for the local elections, viz noon to 8pm. Owing to the increased number of electors it was decided to ask the County Council to order polling to take place from 8am to 8pm.

Finally, the chairman was authorised to accompany the chairmen of Finedon and Irthlingborough Councils to interview the postmaster at Wellingborough, to ask for a second delivery daily.

It was reported that the Children's Home Committee of the Thrapston Board of Guardians had on Tuesday, **17 December**, received the resignation of the superintendent and matron of the Children's Home at Raunds. The couple had been appointed to a position at Romford, Essex.

The Raunds woman accused of bigamy made a return appearance at the Thrapston Court today and after the delivery of more prosecution evidence, she was committed for trial at the Assizes for feloniously marrying again while her husband was still alive. During the hearing it was stated that she had told the officials at the Baptist Chapel, Ringstead, where the marriage took place, that she had been divorced.

The death of Mrs Atkins, aged 51, wife of Mr Thomas Atkins, of the "Wheatsheaf Inn", was announced on Friday, **20 December**. In addition to her husband, she left two sons (one of whom was serving in Mesopotamia), and a daughter.

The annual prize distribution took place at the Church Schools this afternoon. The vicar presided, and 26 "old boys", Army men on leave, were present, including five Military Medal holders, several war prisoners recently returned from Germany, and a Zeebrugge Mole hero! Carols and part-songs were sung and 36 prizes were awarded for attendance, progress and conduct. All scholars also received an orange, the gift of Mr A Camozzi, chairman of the School Managers.

It was revealed today that of the 22,000 men of the Midland Railway who joined the Colours, 1,987 were killed, 4,000 were wounded, 268 were reported missing and 452 were prisoners of war. Medals or orders had been awarded to 331 men.

"Thanks – Mrs Jesse Lawman and family, 14 Beech Hill, desire to thank most sincerely all friends for the sympathy shown in their sad and sudden bereavement; also for the beautiful flowers sent."

The Independent Order of Rechabites, in connection with their Juvenile Tent, held a tea and social in the Temperance Hall on Saturday afternoon, **21 December**. Bewteen 60 and 70 sat down to the tables; and after they had been cleared songs, recitations, and instrumental items were given by the members. During the evening an initiation service was held, followed by games and amusements.

A dance was held in the Church Institute this evening, the music being supplied by Mr J H Stubbs (piano) with Mr E Eaton carrying out the duties of MC.

"Northants War Agricultural Executive Committee – Notice to Bee-Keepers, the Royal Commission on the Sugar Supply have decided that Bee Food shall be rationed. All Bee Keepers who will require Food for Spring feeding must register not later than 31 December, 1918."

The annual musical meeting was held in the Wesleyan Church on Sunday afternoon, **22 December**, when the church was well filled. The usual carols were sung and a solo was rendered by Miss M Sanders, Mr J W Hall accompanied at the organ. An instrumental quartette was given by members of the Temperance Band (Messrs O Pentelow, F Jeffkins, E Vickers, and W Groome). Mr W F Corby read the letter sent with the monetary gift from the Town War Charities Committee to the men of the town serving with H M Forces, and also some extracts from the replies, which proved of a very interesting character. The collection for Northampton Hospital amounted to £5-4s-6d.

The Admiralty and War Office announced on Monday, **23 December**, that officers and men already awarded the 1914 Star would not also be eligible to receive the new decoration (the 1914-15 Star) which embraced service in a theatre of war for the period up to 31 December, 1915.

A quiet wedding was solemnised at the Primitive Methodist Chapel today, the contracting parties being Miss Lilian Bertha Harrison, the only daughter of Mr and Mrs John Harrison, Sackville Street, and Pte George William Parker, youngest son of Mr and Mrs J Parker, Marshall's Road. The Rev W Bridge (Wellingborough) officiated and Mr J Tanner presided at the organ.

The following day, **Christmas Eve**, it was reported that the question of war medals was now under official consideration; the main one being whether one general war medal should be issued, or whether precedent should be followed to the extent of issuing separate medals for each theatre of war.

Through the generosity of the Guardians and local friends, the children of the Children's Home enjoyed **Christmas Day** in the good old-fashioned style. The dining hall was tastefully decorated by the master and matron, and a huge Christmas tree was heavily laden with useful presents and toys. The children sat down to a substantial dinner of roast goose, potatoes, vegetables, sweets, and mince pies, to which ample justice was done. For tea, bread and butter, cake, pastries, blanc-mange, and jellies were provided. Mrs G E Smith, chairman of the Homes Committee, generously supplied a quantity of sweets and oranges.

Through the kindness of Mr William Richards and members of the Woodbine Working Men's Club, for the third consecutive Christmas each child was presented with a bag containing sweets, nuts, oranges, bananas, and fourpence. Five large cakes were also provided. Great credit is due to Mr Richards and his fellow-members for contributing in such a lavish manner to the happiness of the children. In the evening, the children were entertained to gramophone selections by Councillor J Hodson and Mrs Hodson and friends, which were greatly enjoyed. The Christmas tree was then stripped, and each child was presented with a useful and pleasing present. Hearty cheers were given for the Guardians, the Woodbine Club, Councillor Hodson and Mrs Hodson, and friends.

On **Boxing Day**, the Wesley Guild held their annual social in the schoolroom which was largely attended. Vocal and instrumental items were contributed, and various seasonal games were also provided. Light refreshments were served during the evening.

Two stories of town interest appeared in the newspapers of Friday, **27 December**: one concerned Pte Hugh Clarke, Northamptons, recently arrived home from Alsace-Lorraine, where he had been in German hands for several months. Pte Clarke had suffered several wounds to his legs but medical attention had been severely lacking, although thankfully it was sufficient to avoid the need for amputation. The soldier, having been forced to work at a German aerodrome close to the lines, had some telling observations on the relative merits of the opposing airmen. He said that the German pilots had something lacking about them, either their training was too superficial or they did not possess the necessary pluck and initiative of our own boys, who displayed such a splendid fighting spirit!

The other, much briefer story was that among the souvenirs brought home from Germany by 1st Air Mechanic Holmes, was an illustrated pamphlet in French designed to be dropped by balloon over Germany.

The good news today from the railway companies for disabled soldiers was the announcement that all accompanying invalid and bath chairs would be carried free.

Starkly contrasting post-war stories from Europe and Britain appeared today. At home, due to the large number being imported, oranges and lemons were removed from the price restricted list; the maximum price of Egyptian dates was fixed at 10d per pound; and from Sunday, 29 December, pork and all kinds of canned meat were to be free from rationing. However, in Vienna it was reported that thousands were dying for want of food, with up to 20,000 out of the population of 2,250,000 expected to die as soon as the cold weather set in; and from Turkey came alarming reports of Christians being murdered by their fellow Turks!

Saturday, 28 December, David Lloyd George, Coalition Party, becomes Prime Minister.

Today, an overwhelming victory in the General Election for the Coalition candidates was declared: Coalition, 477 seats; others, 229; an overall majority of 248. However, the Labour Party was successful in the East Northants division, with Mr W R Smith edging out Mr Milner Gray by 10,290 to 9,313.

Meanwhile in Rance, a largely-attended dance was held in the Central Hall of the Church of England School this evening, arranged by the teachers of the Sunday School for the benefit of Miss Rose Merrill, who had been ill for over two years. Dancing was indulged in, the music being supplied by (*Yes, you've guessed it!*) Mr J H Stubbs (piano) and Mr Bert Clarke (violin). Mr E Eaton was the MC and the proceeds amounted to the sum of £8.

The Young Leaguers Union held a bazaar and entertainment in the Wesleyan Schoolroom on Monday afternoon, **30 December**, in aid of the National Children's Home. The stalls were arranged by Mrs Green and friends and a musical programme was given. The proceeds were £20.

A "Masked Ball" was held in the Church Schools this evening, in aid of funds of the Church Lads Brigade; the MC was Mr Herbert Betts. Prizes for fancy dress were won by: *Ladies*, 1st, Miss E Pettit; 2nd, Miss E Butler; 3rd, Miss D Wilkins; *Gentlemen*, 1st, Mr E March; *Special Prize*, Miss E Pettit.

"In Aid of the YMCA – a Fancy Dress Dance will be held in the Church Rooms, Stanwick, on 1 January, at 7.30pm; Prizes Given, Admission 1s-0d; Messrs Stubbs and Clarke's Orchestra!"

The full list of the staff of the Church of England Schools, as recorded on Tuesday, **31 December**, was: Mixed School: *Headteacher*: Arthur David Rawlings; *Certified Teachers*: John Henry Stubbs, and Dorothy Louise Tether; *Uncertified Teachers*: Elsie Mackenzie Ash, Florence Kirk, and Florence Hall; Infants School: *Headteacher*: Lilian Mary Manley Hull; *Certified Teacher*: Gladys Lodder; *Uncertified Teachers*: Florence Ethel Spicer and Gertrude Jane Spicer.

The Director of Raw Materials gave year-end cheer to all with the news that a revised list of "war time" boots and shoes had been issued providing for an advance in the manufacturers prices and the consequent increase of the retail selling prices. The advance had been made as a result of recent wage increases to factory operatives.

And so the town enjoyed its first peacetime Christmas and New Year celebrations for five years. One hundred and twenty seven Raunds men or men of Raunds who had lived and loved at the beginning of 1914, had perished during the fifty two months of war that followed; and the death toll would rise even higher before the town's memorial to the fallen was unveiled in October 1921.

9 – January to December 1919

The first council houses and "Peace Day".

JANUARY – The Rev C Curtis wrote in his Parish Notes "We enter upon the New Year under the conditions of an armistice, which we hope and pray and fully believe will lead to a right and lasting peace. We entered upon the year 1918 under the gloomy conditions of war, how very differently we enter upon 1919!

He then added to the list of those who had "Died in the Service of Their Country" the names of **Herbert Bates (22)**, **James Bond (23)**, **Jesse Lawman (70)**, and **George Orton (85)**.

The local newspapers of Friday, **3 January**, carried several military stories of local interest: Pte Bert Nunley, Cambridgeshires, the son of Mrs O Nunley, Wellington Road, had been awarded the Military Medal for gallantry and devotion to duty on the Western Front; Pte S Cuthbert, Gloucestershires, wrote of his weird experiences as a prisoner of war, working in an iron mine, and surviving on starvation rations; the Higham Ferrers VAD Hospital had closed on Tuesday, 31 December, 1918; and the men of the 1st Battalion, Northamptons, captured at the Battle of the Dunes had been released from their prison camp in Bavaria and had recently crossed the Swiss frontier into France.

A Raunds married woman was summoned to the Thrapston Petty Sessions on Tuesday, **7 January**, charged with common assault on the headmaster of the Council School. Found guilty, she was fined £1. And making yet another return appearance before the Bench today was the town clicker, who this time had amassed maintenance order arrears of £2-10s-0d; an order for payment was made.

Friday, **10 January's** newspapers all reported on a Raunds woman who had complained that though she had voted for the "Coal" candidate in the recent general election, she still had not yet received any coal!

The Co-operative Women's Guild held an entertainment in the Temperance Hall on Saturday evening, **11 January**. The programme was provided by the members and children, who were trained by Miss Gladys York. Dancing followed, the music being supplied by the veritable duo of Stubbs and Clarke.

Sunday, 12 January, the Paris Peace Conference begins.

While at home on leave on Tuesday, **14 January**, 1A/M Harold Holmes, RAF, the second son of Mr and Mrs W Holmes, "Lawson House", heard that he had been demobilised and quickly arranged to resume his former civilian employment.

Pte G W Agutter's return from Germany was reported on Friday, **17 January**. The Military Medallist told how, after being captured, he was taken to a camp near to Berlin. There he found the hardships at times inhuman and for little or nothing, he was clubbed with the butt end of a rifle. It was only after he began receiving parcels of food and money that he was no longer in danger of starving.

On Monday, **20 January**, the Urban Council heard that the surveyor had been discharged from the Army. The medical officer, Dr McInnes, advised that six births and three deaths were registered during December; and the Sanitary Inspector reported on the poor condition of houses in the Newtown area where four cases of diphtheria had been reported.

The Cecilia Choir held a whist drive and dance in the Church Institute on Friday evening, **24 January**, for the benefit of an old member of the choir, Mr H Cox, who had been ill for a long time, and raised £9. First prizes in the Ladies' and Gentlemen's competitions were won by Miss G Essex and Mr J Vorley.

Saturday, 25 January, the Paris Peace Conference accepts the principle of the League of Nations.

Mrs A Camozzi arranged another successful flag day today in aid of the YMCA Hut Week Fund. A dance was also held in the evening in the Church School. The proceeds of both efforts totalled £20.

The Independent Order of Rechabites held a meat tea and social in the Temperance Hall this afternoon when twenty new members were enrolled.

A large company assembled in the Wesleyan Church for a special service on Sunday afternoon, **26 January**, in aid of funds for the YMCA. The Temperance Band was present and a solo was rendered by Pte C Coles, home on leave from France. Mr J W Hall provided the accompaniments and the collection realised £14.

Percy Ashby, a lad in the employ of Messrs Neal and Gates, was working on a Hercules leveller on Monday, **27 January**, when he got both his thumbs crushed. He was taken to Northampton Hospital where he was said to be satisfactory.

The young women employed at the Regulation Boot Co held a very successful dance in the Temperance Hall on Wednesday, **29 January**. The proceeds of £8 were in aid of the St Dunstan's Hostel for Blinded Soldiers and Sailors.

Mrs A Hazeldine received on Friday, **31 January**, a note from Lt E O Davies, South Wales Borderers, concerning the death of her husband, Pte **Arthur Hazeldine (61)**, in November 1917. The officer had been given her husband's papers on the battlefield but had subsequently been captured and held prisoner, and so had been unable to forward the items to her until now.

* *

FEBRUARY – The Raunds branch of the Labour Party held a tea and social in the Temperance Hall and the large room of the Woodbine Working men's Club on Saturday, **1 February**, to celebrate the victory of Mr W R Smith in the general election. A sandwich tea was provided to which about 420 sat down; the catering being admirably carried out by the Raunds Distributive Co-operative Society. A dance was held in the Woodbine Club, the music being supplied by Miss Gladys York (piano) and Mr F S Harris (violin); Mr J Coles was the MC.

At the Thrapston Petty Sessions on Tuesday, **4 February**, five lads, shoehands of Raunds, were summoned for obstructing the public footpath, causing a number of persons to get off the footpath on to the road, including people going to divine service. The incident took place after the lads had been given several cautions; as a result, four were fined 5s-0d, and the other 2s-6d.

On Friday, **7 February**, it was announced by Mr J Gribble that a mutual agreement had been reached by the Boot and Shoe Union and manufacturers to reduce the working week to 48 hours, commencing at the end of March. Whether this would mean Saturdays becoming "off days", longer meal times, or a later start in the mornings, was left to the "localities" to decide.

It was recalled today that, 50 years ago (1869) in the important village of Raunds, the inhabitants had at last decided to adopt the Lighting and Watching Act and place street lamps in their "sinuous and winding streets".

A town meeting was called by the Urban Council on Monday, **10 February**, to consider the question of housing for the working classes. In addition to the councillors, about 40 others were present. The Council proposed the building of 44 houses on suitable sites viz land adjoining the Council Schools, near Messrs Neal and Gates factory, and on building land in Clare and Lawson Streets.

Friday, 14 February, the draft covenant of the League of Nations is completed.

Today, it was reported that the name of Miss Marie Yorke, late of Hill Street, had been brought to the notice of the Secretary of State for valuable services rendered to the Air Ministry in connection with the war.

Also today, it was revealed that the Raunds Wesleyan Methodist Circuit had had a record year in 1918 for Foreign Missions, some £200 having been raised. Mr T C Jeeves had collected the impressive sum of £71-18s-0d and £15 had also been contributed for the "Transvaal work".

"For Sale – Six newly built dwelling houses in Brooks Road, Raunds; Apply to W F Corby, Raunds."

Saturday, 15 February, Frederick Athol White (127), died.

A benefit dance for disabled soldiers (not discharged) was arranged by the Misses A Coles and M Lawrence today and together with a "sugar-guessing" competition, realised £8-8s-6d, which was divided between seven disabled soldiers and two widows. Messrs Stubbs and Clarke provided the music with Mr W Millard as MC.

At the council meeting on Monday, **17 February**, the housing scheme proposed at the town meeting was adopted; the acting surveyor reported that a part of the culvert in Newtown had collapsed, and it was decided to take the question of reconstruction of the culvert in the next estimates. The medical officer, Dr McInnes, reported five deaths and four births during January, there were also nine cases of infectious diseases notified during the month.

The Temperance Society held their annual meeting in the Temperance Hall on Thursday evening, **20 February**, when the officers for the coming year were elected; Miss Pulpher was again chosen as president.

It was announced on Friday, **21 February**, that Bombadier Charles A Mansbridge, Royal Garrison Artillery, had been awarded the French "Croix de Guerre" for devotion to duty during the great retreat in March 1918. The Prince of Wales was present at the awards ceremony.

"Notice – Any person damaging Osiers in my occupation in the parish of Raunds by shooting in the same, will be prosecuted without distinction. £1 reward offered for information leading to the conviction of the offender; George Shaw, Raunds, 19 February, 1919."

Sunday, 23 February, Benito Mussolini forms the Italian Fascist Party.

On Monday, **24 February**, the Council Schools managers decided to present a book to a scholar who had made six years full attendance.

News reached Raunds on Friday, **28 February**, of the death in a French hospital on 15 February, of Pte **Fred White (127)**, 4th King's Liverpools, the son of Mrs Walter Hales, of Wellington Road. The first war casualty for the town of 1919, he had become another victim of the influenza pandemic sweeping the globe.

It was also announced today that the Raunds seat nominations for the upcoming County Council elections were William Fellowes Corby, assistant overseer (Independent), and James Coles, foreman boot-finisher (Labour).

"New Companies – Wellington Chrome Tanning Co (Raunds) Ltd (153183); Private Company, Registered 15 February, Capital £10,000 in £1 shares." All of the first subscribers and directors were Kettering men.

* *

MARCH – Miss Pulpher celebrated her diamond jubilee as a teetotaller by giving tea on Saturday, **1 March**, in the Temperance Hall to inaugurate the scheme for raising a special fund for 1919 for the Northamptonshire Temperance and Band of Hope Union. About 60 were present. ***(Plate 4)***

At the monthly meeting of the Boot Operatives Union on Monday, **3 March**, a proposal was carried unanimously that "The time has arrived for the introduction of a national annual summer holiday of 10 days duration, wages to be paid, and any workers foregoing this to have the right afforded to them of an alternative date by arrangement." Strong dissatisfaction was also expressed at the smallness of the female minimum wages, and the minimums fixed for boys and youths. Finally, the committee set up to deal with demobilised soldiers and sailors in men's departments and the displacement of women working in men's departments, proposed that married women, whose husbands were working, should be the first to leave before single girls who depended on their own earnings for a living.

On Friday, **7 March**, it was reported that rain had fallen on Raunds on 129 out of the 191 days from 25 August to Tuesday last.

The result of the County Council elections announced today produced a victory in the Raunds Ward for Mr W F Corby over Mr J Coles, by 873 votes to 744.

A social in aid of funds to carry on the work of the British Women's Temperance Association's "Little White Ribboners" was held in the Temperance Hall on Saturday, **8 March**, when £4-13s-7d was raised.

The members of the Wesleyan Church entertained 70 demobilised soldiers connected with the Church, Sunday or Day School on Monday, **10 March**. In addition to the 70 guests, about 200 other friends sat down to tea.

On Friday, **14 March**, the War Office announced that since the date of the armistice, 48,717 officers and 1,613,449 other ranks had been demobilised.

"In Memoriam – In ever loving memory of **John Brackley Higby (63)**, Bedfordshire Regiment, who died of wounds in France, 15 March, 1917, aged 26 years. Also **Ralph Higby (64)**, Bedfordshire Regiment, reported missing, 3 May, 1917, aged 19 years:

Days of sadness still come o'er us, Hidden tears often flow,
For memory keeps our loved ones near us; Although they died two years ago.

From mother, father, sisters, brothers, Ida and Minnie, High Street, Raunds."

When the twenty-six nominations for the twelve seats on the Urban Council were received on Thursday, **20 March**, that of Mr L G H Lee, a present member who had long been away in the war, was declared invalid on the grounds that he had not resided in the district for the qualifying period of twelve months! Fear not, such a perceived injustice would never be tolerated by the folks of "Red-Rance".

Friday, **21 March**, "In Memoriam – In loving memory of Pte **George Webb (122)**, who died from the effects of gas in France, on 23 March, 1918:

One year has gone, but oh! we miss him; Some may think the wound has healed,
But they little know the sorrow; That's within our hearts concealed,
There's one link death cannot sever; Fond remembrance lasts for ever.

From his wife and children, parents and sister."

"In Memoriam – In ever loving memory of Lance Corporal **Fred Norris (81)**, eldest son of Mr and Mrs G Norris, of 48 Marshall's Road, Raunds, who fell in action in France, 22 March, 1918:

Though his grave I may not see; My boy will ne'er forgotten be,
My real son can never die; 'Tis but his body that may lie,
In foreign land, and I shall keep; Remembrance fond forever, deep,
Within my heart of my true son; Because of triumphs that he won."

The Rev J Crowle Smith, of Letchworth, was the speaker at a special meeting at the Wesleyan Church on Sunday afternoon, **23 March**, on behalf of the Palestine and Syria Relief Fund. Solos were sung by Mrs J W Hall and Mr O D Hall, the latter having only just arrived home from Egypt that morning; both were accorded hearty receptions. The collection, on behalf of the Fund, realised a good sum.

The Urban Council met for its final session on Monday, **24 March**, and confirmed the appointment of Mr H Nichols of Oundle as the new veterinary inspector for Raunds at a salary of £20 per annum. The medical officer, Dr McInnes, reported three births and two deaths during February.

On Friday, **28 March**, it was announced that the Military Medal had been awarded to Pte F Burton, of the 6th Northamptons.

Another County Regiment man appeared at Thrapston Police Court today, in a sequel to the recent bigamy case, charged with abetting; fortunately for him, the case was dismissed.

And in another sign of the gradual return of normal life, it was announced that the daily bus service between Wellingborough and Raunds would shortly be resumed.

Saturday, 29 March, Einstein's theory of Relativity is confirmed experimentally during a solar eclipse.

* *

APRIL – The vicar began his Parish Notes with the news that a recent congregational meeting had decided to purchase some "parochial crockery", and the committee duly formed for the purpose had recommended that enough crockery and spoons be purchased to supply 16 tables; each article to be stamped with a badge bearing the words "Saint Mary's, Raunds". Donations towards the £20 total cost were requested, with Mr A Camozzi offering to pay in advance for the goods, to be repaid in installments as funds were forthcoming.

Another decision taken was to give a "tea of welcome" followed by a social to all of the demobilised men of the Parish; to be held on Friday, 2 May. Bills were to be printed and distributed in the shops and factories to find out the names of all who had returned.

Sweet-toothed locals would have been delighted to read on Friday, **4 April**, that Easter eggs were to be sold this year free from all restrictions.

The Urban Council elections took place on Saturday, **5 April**. Of the 1,600 on the electoral roll, 1,180 voted and L G H Lee, whose nomination was the subject of some dispute, ironically emerged as the most popular candidate, collecting 681 votes. Taking the other eleven seats were, in order of votes received: G E Smith, E Batchelor, J Hodson, A Camozzi, A D Rawlings, J Coles, W Cobley, A Hazeldine, H W Lawrence, E C Martin, and A Lawrence.

The Northants Football League met at Wellingborough on Thursday, **10 April**, and decided to resume the competition in autumn. Although many clubs were represented at the meeting, no word was heard from Raunds or Irthlingborough.

Friday, 11 April, Leonard Whitney (132), died.

"In Memoriam – In loving memory of Pte **Ralph Pentelow (91)**, of the 12th Suffolk Regiment, who was killed in action in France on 9 April, 1918:

We often think of days gone by;When we were all together,
A shadow o'er our life is cast;A loved one gone forever.

From his sorrowing wife and children, father and mother, brothers and sisters, Raunds."

"In Memoriam – In loving memory of Pte **George W Thurlow (115)**, the dearly beloved son of Sarah Jane Hall, 5 Harcourt Street, Raunds, who was killed in action on 11 April, 1918, aged 18 years and 11 months:

We could not clasp your hand, dear George;Your face we could not see,
We were not there to say farewell; But we'll remember thee,
Far and often our thoughts do wander;To the grave so far out yonder,
From memory's page we'll never blot;Three little words,"Forget you not",
When duty called and danger came; He was not wanting there.

From his loving mother and brother."

"New Companies – Advance Motor Repair & Hire Co (Raunds) Ltd (153947), Private Company, Registered 29 March, Capital £3,000 in £1 shares; First Directors: A Lawrence, "The Hall", boot manufacturer; T L G Coggins, "The Hall", tanner and currier; W F Corby, "Hawarden House", assistant overseer; Secretary, W F Corby."

A flag day and concert were held in aid of the Northampton and County Crippled Children's Fund on Saturday, **12 April**, arranged by Mrs A Camozzi, the proceeds amounted to £31.

Also today, the Raunds Labour Party held a tea in the Temperance Hall, when about 250 sat down. Mr George Lee made a presentation to Mr Ernest Harris of the Military Medal, awarded to him for devotion to duty and bravery in the field. A social evening followed.

On Friday, **25 April**, came the news that Mrs W Archer, 17 Sackville Street, had just received official confirmation from the Infantry records Office that, as no further news had been received relative to her son, Pte **J Archer (14)**, 9th Norfolk Regiment, the Army Council had regretfully concluded that his death had taken place on 21 March, 1918 or since.

Today it was reported that no fewer than 230 persons at Raunds were receiving the unemployment dole.

And it was also recalled that 50 years ago (1869) in Raunds, the annual entertainment given by Mr W H Lovell, assisted by Miss Knowles and Messrs Knighton, Rooksby and Pulpher, had been given in the Temperance Hall that Monday evening, and repeated on Thursday.

At the Urban Council meeting on Monday, **28 April**, the clerk reported that improved postal facilities would be granted, and that a second delivery had already commenced. Dr McInnes advised that the number of infectious diseases in March were: Measles 11, scarlet fever 1, pneumonia 1. A cemetery caretaker, Mr Thomas Smith was appointed part-time, 30 hours a week at 26s-0d per week. The estimates for the year were presented, and a rate of 5s-4d in the £ per year was set. Finally, the question of the celebration of the signing of peace was considered, and it was decided to hold a meeting on The Square on the day of the signing.

* *

MAY – In his Parish Notes this month the vicar said "the time has arrived when we ought to think seriously what permanent memorial we will place in the Church to those brave and devoted sons of Raunds who have fallen in this war." In view of this, a congregational meeting in the Institute was arranged to follow the evening service on 11 May, to discuss the initial steps of this important matter.

Two more names were also added to the roll of those who had "Died in the Service of Their Country": **John Archer (14)** and **Leonard Whitney (132)**.

On Thursday, **1 May**, at the Parish Church, Sgt H Betts MM, of Thorpe Street, was married to Miss Ethel M Major, of Louth.

The vicar and congregation gave a welcome tea and social to demobilised men on Friday evening, **2 May**. About 210 returned soldiers and sailors sat down, amongst whom were several wearing decorations gained on service, and returned prisoners of war. After tea, the vicar extended a hearty welcome to all the men. A social and musical evening followed and Mr L G H Lee, JP, on behalf of the demobilised men, thanked the Church for the "splendid repast and social".

Looking back 50 years today to 1869, it was recalled how the town's Temperance Society had expressed their sincere thanks to Messrs J Hasseldine and L Eagle, who were leaving Raunds, for the cheerful and willing services they had rendered; Mr H as secretary of the Society and Mr E as treasurer of the Band of Hope.

A staff crisis loomed at the Church School when on Monday, **5 May**; the managers received resignations from Mr Stubbs, Mrs Ash, and Miss Tether, with effect from 31 May. They reluctantly accepted each notice and immediately wrote to the Local Education Authority requesting that the vacancies be advertised.

Saturday, **10 May**, saw a cricket match take place between the Raunds Married XI and the Raunds Single XI; the husbands running out victors by 145 runs to 59.

At the Urban Council meeting on Monday, **12 May**, the Housing Committee recommended: 1) that provisions be made for 50 houses; 2) that the first site recommended by Caley Piece, or Hill Close; and 3) that the houses be of the six room type. Items 1 and 3 were carried, item 2 was carried over and the Committee asked to submit other sites for consideration.

Two Raunds men appeared at the Thrapston Police Court on Tuesday, **13 May**. A soldier, charged with being a deserter from the Cambridgeshire Regiment, was remanded to await a military escort; while a town labourer was fined £1 for keeping a dog without a licence.

The local newspapers of Friday, **16 May**, carried the sad story of a 79 year old agricultural labourer, of the "Cock Inn" Yard, who had been found dead in his home. The inquest verdict was "Suicide by hanging", there not being sufficient evidence to show the state of his mind.

Looking back 50 years to 1869, the journals remembered the annual exposition of the methods of instruction employed in the Raunds Wesleyan School when demonstrations on various subjects were given by Mr G Lee, headmaster.

On Saturday, **17 May**, an open air meeting was held on The Square under the auspices of the Discharged Soldiers' and Sailors' Association, Raunds Branch. The Rev C Curtis presided and introduced the Rev Ian Carroll, of Rushden, who spoke at length, urging those who had not already done so, to join the association, as they could achieve so much more in a united effort.

A town meeting was called by the Urban Council in the Temperance Hall on Tuesday evening, **20 May**, to consider what form a permanent war memorial (if any) should take. Various ideas were put forward: a park for workers games and amusements, a public library, a gymnasium and memorial, and a recreation ground with facilities for bathing. The latter suggestion was formerly proposed, seconded and unanimously carried and the council was asked to form the nucleus of a committee together with representatives from other town bodies.

Friday, **23 May**, "For Sale – By private treaty, Freehold Dwelling-house and Shop, together with outbuildings and paddock, and three Copyhold Dwelling-houses, the whole situate and being Nos. 35 to 41 High Street, Raunds; For further particulars apply: W F Coles, Raunds."

The "Annual Treat" to the children of the members of the town's Co-operative Society was held on Saturday, **24 May**. At 1pm a procession formed, headed by the Temperance Band, about 1,000 children under 14 taking part. The boys were taken to the National School, and the girls to the Wesleyan School for tea. Following the tea the children proceeded to a field in Thorpe Street for sports.

Raunds Town Cricket Club took on Wellingborough Wesleyans this afternoon and were victorious by 1 wicket; the Wesley boys 95, the town 96 for 9.

The Women's Adult School held a musical service on Sunday afternoon, **25 May**. Miss Pulpher presided, the proceeds being in aid of the War Victims' Fund.

On Thursday, **29 May**, Mr R Thompson's six hens laid eight eggs. Once previously he had seven eggs in one day from the same hens.

"Notice of Sale – Raunds, Saturday, **31 May**: Furniture and effects, upon premises at Kingswood Place, by instructions from the Representatives of Mrs Pendered; Sale at 3pm. Full details from Arthur G Brown & Son, Auctioneers"

The following conundrum was asked at a recent entertainment in the town: "Why is an analytical chemist always a woman? Because if she is not an Ann Eliza, she is always a Charlotte Ann!"

* *

JUNE - The vicar opened his Parish Notes with the news that at the congregational meeting of 11 May, it was decided to erect in the Church a memorial to those who had given their lives for freedom and honour. Since then donations had been collected throughout the town for a follow up meeting on 2 June, when they would know how much money they had for the purpose.

He closed with the news that a service for ex-servicemen was to be held in the Church on Trinity Sunday afternoon, 15 June, when the Rev Ian Carroll, Vicar of St Peter's, Rushden, would give the address; and that the names of **Charles Henry Spriggs (111)** and **Ernest White (126)**, had been added to the list of those who had "Died in the Service of Their Country".

There were contrasting fortunes for the Town's cricket teams on Saturday, **1 June**: the First XI were beaten at home by Wollaston by 9 runs; whereas the 2nds travelled to Stanwick and were victorious by 34 runs.

The annual meeting of the Raunds Nursing Association was held on Monday evening, **2 June**, with Mr A Camozzi presiding. The secretary, Mrs J V Spicer, presented the report and balance sheet which showed receipts of £162-9s-11½d, expenditure of £116-5s-7d, leaving a balance in hand of £46-4s-4½d.

The Boot Operatives Union monthly meeting was held at the Woodbine Club on Tuesday, **3 June**, and it was resolved to ask the Council of the Union, in view of the Government unemployment pay being reduced, to bring into operation the Union out of work pay.

At the meeting of the Church School managers on Monday, **5 June**, a letter was read from Miss Lodder stating that she was to be married in August but wished to stay on as a married assistant teacher for a short time. The managers opinioned that they did not agree with retaining married assistant teachers but would allow her to remain until 31 October. The Headmaster reported that he had today received twelve new desks, the completion of an order placed previous to the outbreak of war! The caretaker was instructed to assemble the desks during the Whitsuntide holidays and to store the old desks on the school premises.

On Friday, **6 June**, it was announced that the town's Sgt G A Walker, 5th Northamptons, had been awarded the Meritorious Service Medal.

Today, the final meeting of the Red Cross Working Committee was held at the Vicarage when the secretary reported that the total number of garments sent to headquarters at Northampton amounted to 3,247.

Also today, the final meeting of the Raunds War Charities Committee was held. The treasurer reported a balance of £180-12s-6d and it was decided to donate £10 to the town's Nursing Association, with the balance being held by the treasurer until a permanent town memorial had been decided upon. Over £2,500 had been raised for war purposes since the committee began in 1916.

The death of Mr Alfred Groom, baker, aged 56, took place suddenly on Sunday morning, **8 June**. He had been far from well during the past winter.

The case of the Raunds man summoned for harbouring and preventing his daughter from returning to the care and control of the Thrapston Guardians raised its head again at the Thrapston Police Court on Tuesday, **10 June**. After considering the latest facts, the Bench adjourned the matter for another fortnight.

Also on the charge list today were two 17 year old town youths, a labourer and a shoehand, charged with stealing a trout fishing rod, value £7-10s-0d, the property of Mr W M Plevins, JP, of Twywell (a bad move!). One youth failed to appear for a second time, but the other was found guilty and bound over with a caution and ordered to pay 10s-6d costs, and £1, half of the damage done to the rod.

At the quarterly meeting of the Raunds Wesleyan Methodist Circuit on Saturday, **14 June**, it was decided that suitable "Peace Services" should be held in each place in the circuit.

Sunday, 15 June, Alcock and Brown complete the first direct flight across the Atlantic.

Thursday, 19 June, the German fleet is scuttled at Scapa Flow.

A new piecework statement with respect to hand-sewn boots for the civilian trade was agreed upon at Raunds on Friday, **20 June**, coming into force tomorrow.

And there was a grim reminder for all today of how the war began with the news that the body of the "Sarajevo murderer" Princip had been recently exhumed with great solemnity and was to be sent home to Serbia.

The town's annual Hospital Week demonstration took place on Saturday, **21 June**, and with beautiful weather, was again a great success. The guests of honour were the Marquis of Northampton and Lord and Lady Lilford; the proceedings included a parade and fancy dress competition; an open air meeting in the grounds of "The Hall"; a Rose Day; a Fire Brigade competition and sports; and an al fresco concert.

Raunds winners in the sports events were: J H Pound, Edith Coles, and Harold Ball; and a hand-painted silk cushion, given by Mrs Coggins, was offered for sale and sold several time over!

Winners in the fancy dress competition were: Edith Cooper, *African Girl*; Edith Nunley's Party, *Six Merry Milkmaids*; Messrs Coggins and Sons, *Victory and Peace*; Miss Milly Pentelow, *Gipsy*; Miss Linda Smith's Group, *Rose Queen and Attendants*; Messrs Coggins and Sons, *Coster's Wedding Party*. ***(Plate 10)***

Raunds Town First XI took part in a benefit match with Rushden Mission this afternoon, on behalf of Harry Madden, an old Mission player, who was ill at Creaton Sanitorium, and won by 6 runs. The Conservative Club bowls team was also in action this afternoon, defeating Thrapston by 52 to 38.

Friday, **27 June**, "Thanks – Mr and Mrs Shrives and Family, of Hill Street, Raunds, wish to thank all kind friends for sympathy shown to them in the loss of their dear son **Frank (Shrives) (103)**, who was reported wounded and missing, 22 March, 1918, now presumed to have died on that date; For his country's sake."

Saturday, 28 June, the Treaty of Versailles is signed by Germany and the Allies.

As the Peace Accord was signed in France, the town's cricketers entertained Rushden Mission again and once more were victorious, this time by 15 runs.

On Sunday evening, **29 June**, a united thanksgiving service was held on The Square, Mr L G H Lee, JP, chairman of the Urban District Council presiding. The Temperance Band rendered selections and all denominations were represented.

* *

JULY – The vicar reported that the amount already collected or promised towards the cost of the Church War Memorial now exceeded £100. He looked forward to the forthcoming School Treat and Garden Fete, noting that with the resumption of peace, it meant a return to the old order and tea would be served to the children. Yet more donations of money and flowers for the War Shrine were acknowledged, and the name of **Frank H Shrives (103)** was added to the roll of local men who had "Died in the Service of Their Country".

On Friday, **4 July**, it was announced that until the ratification of the Versailles treaty was made by the German National Assembly and probably the Prussian and Bavarian Districts, a modified blockade of Germany would continue.

The new Memorial unveiled in Rushden Parish Church included Raunds men: **"Jack" Bamford (19)**, **Horace Gunn (57)**, **Arthur H Jervis (65)**, and **Arthur Wheatley (125)**.

At the Thrapston Police Court on Tuesday, **8 July**, an application by a Raunds woman for a variation in the amount of maintenance under an order against a Wellingborough man was granted, being increased from 1s-9d to 3s-6d per week.

A dance was held on the lawn of "The Hall" on Thursday, **10 July**, in aid of new uniforms for the Temperance Band, who supplied the music.

The Church School managers reviewed an application from Mr George F Knight for the post of certified teacher on Tuesday, **15 July**, and agreed that he be recommended to the Education Authority for the vacancy at a salary of £165 pa.

On Friday, **18 July**, it was reported that Mr and Mrs Groom, 24 Brooks Road, had received official confirmation that their eldest son, Pte **W H Groom (56)**, Northumberland Fusiliers, was now presumed killed on or after 28 March, 1918.

And today the results of the recent examinations for a scholarship to a secondary school produced success for Nellie Stubbs and Ralph Burton.

"Belgian Battlefield Tours – Conducted tours every Tuesday, Saturday, visiting Ostend, Bruges, Zeebrugge, Ypres; Competent lecturer in each party; Grand Local Tour, 16 August, Fare including travel, excellent accommodation, excursions, Nine Pounds, no extras; Turland's Agency, Wellingborough."

Saturday, 19 July, the Cenotaph is unveiled in London.

Today the town celebrated **"Peace Day"**. In the morning the ringers were early in the Church, and the bells were soon ringing merrily. At 12 o'clock most of the parishioners who were able assembled on The Square, where a massed choir, under the conductorship of Mr Walter Hall, rendered the hymn "All people that on earth do dwell" and the "Hallelujah Chorus". ***(Plate 13)***

A procession was then formed, and, headed by the band, marched to the top of the Wellington Road, where the competitors in the fancy dress competitions assembled in the field opposite the "Red Lion" Inn for the judging.

The procession then moved off in the following order: Discharged and crippled soldiers in a brougham kindly lent and driven by Mr Wm Peck; demobilised soldiers and sailors; the Temperance Silver Band; members of the Council; tradesmen; the town Fire Brigade; the fancy dress competitiors; the Church Lads' Brigade; and non-competitors in the fancy dress.

The procession marched to The Square, where songs were sung by the children. The fancy dress winners were: G Collins, *Derby Winner*; Reggie Eaton and Colin Hodson, *Looking for a House*; Mrs Campbell's Group, *The Fate of Nurse Cavell*; Messrs Coggins and Sons, *Victory and Peace*; Mrs H Cuthbert, Father Christmas; and Mr F Martin's Group, *The Coster's Wedding*. ***(Plate 14)***

After the announcement of the awards Capt V H Sykes, in a few appropriate remarks, said that it was the greatest day in their lifetime, and they all ought to feel glad to be alive. While they rejoiced, they must not forget those who would never come back, and he asked all the men to take off their hats for a minute while the band played a few bars of appropriate music as a tribute to their memory.

The boys and girls then marched to the schools where they were entertained to tea. At 3 o'clock a tea for all people over 60 was held in the Temperance Hall and the Church Institute, when there were about 300 present. At 4.15 a meat tea for the demobilised men and those home on leave was served in the Wesleyan School.

Unfortunately, while tea was being held it came on to rain, and as it did not look favourable for outdoor amusements it was decided to adjourn the sports etc, until Monday. A dance was then arranged for 8 o'clock in the Temperance Hall, which was largely attended, the music being supplied by Mr C Cox (piano).

At the Thrapston Police Court on Tuesday, **22 July**, a Raunds fruiterer was fined 2s-6d for allowing his dog to be at large without the owner's name on its collar.

On Friday, **25 July**, it was revealed that the total of deaths last year exceeded births in Higham Ferrers, but in Raunds births exceeded deaths.

* *

AUGUST – The vicar tackled a controversial subject in this month's Parish Notes – Lady Choristers! He lamented on the current standard of singing and blamed it on the lack of boys coming forward and the irregularity of choir practice attendance of the existing young male members. His answer was, very reluctantly, the introduction of a few ladies, although his personal preference would always be for boys; "If we cannot get suitable singing out of boys but can get it out of ladies then we must welcome them with open arms!"

He also extended congratulations to Margaret Streather, Kathleen Kirk, and George Kirk who had passed the Probationer Pupil Teacher's written examinations.

The boot factories closed for the holidays from Friday, **1 August**, until Tuesday, 12 August. A large number of the townspeople left for the various seaside resorts, Yarmouth and North Wales being the most popular.

"In Memoriam – In loving memory of our Cyril, who died of wounds in France, 3 August, 1917; Pte **C J Clarke (38)**, 2nd Northants: "Gone, but never forgotten";

From his loving Mother and Dad, brothers and sisters, 13 High Street, Raunds."

Amongst the results for Classes in Boot and Shoe Manufacture announced on Friday, **8 August**, was an Advanced Stage, 2nd Class Certificate and pass in practical hand lasting (with a County Council prize for a well-kept notebook), and an Elementary Stage pass, for Walter Lack from the Raunds Centre.

The annual balance sheet of the Raunds Hotel and Coffee Tavern for financial year just ended showed the sum of £37-8s-7½d available for dividend after the deduction of the previous year's losses. A dividend of 3¾% was decided upon plus a bonus to the manageress and assistant in appreciation of their services.

The half-year balance sheet of the Distributive Co-operative Society showed an increase in sales of £6,684 over the corresponding period in 1918. From the surplus in trading of £1,149-5s-8½d, a dividend of 1s-0d in the £ was agreed. The committee regretted that the coal department had not contributed to the surplus, however, the poultry farm had produced 24,425 eggs during the period.

Friday, **15 August**, "In Memoriam – In loving memory of Ptes **Sam Brayfield (27)** and **Percy Watson (119)** of Raunds, of the East Anglian Casualty Clearing Station, lost on board the "Royal Edward" in the Aegean Sea, 13 August, 1915, who, at the call of duty, left everything that men hold dear – C.W.W."

At the Wesley Guild meeting on Monday evening, **18 August**, the members presented the Rev E P Blackburn (who was about to conclude three years ministry at Raunds) with a walking stick, and Mrs Blackburn with an umbrella. The Blackburns were leaving the town next month for Leighton Buzzard.

There was a rare happy outcome to an appearance of a Raunds woman at the Thrapston Petty Sessions on Tuesday, **19 August**. An Irthlingborough man had been charged on remand with non-payment of £5-14s-6d arrears of a maintenance order to support the woman (his wife) and their child. However, the woman announced to the Bench that she and her husband had reunited and she wished to thank Inspector Campion for his kindness in bringing them together again!

The Raunds Boot and Shoe Manufacturer's Association entertained their demobilised workmen and wives to a meat tea on Saturday, **23 August**. About 380 sat down, after tea they all adjourned to the grounds of "The Hall". A concert was given by the "Bachelor Boys" Concert Party from Northampton, followed by a whist drive and the Temperance Band played for dancing.

On Sunday, **24 August**, the 107th anniversary of the Wesleyan Sunday School was celebrated. At the afternoon service, gifts from the children included 517 eggs and fruit etc, which were sent to the Northampton Hospital. At the evening service a solo and chorus "There's a beautiful land" was rendered by Miss Miriam Sanders.

On Friday, **29 August**, worrying developments for local boot factory owners were reported. The effect of the new piecework rates in the trade meant that even the slowest clickers could now earn £4 pw, and the "scrats" up to £8. Consequently, the manufacturers had seen their outgoings on wages rise by up to 130%!

The Town Football Club confirmed that the ground at Carter Hill had been secured for the coming season and the Northants League promised some good matches. All the old players who were home had signed on although the war had accounted for two good players; several promising youngsters had also signed on.

"In Memoriam – In loving memory of Cpl **Henry Allen (9)**, killed in action, 25 August, 1918, buried at Grevillers British Cemetery, France:

Not dead to thee that loved him; Not lost but gone before,
He lives with us in memory still; And will for evermore,
Oh for the touch of his loving hand; And the sound of his voice that is still.

From his loving Mother, Father, Sisters, Brothers and Floss, Raunds."

An organ recital was given in the Parish Church on Sunday afternoon, **31 August**, by Mr J P Archer, assisted by Messrs J W Rendall (Higham Ferrers) and F E Plackett (Wellingborough). Mr Rendall's violin solos and Mr Plackett's vocal renderings were listened to with keen attention. The Choir Fund collection was £4.

SEPTEMBER – The bee in the vicar's bonnet this month was parents not giving him sufficient notice of their wanting him to baptise their children. He pleaded: "Will parents kindly read the covers of their parish magazines on which are printed, month after month, the relevant information on arranging a baptism!"

The recent successful choir outing to Aldwincle was recalled: the ride there and back in the two brakes, cricket in Mr Bream's field, a picnic tea, a stroll down to the river, races, and singing songs all the way home despite the shower.

The gift of six new purifacters, the work of Miss Edwards, was acknowledged and finally, the names of **William Henry Groom (56)** and **George James Whitmore (131)** were added to the list of those who had "Died in the Service of Their Country".

Wednesday, 10 September, the Treaty of St Germain results in the break-up of the Austro-Hungarian Empire.

At the monthly meeting of the local branch of the Boot Operatives Union on Monday, **1 September**, it was said that "trade in August had been good as, except for Raunds and Ringstead, there had been very little unemployment".

Five Raunds men appeared at Thrapston Police Court on Tuesday, **2 September**, summoned for gaming with cards on a public footpath at Raunds on 24 August. All were found guilty, the ringleader being fined 15s-0d, the rest 5s-0d.

Friday, **5 September,** "In loving memory of Pte **Evelyn Wood (135)**, 12th East Surrey Regiment, killed in action in France, 3 September, 1918:

We little thought when you said goodbye,
You were leaving us then, dear one, to die,
Though too far off your grave to see,
But not too far to think of thee.

'Ever in our thoughts',

From his loving Wife and Children, Ringstead, Thrapston."

Stanwick Hill claimed another victim this week when a Northampton man, who was returning home from Raunds, lost control of his bicycle when his brake failed and was thrown from his machine. He was badly cut about the face and hands, and sorely shaken. He was conveyed back to Raunds for treatment by the doctor. The man, an ex-soldier, had been to France and was twice wounded.

Friday, **12 September**, "In Memoriam – In unfading memory of Pte **Ernest Webb (121)**, 9th Yorkshire Regiment, who died of wounds, 8 September, 1918, at the 24th Casualty Clearing Station, aged 25, buried in Cavalletto British Cemetery:

Could we have raised his dying head; And heard a last farewell,
The blow would not have seemed so hard; To us who loved him well.

From his loving Wife, Irthlingborough, and Mother, Father, and Family, Raunds."

Mr and Mrs Amos Lawrence entertained the employees of the "Nene Works" to celebrate their silver wedding on Saturday, **13 September**, when over 200 sat down to tea in "The Hall" grounds. The Temperance Band played selections and for dancing in the evening, when games and amusements were also indulged in.

At a busy council meeting on Monday, **15 September**, the members decided to appoint a committee under the Profiteering Act; it was decided to press for an additional 500 tons of coal for the town; it was also resolved to try to form a Division of the St John Ambulance Brigade in Raunds.

On Tuesday, **16 September**, the Thrapston Petty Sessions passed judgement on no less than four separate Raunds cases! A motorcyclist was fined 5s-0d for riding a motorcycle on the highway at midnight without having a lighted headlamp; a tinsmith was fined 10s-0d for allowing a dog to be on the public highway and not under control; two twelve year old boys were summoned for wilful damage to kohl rabi to the value of 1s-0d, the property of Thomas C Jeeves, farmer. The case was withdrawn; and finally the "boomerang" clicker (he always came back!) was summoned for non-payment of reformatory arrears to the amount of £2-15s-0d, and yet again he was given a fortnight to pay.

A Forget-Me-Not day in aid of the Rushden District United Club's Blind and Crippled Children's Fund was held on Saturday, **20 September**. Flowers sold raised £13-11s-7d, and a corresponding number competition realised £14-8s-0d. Tea was given to the members' children in the Woodbine Club.

On Monday, **22 September**, the recognition meeting of the new superintendent minister, the Rev J Wells, was held at the Wesleyan Church, when the choir sang an anthem.

On Friday, **26 September**, the Town Cricket Club averages for the 1919 season were issued: Played 12, Won 6, Lost 6; J Allen topped both batting and bowling, averaging 36 runs including 56 not out and taking 14 wickets at 5.78 each.

Nationally, the railwaymen came out on strike in all parts of the country at midnight after talks with the Government broke down.

The Shopmates played Northampton Town Reserves in the First Round of the County Senior Cup on Saturday, **27 September**, and were thrashed 10-0!

The annual gathering of the Temperance Society, including a tea and public meeting, was held on Statute Monday, **29 September**, in the Temperance Hall. The speaker was the Rev T Greener Gardner of Kettering, and solos were rendered by Miss Winnie Abbott, Miss Olive Abbott being the pianist.

A Raunds shoehand was summoned at the Thrapston Petty Sessions on Tuesday, **30 September**, for leaving his wife, who had gone to live with another while he was away. Col Stopford Sackville said the most satisfactory thing would be for them to get a divorce, however, the Bench could not make any order upon the defendant to pay to maintain his wife.

OCTOBER – The new session of Evening Continuation Classes opened on Thursday, **2 October**, with a prize distribution to successful students of last session. The chairman of the managers, Mr W F Corby, said that now the parish had at its disposal a motor ambulance, it had been decided to get it for the Raunds branch of the St John Ambulance Association, in order that assistance might be at hand for the removal of local cases to the Hospital.

Friday, **3 October**, "In Memoriam – In loving memory of Pte **J G Cooper (42)**, 42614, killed in action, 29 September, 1918, aged 19 years:

A loving son, a brother kind; A beautiful memory left behind,
We know, dear son, you did your best; And may God grant you eternal rest,
One year has passed, our hearts still sore; As time goes on we miss him more,
His loving smile, his welcome face; No one can fill his vacant place.

From his loving Mother and Brothers and Sisters."

At the Wellingborough Police Court on Friday, **10 October**, a Raunds man was fined 15s-0d for using improper language!

Also today, it was recalled how, this week in 1869, a rich and easily workable bed of iron ore had been discovered in fields known as "The Cottons" contiguous to the River Nene on land the property of Mr John Knighton Nichols.

"In Memoriam – In loving memory of **Charles Henry Spriggs (111)**, dearly loved son of Mr and Mrs J Spriggs, 31 Gordon Road, Wellingborough, who was killed in action, 10 October, 1918:

There is a link death cannot sever,
Love and remembrance will live forever.

From his loving Mother, Father, Sisters and Brothers."

Monday, **13 October**, "Notice of Sales – The whole of the Superior Household Furniture and other effects, upon the premises of "Banff Villa", Raunds, late in the occupation of Miss E Mackenzie, deceased; Sale at 11 o'clock prompt.

Also, At an early date: 4 Dwelling houses in Marshall's Road and Valuable Building Land, by instructions from the Trustees for Sale under the will of the late Dr Wm Mackenzie; Full particulars from Arthur G Brown and Son, Auctioneer."

Two Raunds men, a labourer and a boot and shoe dealer appeared at Thrapston Police Court on Tuesday, **14 October**; the former charged with stealing leather and heel plates, the property of C E Nicholls and Co, and the latter charged with receiving the items in question, knowing them to be stolen. Both men were remanded in custody and committed for trial at the next Quarter Sessions.

Disturbing news emerged for the local boot trade on Friday, **17 October**, when the Government announced that "owing to the changed conditions they desired to cancel the contracts for Army boots". Not surprisingly, the news caused much consternation for the contractors and many households in Raunds would especially be hit as the whole of their work depended on Government orders.

"Notice of Sale – Raunds, Monday, 27 October – Household Furniture, Oak and Mahogany Articles, and numerous effects, upon the premises at 'The Laurels', Grove Street, by instructions from the Executors of the late Mr John Corby; Sale at 12 o'clock prompt."

A flag day, arranged by Mrs A Camozzi, and concert, arranged by Mrs J V and Mrs W H Spicer and Mr Leslie Horrell, in connection with the Raunds Nursing Association, took place on Saturday, **18 October**. In total £35 was raised.

On Thursday, **23 October**, the Church School managers discussed the "King's Peace Holiday Week" and came out strongly in favour of granting the week beginning 9 November as the Peace Holiday. However, they felt they would like to fall in line if possible with the Council School, it was therefore agreed that the chairman would write to the Council School managers and ask them to reconsider their decision to only give two days, and extend this to a whole week.

Friday, **24 October**, "In Memoriam – Lawrence – In ever loving memory of Pte **Herbert Lawrence (72)**, 1st South Staffs, reported missing, 26 October, 1917, aged 19 years:

The shock was great, the blow severe,
We little thought his death so near,
Only those who have lost are able to tell,
The pain that we felt at not saying farewell,
His cheery ways, his smiling face, are pleasant to recall,
He always had a kindly word, and died beloved by all.

From his loving Mother, Father, Brothers and Sisters, 12 Grove Street, Raunds."

Friday, **31 October**, "Official Notice – Miss Elspet Mackenzie, Deceased: All persons having any Claim against the estate of the late Miss Elspet Mackenzie, Raunds, in the County of Northampton, who died on 16 September, 1919, are requested to send particulars thereof to us, the undersigned; and all persons Indebted to the deceased are required to pay the amount of their debts to us. Hunnybun and Sons, Solicitors, Thrapston."

* *

NOVEMBER – The Vicar, in his Parish Notes, talked of the cost of producing the parish magazine, that expenditure far exceeded the receipts, and that they faced two alternatives: either disbandon the publication altogether, or raise the price, adding wryly that he thought that they could do this without any fear of the Profiteering Act! He also mentioned recent donations to the War Memorial Fund, highlighting the gift of 30 dollars (£6-17s-6d) from a family "across the water".

The annual parochial tea was held on Saturday, **1 November**, in the Church Schoolrooms. After tea the parochial accounts were presented, followed by a sale of work. Dancing followed, the music being supplied by Messrs F Kirk, K Kirk, and E Bamford. The proceeds were in aid of Church funds.

And this evening, a dance was held in the Temperance Hall for the benefit of Miss E Cunnington. Mr C Cox (piano) supplied the music, assisted by Mr R Cox.

At the Wesleyan Church on Sunday evening, **2 November**, the choir sang the music as given at the recent Non-Conformist Choral Festival at Wellingborough. Mr W W Hall conducted and Mr J W Hall presided at the organ.

The monthly meeting of the local branch of the Boot and Shoe Operatives Union was held at the Woodbine Club on Monday, **3 November**, when members expressed great dissatisfaction at the wages being paid to day workers and decided to hold a mass meeting on the subject. A resolution was then passed demanding 70s-0d minimum per week and to have a "show card" day at an early date.

The Church School managers met on Tuesday, **4 November**, when a letter was read from the Council School managers regarding the "King's Peace Holiday" confirming that they would adhere to their decision to grant only two days holiday. Although a proposal was then made that the Church School should still close for the full week's holiday, this was defeated and the managers reluctantly agreed to fall in line with the Council School.

At the monthly council meeting on Monday, **17 November**, Dr McInnes reported seven deaths and eight births registered in October and that five cases of infectious diseases were notified. The Sanitary and Waterworks Committee recommended that the land requested by the town's Allotment Association be acquired by the council although private arrangements should be made if possible.

The members decided that urgent improvement needed to be made to the "dangerous corner" at the bottom of Chelveston Road. And finally, the plans relating to the layout of the proposed housing scheme were submitted and the amended plan suggested by the Housing Commissioners was approved.

A town meeting was held in the Temperance Hall on Tuesday, **18 November**, in support of the League of Nations. Mr L G H Lee, JP, presided and explained the objectives of the League.

On Friday, **21 November**, it was announced that the Government were about to order a million pairs of new boots, of the same standard as those made during the war. The order would be divided among several firms and it was expected to appeal especially to Raunds and Kettering manufacturers.

On Monday, **24 November**, at the final Church School managers' meeting of the year, a letter was read from Mr Rawlings on behalf of the teachers of the Council and Church Schools asking for a conference of teachers and managers of both schools to discuss "certain things which have arisen". The managers resolved to respond to their headmaster saying "The Managers would be willing to comply with the teacher's request, provided that such a meeting would be advantageous to teachers and managers and, on receiving the agenda of the meeting; they will give it their further consideration".

In an unusual twist to the never-ending saga of the town clicker and his continuing maintenance order arrears, the Thrapston Petty Sessions Bench were told on Tuesday, **25 November**, that the amount had since been paid. As a result, the associated demand for 8s-0d costs was withdrawn.

* *

DECEMBER – Opening his Parish Notes, and without any further explanation, the vicar announced that "for the present time there is no need to increase the price of the Parish Magazine". He then went on to say how many folk had taken the opportunity to inspect the design for the proposed War Memorial, and given their general satisfaction with the plan. The cost, without Faculty, would be approximately £150, and to date nearly £130 had been collected or promised.

Finally, a hearty welcome back again in their old places at the Vestry Class was extended to all members who had returned home and were now settled down in civil life; and acknowledgement was given of more monetary and floral donations for the War Shrine, notably including the names of bereaved families: **Ball (18)**, **Knighton (68)**, **March (75)**, **Shrives (103)**, **Stubbs (113)**, and **Warner (118)**.

At a local branch meeting of the Leather Workers Union on Monday, **1 December**, the divisional secretary said that although he was glad so many had come back safe, he believed that many promises that had been made to induce them to join up were far from being redeemed; as he believed that the Government were trying to set soldier against trade unionist and so urged members to stand loyal together.

On Tuesday, **2 December**, two town shoehands appeared before the Bench at Thrapston charged with stealing a quantity of seed beans, value £3, the property of Thomas Henry Bletsoe, on 25 November. Found guilty, the prisoners were each sentenced to three months hard labour!

"A Diamond Jubilee – Raunds Lady's Sixty Years of Total Abstinence" was a story appearing in all the local newspapers on Friday, **5 December**. It told of Miss Pulpher, a well-known temperance worker in the district for many years; over £70 being subscribed by her friends and admirers at a tea and social evening in order to renovate the Temperance Hall in celebration of her achievement. ***(Plate 4)***

At the Salvation Army meeting at Kettering on Saturday, **6 December**, a motor cyclist ran into the big drum, and later, the concertina player fell off the stage!

In his report given to the Urban Council on Monday, **8 December**, Dr McInnes advised that during November, nine infectious cases had been notified, and one death and twelve births had been registered.

A gloomy outlook in the boot trade was forecast on Friday, **12 December**, with the news that many retailers and factories were cancelling boot and shoe orders. Unless an improvement was seen soon, short time working appeared inevitable.

And at a meeting in the Temperance Hall this evening, Mr W R Smith, MP, described the Coalition as consisting of financial and vested interests which were opposed to the interests of the workers – *what goes around, comes around*!

At the Northants Education Committee meeting on Saturday, **13 December**, an application was submitted from Mr L G H Lee, head teacher of the Raunds Council Mixed School, for leave of absence to attend Gray's Inn for six days in each of four terms per year for three years in order to qualify as a barrister. It was resolved that leave, without salary, be granted, the attendances at Gray's Inn to be made, as far as possible, out of school sessions.

On Thursday, **18 December**, a Raunds boot operative was granted a decree nisi in the Divorce Court having alleged misconduct by his wife. The father of two had joined the Army and while in France in the summer of 1918, his wife had written saying she was miserable and confessed to misconduct with a Rushden man.

In an "act of pure humanity", a Bill was passed through all Stages in one Sitting in the House of Commons on Friday, **19 December**. The proposal to increase the pension to 10s-0d per week for all who had no means exceeding £31-10s-0d per annum in gross value was duly carried through all its stages without examination.

An official notice of 50 years ago (1869) was recalled today: "In Liquidation – The Nene Valley Co-operative Society Ltd, to be disposed of by valuation, all the stock-in-trade, and fixtures and utensils-in-trade, belonging to the above-mentioned Society at their several stores in the villages of Raunds, Stanwick, Irthlingborough, and Woodford."

With Christmas approaching, and showing exemplary timing, an Army Board Court of Inquiry decided on Monday, **22 December**, that all females who were currently employed in men's departments of boot factories should cease to work in those departments by the end of first week of the New Year. The decision referred to Raunds, Stanwick, and Ringstead.

On Boxing Day, **26 December**, the Rushden District Clubs work for the Crippled Children and Blind announced that they had raised £427-9s-6d during 1919, of which the following came from Raunds: £14-3s-0d from the sale of Forget-Me-Nots; £1-0s-6d donated by the Conservative and Woodbine Clubs; and £24-3s-0d from the Special Appeal through the town made by Messrs Hodson and Bass (all factories and the Co-operative Society contributed).

The year closed with the funeral of the town's oldest inhabitant, Mr James Dickerson, Thorpe Street, aged 91, on Wednesday, **31 December**.

A new decade dawned, and though for many civilian life in the town had steadily returned to some kind of normality, for a few the spectre of the war still lingered, and for that tragic minority it would continue to haunt them.

10 – January to December 1920

The residents decide and a century for Betts.

JANUARY – On **New Year's Day**, the Wesleyan Church entertained "another batch" of 260 demobilised servicemen and friends to a meat tea.

Monday, **5 January**; among the entertainment temptations on offer this week, at "The Palace, Rushden", the Royal Syndicate presented the screamingly funny musical revue "A Trip to Paris", with Full Beauty Chorus; 4d to 1s-8d; whilst their upmarket rivals at the "Royal Theatre, Rushden", presented the Grand Xmas Pantomime "Dick Whittington", with a Star Company of Panto Favourites including the "Six Bourbells" in Song and Dance; 1s-3d to 4s-3d.

At Northampton Quarter Sessions on Thursday, **8 January**, the Raunds labourer and bootmaker, remanded at Thrapston in December, were charged respectively with stealing leather and grindery and receiving the same. The "receiver" case was taken first and it was heard that he was a man of a former upright and respectable character who had fallen on evil times some years ago which had affected his health. After hearing more testimonials on the man's behalf, he was sentenced to two months in the second division.

The case of the 72 year old labourer was then taken. A witness told of how he saw the defendant take a bag of sole leather and heel tips into the bootmaker's factory, another said that he saw a quantity of uppers, the property of Messrs C E Nichols, at the factory. The prisoner was found guilty, but recommended to mercy on account of his age, and sentenced to three months in the second division.

On Friday, **9 January**, local newspapers recalled how, on this date 25 years ago, twelve degrees of frost had been recorded in the district, and there had been several fatal ice accidents including at Raunds, where a lad was sliding on a pond when the ice broke and he was drowned.

The "Veterans" connected with the Primitive Methodist Church conducted the services on Sunday, **11 January**; the following day a recital was given by Miss Elsie Bicheno, elocutionist, with Mr W Smith presiding. Whilst at the Wesleyan Church, Mr Milner Gray, CC, of Luton, preached to good congregations; at the evening service solos were rendered by Mr O D Hall and Miss Miriam Sanders.

At the Church School managers' meeting on Thursday, **15 January**, it was agreed that Miss Hall act as a supply teacher in the Infants Department until the vacancy there was filled by a certified teacher. Mr Rawlings submitted his agenda for the proposed conference of teachers and managers; to which the managers agreed to hold the conference in the Council School on Thursday, 22 January, at 6.45pm.

The London Joint City and Midland Bank opened a branch in Raunds on Monday, **19 January**.

On Tuesday, **20 January**, the annual box opening of the Young Helper's League was held and Mr and Mrs Camozzi invited the helpers and friends to a tea and social in the Church Institute.

Friday, **30 January**, "Official Notice – Notice to Bee-Keepers in the County of Northampton – The Spring Feeding of Bees in 1920 – The Ministry of Agriculture and Fisheries, by arrangement with the Royal Commission for Sugar Supply, have been able to secure for registered Bee-Keepers, a ration of 6lbs of sugar per stock for the period January to May 1920."

* *

FEBRUARY – The divisional coroner (Mr J T Parker) held an inquest on Thursday, **5 February**, on the body of Mary Ann Streather, widow, of the "Globe Inn", Raunds, at the home of the deceased. Dr McInnes testified that the deceased, who was 73 years of age, had had a fall on 22 January at her home which had caused a dislocation of her right shoulder. As the injury was so painful he administered chloroform before setting the limb. The patient, who was suffering from shock, improved at first but a relapse followed and she died. The coroner returned a verdict in accordance with the medical testimony.

The Urban Council met on Monday, **9 February**, passing plans for a new organ factory for Mr J Tanner; the Highway Committee were empowered to acquire land and proceed with improving the corner opposite the "Red Lion"; and the medical officer reported ten births and six deaths registered during January.

Friday, **13 February**, "William Mackenzie, Deceased: Notice is Hereby Given that all Creditors and other persons having any debts, claims or demands against the Estate of William Mackenzie, late of Raunds, in the County of Northampton, Physician and Surgeon (who died on the 13th day of July, 1917), and whose will was proved by the Rev Cyril Clowes Aldred and Gerald Hunnybun, Executors, are hereby required to send particulars in writing of their debts, claims or demands, to us, the undersigned, as Solicitors of the said Executors, on or before the 1st day of March, 1920; Hunnybun and Sons, Thrapston and Huntingdon."

The Temperance Band and friends had their annual tea on Saturday, **14 February**. The secretary reported that there were 29 members in the band; the new uniforms had cost £96-10s-0d; and £71-13s-5d was in hand; a concert followed.

A town meeting was held on Monday evening, **16 February**, in the Temperance Hall to receive the report of the sub-committee appointed to consider schemes for a Town War Memorial. Mr L G H Lee, JP, chairman of the Urban Council and the Memorial Committee, presided over a large and representative attendance. The sub-committee's proposal was to clear away the existing buildings on The Square, which comprised the Urban Council's stables and fire station, and certain tenements and shops, and to plant a border of trees, with a low fence, placing the cenotaph in the middle of The Square.

The chairman said that although there would be difficulties in carrying out the proposed scheme, the first of which was the matter of expense, if approved, it would give a memorial to the dead in the centre of the town, besides effecting a town improvement and beautifying the centre of the town. This was a matter, above all, of sentiment, and, deep down, it was a matter that touched the sacred.

Various speakers then had their say on the pros and cons of the proposed scheme and there was a quite vociferous faction in favour of a proposal for a recreation ground with a memorial. Mr Corby explained that this idea had also been investigated by the committee but found to be, in their opinion, impracticable.

Ultimately a vote was taken, Messrs H Betts and J H Haynes being appointed counters, and 69 voted in favour of the proposal, with 15 against.

The Rushden Echo's report on the meeting appeared on Friday, **20 February**, as follows: "All who know Raunds will cordially approve the town's scheme of a War Memorial. The Square, at present little better than empty ugliness, is to be cleared of the few buildings on it and beautified by planting trees with a cenotaph to the fallen in the centre. With that scheme effected, the heart of the town will present a strikingly decorative appearance."

"Northamptonshire County Council – Rats and Mice (Destruction Act) 1919 – Applications are invited for the appointment of a Rat Officer for the Administrative County of Northampton, at a salary of £250 per annum."

* *

MARCH – At the Thrapston Petty Sessions on Tuesday, **2 March**, a Raunds man was summoned by a town widow for common assault on 24 February; and the widow was reciprocally summoned by the man! Both were found guilty and were each bound over for six months in £10.

At the Church School managers' meeting on Thursday, **4 March**, it was agreed that the chairman should write to the Local Education Authority to the effect that if help was not sent to the Staff of the Infants' Department, it might be necessary to close the school, as the strain of the extra work was being felt in no small degree by the existing staff, especially the Headmistress!

Finally, the School Garden was discussed, the land having been sold and notice to quit in October received. It was decided to forward to the LEA, the letter from Mr Rawlings suggesting that either a plot of private ground near the school be obtained for a school garden, or apply for a plot from the Allotment Association.

A Raunds organ builder appeared at Thrapston County Court on Friday, **5 March**, to contest a claim from his Northampton landlord for possession of the factory he rented. The plaintiff insisted that he had a quarterly tenancy agreement whereas the defendant claimed that he was a yearly tenant. After hearing all the presented evidence the Bench ruled in favour of the plaintiff and an order was made for the defendant to vacate the premises within six weeks.

The Northants District Rechabites on Saturday, **6 March**, presented Brother H W Lawrence, of Raunds, the district secretary, who was retiring from the position, with a silver tea and coffee set, a salver (inscribed), a pair of silver candlesticks, and an emblem of the Order. The Raunds branch held their jubilee celebrations the following Monday, when the High Chief Ruler, Bro. Coton, gave an address.

A concert arranged by the Raunds branch of the Demobilised Sailors and Soldiers Association was held in the Palace Theatre on Sunday evening, **7 March**. Mr L G H Lee, JP, took the chair, and the proceeds, about £23, went to the Lord Kitchener's Convalescent Home for Ex-Servicemen.

On Sunday, **14 March**, Chelveston's "Perpetual Tribute to Its Fallen" was unveiled as a War Memorial in the Parish Churchyard.

Monday, **15 March**, "Auction Sales – Raunds, Thursday, 1 April: Household Furniture and Bedroom Requisites at 29 Wellington Road, by instructions from Mr Joseph Bass, and also at 7 Thorpe Street, by instructions from Mrs A Doran; Sale at 12 o'clock prompt; and at Raunds, Early in April: The whole of the Valuable Freehold Properties in Manor Street and Park Road, by instructions from A W Hollis Esq, the owner; Full particulars from Arthur G Brown, Auctioneers."

On Sunday, **21 March**, Memorial Crosses were unveiled at Wadenhoe and Warkton.

Another town man "went a courting" on Friday, **26 March**, when he was summoned at Wellingborough Petty Sessions for driving a motor cycle with the indentification disc obscured, at Chelveston, on 4 March. In his defence it was said that a passenger's coat had accidently covered up the plate and the defendant was unaware of the fact. The case was dismissed on payment of 4s-0d costs.

"In Memoriam – In fond and loving memory of our dear son, Pte **W H Groom (56)**, Northumberland Fusiliers, Killed in France, 28 March, 1918:

Two years have passed, but still we miss him,
Some may think the wound has healed,
But they little know the sorrow; Deep within our hearts concealed,
Forget him, no we never will; We loved him then, we love him still,
His memory is as fresh today; As in the hour he passed away.

From his loving Mother, Dad, and Brother, also Ede, Brooks Road, Raunds."

Friday, **26 March**, in the final of the Conservative Club billiards handicap held this week, Mr V Spicer beat Mr B Maddock.

A concert was held in the Wesleyan Schoolroom on Saturday, **27 March**, in aid of the Crippled Children's Fund. Solos and quartettes were rendered by "Mr Max Stringer's Concert Party", of Rushden.

On Sunday, **28 March**, the Glapthorn War Memorial was unveiled.

APRIL – As the state of the boot trade in the district continued to deteriorate, the local Boot Operatives Union reported on Friday, **2 April**, that the position in Raunds was much worse than in the previous month; with no less than £130 in "Out of Work Pay" having been paid out to town men during March.

"In Memoriam – In loving memory of **Ernest White (126)**, private, 6th Northants Regiment, the only son of Mrs E White, High Street, Raunds, who was presumed killed in France on 5 April, 1918:

You are always in our thoughts, dear Ern; It is sweet to breather your name,
In life we loved you dearly; In death we do the same. R.I.P.

From his loving Mother and Sisters."

"For Sale – About 4 tons of well-got Hay, £16 per ton, delivered in 8 miles radius free; Yorke, Brickyard, Hargrave."

Two more War Memorials were unveiled in the county on Sunday, **4 April**: a Tablet in Gretton Church and the restored Old Cross at Higham Ferrers.

The Thrapston Board of Guardians meeting on Monday, **5 April**, received the revised tender of Mr Beeby for bread and flour for the Raunds Children's Home, the original submission having been referred back as it was considered that the tenderer was not aware of the impending increases in prices of the commodities. He had now tendered: Bread, until 10 April, 8½d per 4lb loaf, and flour 2s-6d per stone; from 10 April to 30 June, 11½d per 4lb loaf, flour 3s-6d per stone. The new tender was recommended by the Contracts Committee and confirmed.

"Wanted – Gentleman requires Bed and Sitting Room with board, in Raunds; Apply to Box 100, 'Journal' Office, Thrapston."

At the Urban Council meeting of Monday, **12 April**, the medical officer reported six births and four deaths registered during March, with four cases of infectious diseases notified; Mr A Hazeldine was elected chairman for the year; and there was a delay in commencing the housing scheme due to the Housing Committee insisting on getting the sanction of the Quarter Sessions for the diversion of a footpath agreed by the Council.

Wellingborough was honoured by a visit from the Rev G A Studdert-Kennedy MC, aka "Woodbine Willie", on Sunday, **18 April**.

With effect from this week, the new minimum weekly wage ranges agreed by the Boot and Shoe Union and Manufacturer's Federation came into force as follows: *Male operatives employed in other than heel building departments, shoe or stock rooms*: Age 16, 22s-0d (was 18s-0d), up to 23 and over, 68s-0d (was 56s-0d); *Male operatives in heel building, and shoe or stock rooms*: Age 16, 20s-0d (was 16s-0d), up to 23 and over, 65s-0d (was 53s-0d); *Female operatives in heel building, shoe or stock rooms*: Age 16, 19s-0d (was 15s-0d), up to 20 and over, 40s-0d (was 30s-0d).

Also this week, the Agricultural Wages Board, under the "Corn Production Act, 1917", announced the following new minimum rates of wages for Male Workers of 21 and over, with immediate effect: Weekly Wage, 42s-0d; Hours, 50 in summer, 48 in winter; Overtime Rates per hour: Weekdays, 1s-1d, and Sundays, 1s-3½d; Overtime to apply to hours over the normal week and all Sunday working.

On Friday evening, **23 April**, a social gathering of great interest, not only to Raunds but also to a wide district, was held in the Wesleyan Schoolroom. The occasion was to celebrate the fact that Mr W F Corby, CC, had recently completed 25 years as clerk to the Raunds Council (Parish Council 1895-1897, Urban Council 1897-1920), an event which could have been described as a festival of local government, the guests, about 120 in number, being nearly all either present or past members of public administrative bodies, or officials, and including Sir Ryland D Adkins, KC MP, chairman of the Northants County Council.

The North Northants Music Competition took place in the Great Hall of Oundle School on Friday, **23** and Saturday, **24 April**, and Raunds contenders were much in evidence; In the Junior section, Evelyn Bailey was second in the "Pianoforte Solo" with No.8 of the 2-part inventions by Bach. ***(Plate 15)***

In the Senior Competition: Dorothy Foster and Wilfred Clarke were first and second in the "Pianoforte Solo" with "Negro Song" and "Alba, Mazurka" respectively; in the choral classes, Raunds Wesleyan Choir were the only entrant in the "Mixed Chorus, towns over 700" class, singing "Call to Remembrance".

On Tuesday, **27 April**, a Raunds labourer was charged at the Thrapston Police Court with stealing wooden fence rails, value 1s-0d, the property of Mr Amos Lawrence. Although the defendant claimed that he only picked up bits of wood by the side of the rails, he was bound over for six months.

* *

MAY – Friday, **7 May**, "For Sale – Valuable Pedigree Blue Persian Kitten; Mrs Johnson, "Bank House", Raunds."

"In Memoriam – In loving memory of Pte **William Ernest Richards (98)**, the beloved son of John and Annie Richards, who was killed in action, France, on the 9 May, 1915, aged 21 years:

One of the gallant defenders of England,
One of the boys who have answered the call,
Now he has laid down his life for his country,
Sad was the message which told of his fall.

From Mother, Father, Sisters, and Brothers, Raunds."

The Women's Co-operative Guild celebrated their second anniversary on Saturday, **8 May**, when a tea and meeting was held in the Co-operative Hall. The guest, Mr H Clayson, of Wellingborough, spoke on "Women's Opportunites".

The Chelveston War Memorial Cross was dedicated at a service this evening.

And Raunds Town FC recorded a notable victory over Stotfold in the Scott Gatty Cup today. The match was played at Hinchingbrooke and the Shopmates ran out winners by 4 goals to 2. ***(Plate 16)***

A solemn ceremony took place on Monday evening, **10 May**, at the Parish Church, when the war memorial erected in the Church to the memory of those who were killed in the war was unveiled and dedicated by the Venerable the Archdeacon of Oakham. The cost of building the memorial, a stone tablet with the Crucifix and the names of the fallen on each side, was £150, and prior to the unveiling the subscriptions collected totalled £115-19s-4d. The arrangements were carried out by a committee under the chairmanship of the Rev Cecil Curtis. ***(Plate 17)***

"Raunds, Northants – Messrs Pendered and Son Ltd, will sell by Auction, at the "Globe Inn", early in June: A Factory of Three Floors, and Four excellent Dwelling Houses adjoining, situated in Hollington Road and Coleman Street; also Stone Pit Cottage, with large gardens, orchard, and appurtenances, situated in Marshalls Road; By order of the Trustees of Mr R Coggins, deceased."

The Urban Council met on Tuesday evening, **11 May**, and Dr McInnes (medical officer) reported that during April there had been seven births and three deaths (ages 78, 75, and 69) registered. No cases of infectious diseases had been reported. The doctor then congratulated the town's inhabitants "upon having got above the 4,000 line in population" adding "we have left the 3's behind forever, I hope!"

"Tenders – Raunds Urban District Council – the above Council invite applications for the following loans, viz: £800 repayable in 80 years, £600 repayable in 80 years. The money is required for the purchase of Sites for the Council's Housing Schemes, the consent of the Ministry of Health having been obtained to raise the loans on security of the General District Rate. Applications to be sent in to the undersigned, stating the rate of Interest required, not later than 12 noon, Saturday, 15 May, 1920; W F Corby, Clerk to the Council."

A profile of the Raunds Coffee Tavern Football Club appeared Friday, **14 May**, under the headline "A Promising Team". It told how the club was only formed at the commencement of the 1919-20 season and had just completed a series of friendly matches for which its record was: P24, W18, D1, L5, F-110, A-38. The club had now gained admission to the newly formed Rushden, Stanwick & District League, and had high hopes of finishing well up in the table. ***(Plate 20)***

Friday, **21 May**, "New Companies – Manor Boot Company Ltd, (167306); Private company, Registered 10 May, 1920; Capital £4,000 in £1 shares; To carry on the business of boot and shoe manufacture etc.; The first directors are: B Green, 21 Harcourt Street, boot manufacturer; P Tanner, 25 Park Road, boot manufacturer; W Smith, 21 Harcourt Street, boot manufacturer; Qualification £100; Solicitor, C W Wing, Rushden."

The anniversary of the Baptist Sunday School was celebrated in the Baptist Chapel on Whit-Sunday, **23 May**, when sermons were preached by Pastor G Smith. The following day the children were entertained to tea.

Selections were played by the Temperance Band today on "The Hill" near "The Hall", under the conductorship of Mr O Pentelow.

The Wesleyan Sunday School held their annual treat on Whit-Tuesday, **25 May**, when the scholars, headed by teachers and friends and the Temperance Band, paraded the town. After this the children partook of tea in the schools, which was followed by a public tea. In the evening, sports etc. were held in the Carter Hill field, and the Temperance Band played selections and for dancing.

On Wednesday evening, **26 May**, a concert, arranged by the members of the Woodbine Club, was held in the "Palace Theatre". The following contributed towards the evening's programme: Misses M Sanders, L Spicer, and W Pentelow; Messrs R Sanders and W Smith. The Working Men's Club Male Voice Choir, under the conductorship of Mr C Cox, and accompanied by Mr R Cox, rendered several items, as did the Temperance Band Quartette Party. Miss Dorothy Foster, winner of the Senior Competition at Oundle, was the accompanist. The proceeds were for the "Blind and Crippled Children's Fund".

The Co-operative Society held their annual treat for members' children on Saturday, **29 May**. The children, headed by the Temperance Band, paraded the town and were entertained to tea in the National and Wesleyan Schoolrooms. A fancy dress competition and after tea sports, were followed by a public meeting.

On Sunday, **30 May**, Irchester's War Memorial was dedicated and unveiled.

* *

JUNE – On Friday, **4 June**, the draw was announced for next season's "English Cup" (*or the FA Cup as we now know it*); in the Extra Preliminary Round, Raunds Town were pitted against the Northampton War Team.

On Monday, **7 June**, at the Boot Operatives Union meeting, a number of members reported that they were not getting the minimum rate of wage recently awarded. After a good discussion it was agreed to advertise and request all members at present working at less than the minimum to report the matter to the branch office.

At the Thrapston Petty Sessions on Tuesday, **8 June**, a Raunds blacksmith was summoned for indecently assaulting and ill-treating a 15 year old Stanwick girl on 10 May. The offence was said to have taken place in a hut on the defendant's allotment in Chelveston Road. However, as a result of an eloquent address by his defence, a letter of good character from his employers, and the apparent conflicting evidence given by the girl and her friend, the Bench gave the man the benefit of the doubt and dismissed the case!

Friday, **11 June**, "For Sale – Mowing Grass and Aftermath, until 11 October, 1920; field known as Berrister's, about 11 acres; Also 4-Wheel Truck, to carry about 15cwt; Offers to Thomas Ferry, "Manor Cottage", Raunds."

In connection with St Mary's Church, a jumble sale etc was held at the Vicarage on Saturday, **12 June**. Hidden number competitions and name guessing etc were run by several young ladies, and were well patronised. The Temperance Band was in attendance and played selections during the evening. The proposed dance on the lawn was postponed until Monday owing to the wet weather, when a good company was present; Mr H Betts was the MC.

At Monday, **14 June's** Council meeting, a letter was read from the War Office saying that they could not see their way to discontinuing the sale of old Army boots, despite the bad state of trade, the Board of Admiralty did, however, promise to further consider the question of new orders.

On Tuesday, **15 June**, about 30 employees of the Raunds Co-operative Society held their annual outing, proceeding to Hunstanton by char-a-banc, where a pleasant time was spent. The party arrived home about midnight.

Further results of Evening Classes shorthand examinations were announced on Friday, **18 June**, as follows: Royal Society of Arts, Passed and gained speed certificates for 50 words a minute – W Coles, Mildred Phillips, and Edna Corby.

The town was favoured with glorious summer weather for its annual demonstration on Saturday, **19 June**, in aid of Northampton General Hospital, and as usual there was a large influx of visitors. Competitors and others taking part in the procession assembled in the grounds of "The Crossways". The procession proceeded round the town, halting in The Square, where selections were played, and terminating at the grounds of "The Hall". The open air meeting once again took place on the upper lawn, the trees overhanging the platform affording protection to a portion of the company from the sun's rays. ***(Plate 19)***

The Mayoress of Northampton then presented the prizes to the winners in the fancy dress competition as follows: *Children's individual get-up*, Lily Stubbs, "a cabbage"; *Children's small group*, Marguerite Dunham, Muriel Williamson, and Elsie March, "Peace, Justice, and Prosperity"; *Children's large group*, I O Rechabites No.1, "Basket of Flowers"; *Best individual get-up*, Mr F Bugby, "Robinson Crusoe"; *Best artistic or historic group*, B W T A 'Y' Branch, "English Games"; *Best comic group*, Finedon Allen Road Club, "Jazz Band"

Winners in the sports competitions were: *Fire Brigade Challenge Cup*, Raunds No.1; *100 yards, boys under 14*, C Ashley, Rushden; *80 yards, girls under 15*, D K Saddington; *100 yards, open*, C Lawrence; *80 yards, veterans*, D Brearley, Grendon; *Half-mile*, S E Coles; *One Lap Obstacle Race*, H Freeman. An al fresco concert was held in the grounds, and the Temperance Band played selections in the sports field and for dancing. The proceeds for the day amounted to about £230.

"In Memoriam – In loving memory of Vacey Stanley Sykes, who died 23 June, 1918, beloved son of Mr W Sykes, Raunds; "R.I.P." From his Mother, Raunds."

Two separate accidents occurred in the town this week; two small boys were knocked down by a car driven by an Irthlingborough man, near the Owen Smith factory, happily, both escaped serious injury; and at Messrs C E Nicholls Ltd, a lad named Lack got his left hand caught in the sole moulding machine, resulting in his finger having to be amputated at Northampton Hospital.

A Raunds roadman appeared at the Thrapston Police Court on Tuesday, **29 June**, summoned for neglecting his eleven year old son at Raunds on 8 June and on diverse previous dates. Dr MacInnes testified that he found the boy undernourished, his clothing was in rags and there were marks of vermin! The father had been discovered drunk in a local public house and earned 53s-0d per week. Found guilty, the defendant was given six months hard labour.

* *

JULY – Friday, **2 July**, "Auction Sales – Brooks Road Lodge, Raunds, A convenient Small Holding comprising House and Homestead, and 48½ acres of Arable and Pasture Land to be sold by auction by Arthur G Brown and Son at the "White Hart Hotel", Thrapston, on Tuesday, 20 July, 1920. The above described Freehold Farm is situated in the parish of Raunds, adjoining Brooks Road, near the Midland Railway bridge and the parish of Denford, and is in the occupation of Mr John Hazeldine, under a yearly Michaelmas tenancy."

"In Memoriam – In ever loving memory of Pte **W Andrews (11)**, who fell in action, 1 July, 1918:

Some may think he is forgotten; When at times they see us smile,
But they ne'er can tell the sorrow; That is held beneath that smile.

From is loving Wife and Children, Mother, Brother, and Sisters."

On Saturday, **3 July**, the Bozeat War Memorial was unveiled.

At the latest Boot Operatives Union meeting on Monday, **5 July**, trade was said to show no signs of improvement and they were very pessimistic as to the immediate future. "Out of Work Pay" for the June quarter had exceeded £1,000, of which £620 had been paid to Raunds men.

At Monday, **12 July's** council meeting, the question of disposal of the Isolation Hospital was discussed, and it was decided to sell the tents and refer the question of repairing the building back to the Sanitary Committee. The medical officer reported six births and one death in June, and no infectious diseases, but one case of diphtheria in North Street, although not likely to prove serious.

A curious case involving two Raunds men came before the Bench at Thrapston on Tuesday, **13 July**; one suing the other for a declaration of ownership on half a poultry house or £35 damages. The basis of the claimant's case was that at auction he had said that "he would stand in with the defendant". However, judgement went in the defendant's favour, who was awarded costs.

On Friday, **16 July**, Northants County Council awarded scholarships for further education to Lucinda Broker, High Street, and Ralph Burton, Sackville Street.

And there was mixed news for the local boot trade today; the Government confirmed new contracts with Adams Bros, R Coggins and Sons, the St Crispin Productive Society, John Horrell and Son, the Regulation Boot Co Ltd, and Tebbutt and Hall Bros Ltd; however, the Board of Admiralty advised that no further orders for boots would be placed during the financial year.

The funeral of the late Mr W Ferry, Hill Street, took place at the Parish Church on Friday afternoon, **23 July**. The deceased, who had been ill for a considerable time, was in the employ of the Regulation Boot Co, and was a member of the Foremen's Association; he left a widow and nine children!

A concert in aid of the Louth Disaster Fund was held by the Women's Adult School this week, raising £5; whereas a similar dance in aid of the Town Cricket Club raised £7!

At the Hospital Week Fund committee's quarterly meeting on Tuesday, **27 July**, the treasurer submitted the accounts for the annual fete showing the receipts to have been £230-3s-2d, expenditure £47-5s-4d, and balance £182-17s-10d. He also submitted the accounts for the quarter showing receipts of £211-19s-2¾d, and expenditure of Nil! A cheque for £200 was therefore sent to the county treasurer.

The half-yearly meeting of the Distributive Co-operative Society was held on Wednesday, **28 July**, declaring sales of £34,069, up £2,589 on last year, and a profit of £1,923, to be paid as a dividend of 1s-3d in the £.

On Friday, **30 July**, it was reported that the second vote of subscribers to the Town War Memorial had resulted in the selection of the site on The Square. Four sites were first voted upon, but as no clear majority was recorded a second vote was taken on the two sites receiving the highest number of votes in the first ballot. The result was: For The Square, 536, for the Cemetery, 284; a memorial is to be erected at an approximate cost of £650.

Raunds and Higham Ferrers families were joined in the wedding which took place at St Mary's Church, Higham Ferrers, on Saturday, **31 July**. Miss Rose Bird, second daughter of Mr W and the late Mrs Bird, Grove Street, Raunds, married Mr Albert Edward Russell, youngest son of Mrs and the late Mr J Russell of 54 High Street, Higham Ferrers.

* *

AUGUST – Thursday, **5 August**, was a red-letter day for the Raunds Town cricket club. In the match against Higham Ferrers, the Town XI made 214 for 7, with H Betts, opening the batting, scoring an unbeaten 104, the first time a Raunds player had made a century for his side. The shellshocked visitors were then dismissed for 37, with W Gibbs taking 5 wickets. A collection was then taken, which realised a good sum, for a presentation to the hero Betts!

The Thrapston and District Athletic Club held their first sports day since 1914 on Saturday, **7 August**, and in the Boys 220 yards, C Whitney, of Raunds, came third.

Tuesday, 10 August, the peace treaty signed at Sevres results in the break-up of the Ottoman Empire.

There was relief for all on Friday, **13 August**, with the announcement of an armistice signed between Russia and Poland, as Britain's position had been that if the conflict had continued, we would have taken Poland's side and conscription would have returned. This would, no doubt, have pleased those who had attended a meeting on The Square, organised by the Independent Labour Party and Women's Co-operative Guild, protesting against Allied intervention in the war.

"In Memoriam – In loving memory of Privates **S Brayfield (27)** and **P Watson (119)**, of Raunds, late RAMC (T), lost in the Aegean Sea, 13 August, 1915, by the torpedoing of 'HMT Royal Edward'."

Stanwick Feast Sunday, **15 August**, would long be remembered as one of the most inspiring for years. At 11 o'clock there was a parade service, the whole of the inhabitants turning out to witness the procession, which included members of the Raunds Urban District Council, and the ex-servicemen of the parish. Following Evensong there was a sacred concert, at which music was given by Mr J P Archer, assisted by Miss Letha Spicer (contralto) and Miss Winnie Pentelow (soprano). In the evening, close upon 1,500 people attended an open-air service in the Manor Park. The Raunds Temperance Band led the singing, and afterwards delighted the gathering with a varied selection of sacred music. The day's collections reached the sum of over £12.

At the Thrapston Police Court on Tuesday, **17 August**, a Raunds bricklayer's apprentice was summoned by a Denford woman in respect to an affiliation order obtained by her on 6 July for the payment of 7s-6d per week plus £1-4s-3d expenses. The amount due was £3-16s-9d and the complainant told the Court that the defendant had not paid anything. The defendant said he would not pay and when sentenced to one month's imprisonment and told that he would be liable to further terms of imprisonment if he continued to disobey the order, he replied "The child is not mine, and I will not pay!"

"Child in Flames!" was the alarming headline in Friday, **20 August's** newspapers. Young Phyllis Bugby was playing beside one of the council's tar heating boilers when her clothes were set alight, badly burning the child. On examination, Dr MacInnes immediately rushed her to Northampton General Hospital, where her condition was reported to be critical.

Also today, the results of the County Council examinations for the classes in boot and shoe manufacture were announced. At the Raunds Centre, Walter Lack gained an Advanced Stage, First Class Certificate and Pass in Practical Machine Lasting; and William L Harris gained a Pass in the Elementary Stage.

And a tragic event 25 years ago in 1895 was also recalled today with the sad tale of 13 year old Sydney Harrison, who was drowned whilst bathing in the River Nene near "The Staunch", in Stanwick Meadows.

Sports arranged by the Raunds Woodbine Club were held on Saturday afternoon, **21 August**, in the field adjoining the Club premises. The meeting was arranged in aid of the Woodbine Football Club, which fell through during the war but had now been restarted for the coming season. The Raunds winners of the various events were: *80 Yards Flat Handicap (girls under 14)*, K Saddington; *200 Yards Flat Handicap (open)*, J Ball; *100 Yards Flat Handicap (WMC members only)*, R Dix; *Musical Chairs on Bicycles*, W Higby. There were also several side-shows, including skittles and penalty kicks. The Temperance Band played selections in the field during the afternoon and for dancing in the evening.

The once-popular Higham Pony Races were held again in the Borough on Monday afternoon, **23 August**, after an interval of 20 years. The event attracted a crowd of over 5,000 to the Duchy Farm Field for the six race card.

The marriage of Mr Albert Manning, goalkeeper for Raunds Town Football Club, to Miss Eva May Robinson, eldest daughter of Mr C Robinson, Denford, took place on Wednesday, **25 August**, at the Denford Wesleyan Chapel, the Rev J L Gillians officiating.

At the Finedon Band Contest on Saturday, **28 August**, the Raunds Temperance Band obtained two seconds and a first for the best cornet solo of the afternoon.

In the evening, a dance in aid of the Coffee Tavern Football Club was held in the Temperance Hall. A good company was present, the music being supplied by Mr C Cox (piano). Mr A S Dickerson carried out the duties of MC.

The 108th anniversary of the Wesleyan Sunday School was celebrated on Sunday, **29 August**. The Rev Walter Hawkin of Brentford was the preacher for the day. In the afternoon a flower service was held and a collection of eggs, fruit etc was made; as a result, 472 eggs and fruit and flowers were sent to Northampton Hospital. Bibles and hymn books were presented to senior scholars, and the collections, in aid of the Sunday School fund, amounted to £38-8s-9d.

On Monday, **30 August**, the annual tea for teachers and friends was held in the Wesleyan School, after which the company adjourned to "Ashfields" where games were enjoyed.

At the Thrapston Petty Sessions on Tuesday, **31 August**, the infamous Rance clicker appeared before the Bench again, summoned for arrears of £2-10s-0d under a Justice Order made in October 1916, towards the maintenance of his son in a reformatory school. Supt Tebbey stated that the defendant was always a source of trouble, never paying without being summoned – this being the 15th such occurence! The man was given 14 days to pay the arrears plus 8s-0d costs, or suffer one month's imprisonment.

A more pleasurable experience was enjoyed today by about 120 employees of the Regulation Boot Co who proceeded by motor char-a-bancs to St Neots and Paxton where they were entertained to dinner by the firm. The day was spent on the river or elsewhere, the party returning home at about 11 pm.

* *

SEPTEMBER – A Court for the revision of the voters' lists for Raunds and Hargrave was held on Thursday, **2 September**, at Raunds by Mr Millington, OBE.

In the evening, the Coffee Tavern FC held their first practice game before a good crowd. A very evenly contested game ended in a win for the Blues by three goals to two. A collection in aid of Northampton General Hospital amounted to 9s-0d.

And on The Square, the Independent Labour Party held a meeting at which the Rev R Sorenson of London, spoke on "Russia first, Armistice next!"

It was announced on Friday, **3 September**, that over five million men had now been demobilised, all but 20,000 officers and 200,000 men were back at work or in training. However, there were still over 20,000 disabled men unemployed.

On the first day of the new football season on Saturday, **4 September**, Raunds Town drew 0-0 with Fletton United; the Woodbine FC lost 4-0 at Higham Town Reserves; and the Coffee Tavern FC went down 2-1 at Higham Wesleyans.

The Wesley Guild staged a cricket match this afternoon between "the men" and "the women" (the men batting left-handed); the men triumphed by an innings and 28 runs. Tea was taken afterwards in the Wesleyan Schoolrooms.

A photograph was published on Friday, **10 September**, of Baby Ina Lucas, the daughter of Pte Lucas, of the Australian Expeditionary Force, whose wife, Elsie (Sanders), a native of Raunds, had died in the town soon after her child's birth. After the war, Pte Lucas returned to Australia with his baby, who was presented to General Birdwood of the Australian Army, a short time later. ***(Plate 18)***

The Shopmates lost their English Cup, Preliminary Round match against the Northampton War Team on Saturday, **11 September**, by two goals to one.

Unveiled on Sunday, **12 September**, was Barnwell's War Memorial.

Tuesday, 14 September, Jack Pentelow (90), died.

Jack Pentelow (90) became the town's latest war casualty when he died in the Devonshire Hospital, Buxton, after a long and painful illness lasting 14 months. The thirty year old had served with the forces in France for nearly four years, and was demobbed in June, 1919. His funeral took place at the Wesleyan Church on the following Saturday, the service being conducted by the Rev J Wells. The Temperance Silver Prize Band, of which the deceased was solo cornet player for a number of years, was present at the funeral, rendering hymns outside his parents' house in Marshall's Road, while proceeding to the cemetery, and by the graveside.

"In Memoriam – In ever loving and undying memory of **Edgar Ellingham (47)**, the dearly loved son of Sgt and Mrs Ellingham, Raunds, who was killed in action in France, 18 September, 1918, while serving with the 17th Field Ambulance, aged 19 years; Buried in Trefcon British Cemetery, Caulaincourt:

Others he saved, himself he could not save,
This was the task he chose,
And he is sleeping 'neath that foreign soil,
As peacefully as here 'neath heather flower,
Knowing that he has answered duty's call,
Knowing that he has died in Engalnd's hour."

On Monday, **20 September**, Mr W R Smith, MP, addressed a Labour Party meeting in the Temperance Hall. He said that the country was faced with the same old problems which they knew of before the war, and which they were told would not come again into their lives. The unemployment problem could only be solved by sensible distribution and production.

And at this evening's Council meeting, Dr McInnes reported that four deaths and ten births were registered during July and one death and one birth during August, one case of diphtheria and one of tuberculosis were notified in July, but none in August. Formal consent was also given to the erection of the War Memorial on The Square, in accordance with the result of the recent ballot of townspeople.

"Thanks – Mr and Mrs G Pentelow and Family, of 65 Marshall's Road, Raunds, desire to express their sincere thanks to the many friends for the expressions of sympathy shown to them during their son's illness and bereavement, and for the floral tributes sent."

On Saturday, **25 September**, a flag day in aid of the Lifeboat Institution was arranged by Mrs A Camozzi, £10-10s-0d being raised.

Harvest Thanksgiving services were celebrated at the Baptist Chapel and the Salvation Army on Sunday, **26 September**.

At the Church School manager's meeting on Monday, **27 September**, the chairman stated that a child had met with an accident in the Infants' Department during playtime necessitating medical attention, and asked the position of the managers in the event of a claim for compensation. It was proposed to write to the Local Education Authority stating the facts and asking for clarification.

The new session of the Evening and Technical Classes was inaugurated by a prize distribution to the successful students of last year on Tuesday, **28 September**. Mr L G H Lee, headmaster of the classes, reported that 161 had enrolled last year and 70% of those continued to attend.

* *

OCTOBER – Rather alarming news emerged on Friday, **1 October**, that, at an open air meeting at Rushden, trade unionists had voted to strike against ex-servicemen being given their old jobs back!

And today, it was announced that a choir was to be started in connection with the Raunds Co-operative Society, under the conductorship of Mr E Lawrence.

Also today, local journals recalled how at Thrapston, 50 years ago in 1870, a lad named Cooper had been knocked down at the station by a Raunds cart, being driven at "head long speed", and having one side of his face completely ripped off!

To celebrate the success of the Temperance Band at the recent Crystal Palace concert, a concert was held in the Palace Theatre on Sunday evening, **3 October**. The artistes were Miss W Pentelow, Mr W Gibbs, and Mr H Hyde. It was said that the judges' remarks on the band's performance in gaining third place in the 'Grand Shield Contest' were "Nicely together to open, and the blend was good, and a very fine finish too; it was a pity they did not show up better in the middle!"

At the meeting of Council School managers on Wednesday, **6 October**, a letter was read from the Church School managers suggesting an earlier time of assembly for the afternoon session during the winter's months. The managers decided to concur with their Church contempories and the start time of 1.30pm was confirmed. Permission was then granted to teachers to have leave of absence for visits to other schools, as recommended by HM Inspector at his recent visit.

Two Raunds firms were represented at the 21st International Shoe and Leather Fair being held at the Agricultural Hall, London on Friday, **8 October**: R Coggins and Sons Ltd – Men's and youth's boots and shoes, Army bluchers, Navy boots and shoes, firemen's boots, sea boots and canvas shoes; and the Regulation Boot Co Ltd – Men's boots and shoes, and Army bluchers.

Today, the German Ministry of Defence announced that the Army had now been reduced to 150,000 men in accordance with the treaty objectives.

A flower, fruit and vegetable show, arranged by the Raunds Allotment and Small Holders' Association, was held in the Temperance Hall on Saturday, **9 October**. After the show the numerous exhibits were sold by Mr W F Corby, CC, and Mr L G H Lee. The proceeds were handed over to the Raunds Hospital Week Committee to be devoted to the maintenance of the motor ambulance.

Two deaths, one from cancer and one from tuberculosis, and four births were registered during September, according to the medical report given by Dr McInnes to the Urban Council at their meeting on Monday, **11 October**. At the meeting, Mr G E Smith resigned his seat on the council as his firm had just contracted to build the new houses under the council's housing scheme. These first ten houses were to be erected at a cost of £9,740.

The Finance Committee made recommendations regarding the bequests made by the late Dr Mackenzie. It suggested that three trustees be appointed to administer the bequest to the poor, and in respect to the legacy to provide prizes for the scholars at the town's schools, that the School Managers be appointed trustees.

There was excitement in Rance on the afternoons of Tuesday **12** and Wednesday **13 October**, when the airship R33 passed over flying in a westerly direction.

Thursday, 14 October, Degrees first open to women at Oxford University.

The local Labour Party celebrated the opening of their winter session with a tea and social in the Co-operative Hall this evening. After the tea the following programme was gone through: Song, Mr C Coles; song, Miss W Pentelow; song, Mr A Kilborn; quartette, Woodbine Quartette Party; violin solo, Mr F Harris; song, Miss Roughton; recitation, Miss Roughton; and pianoforte solo, Mr G Finding.

The final cricket tables of the Kettering and District League, Division 2 South, were published on Friday, **15 October**, and showed the Raunds Town 2nds finishing sixth out of nine, having played 13, won 5, lost 7, and drawn 1.

"Official Notice – The Ministry of Agriculture and Fisheries have arranged to hold a 'National Rat Week' from 1 to 6 November, 1920, during which they desire that co-ordinated and simultaneous attacks shall be made on the Rat and Mouse population; S Benyon, Rat Destruction Officer, County Hall, N'pton."

"Auction Sales – Raunds: Furniture, Bedroom Requisites and Other Effects to be sold by Arthur G Brown and Son on Saturday, 23 October, 1920, upon the premises at Midland Road, by instructions from Mrs Fuller, who is leaving; including Chaffonier with glazed bookcase over, 6′ by 3′6″. Also to be sold immediately after the above by instructions from Mr Thomas March, similar items removed from 52 Thorpe Street to the above premises for convenience of sale."

A serious accident occurred at St Crispin's factory on Wednesday, **20 October**, at about 11.30 in the morning; Mr H Harrison, of Thorpe Street, having the misfortune to get his hand caught in the press, which cut a part of it off.

A dance arranged by the Manor House Tennis Club was held on Friday evening, **22 October**, in the Church Schools. Light refreshments were provided, the music being supplied by, surprise surprise, Mr C Cox on piano, while Mr C R Abbott carried out the duties of MC. The proceeds were for the Hospital Week Fund.

On Saturday evening, **23 October**, a dance for the benefit of Miss Annie Bates, who had been ill for some considerable time, was held in the Temperance Hall. Inevitably, Mr C Cox (piano) supplied the music, and Mr L Kirk was the MC.

It was Foreign Missions anniversary at the Wesleyan Church today, when a visit was paid by the Rev Stanley E Watson, of British Guiana, who had spent ten years in the British colony. A special service was held in the afternoon for the children; and on Monday, **25 October**, Mr Watson spoke at a public meeting on "Sir Walter Raleigh's El Dorado, Demerara, its people, and their customs".

"Wanted – Dogs, every description; high prices paid for good dogs; dogs only; Smith, 'Hilltop', Stanwick."

Stanwick paid tribute to its brave sons on Sunday afternoon, **31 October**, when a service was held in St Lawrence's Parish Church in thanksgiving and in memory of those who were killed in action or died of wounds or sickness during the war. Before the service about 60 ex-servicemen paraded the village headed by the band of the 4th battalion, Northamptonshire Regiment.

The Tichmarsh War Memorial was also unveiled today, by Lord Lilford.

* *

NOVEMBER – On Friday, **5 November**, it was suggested that the boot trade had recovered slightly after a period of severe depression; and a good downfall of snow all over the country, it was said, would give a much needed impetus to trade.

On Sunday, **7 November**, Brigadier-General Ferguson unveiled the Finedon War Memorial.

At the Higham Ferrers Police Court on Monday, **8 November**, a Raunds blacksmith was charged with an indecent assault on an eight year old Stanwick girl, on 6 November. The police asked the Bench to remand the defendant until Friday so that the case could come before the Wellingborough Petty Sessions. The defendant raised no objections and was remanded on bail of two suretees of £5.

The accounts of the Hospital Week Fund for the quarter were reported at the committee's meeting on Tuesday, **9 November**; receipts were £55-17s-0d and expenses nil! It was therefore decided to forward a further cheque for £55 to the hospital treasurer. The treasurer reported the receipt of £17-13s-9d from the Allotment and Smallholders Association, being the net proceeds of their show; this was for the motor ambulance fund, against which there was previously a defecit balance of £5-15s-0d, thus leaving a balance in hand of £11-18s-9d. The Manor House Tennis Club had also sent £11-5s-6d, being their membership fees and proceeds of a social. This amount was made possible by Mr and Mrs A Camozzi lending their tennis court to the club free.

The death of Mr John Bunyan Clark, one of the leading tradesmen in the town, took place on Wednesday, **10 November**, after an illness of short duration. The deceased, who was 65 years of age, left a widow and one son, his elder son, **Arthur Clark (35)**, having been killed in France during the war. Mr Clark was an ardent temperance worker, and a member of the Wesleyan Church and a lay preacher; he also claimed to be a lined descendant of John Bunyan.

The burial of the "Unknown Warrior" took place in Westminster Abbey on Thursday, **11 November**, in a great ceremony during which the King unveiled the Cenotaph.

On Friday, **12 November**, it was announced that Mr F H Ellis had been appointed Sanitary Inspector for Raunds at a salary of £230 per annum.

Over at Oundle, the town's War Memorial was unveiled by the headmaster of the School on Sunday, **14 November**.

Nominations for the vacancy on the Urban District Council, caused by the resignation of Mr G E Smith, were made on Thursday, **18 November**: Mr George Cooch, publican; and Mr Ralph Lawrence, Co-operative Society manager.

At the Wellingborough Petty Sessions on Friday, **19 November**, the case against the Raunds blacksmith, charged with indecent assault on an eight year old Stanwick girl, was dismissed through insufficient evidence. The defendant had also survived a similar charge at Thrapston some months earlier!

At Stanwick, the second Church Social was held in the Church Rooms on Saturday, **20 November**. It began with a concert, the artistes being the Misses Willmott and W Pentelow, and Messrs J W Hall, O D Hall, A Tebbutt, and W Coles. Songs, duets, and musical monologues were well rendered before a crowded audience; after refreshments, the rest of the evening was spent in dancing.

Two town men appeared before the Thrapston Bench on Tuesday, **23 November**, charged with stealing two ducks belonging to William Enoch Eady. Amongst the evidence presented were tail feathers, allegedly from the canards, found on the men. Pleading guilty, both men were sentenced to one month's hard labour.

About 80 unemployed men, mostly demobilised soldiers, attended a meeting on The Square on Wednesday, **24 November**. It was decided to write to Field Marshall Earl Haig on the matter and also to request that the War Office and Admiralty reinstate the old standard hand-sewn boots.

On Friday, **26 November**, it was announced that, owing to Mr G Cooch having withdrawn his nomination, Mr Ralph Lawrence had been returned unopposed for the vacant seat on the Urban District Council. This was the first time in the council's history that a vacant seat had been filled without needing a by-election.

The Irthlingborough War Memorial was unveiled on Sunday, **28 November**.

* *

DECEMBER – Friday, **3 December**, "In Memoriam – In ever loving memory of Pte **Arthur James Knighton (68)**, 2nd Royal Inniskilling Fusiliers, who was killed at Passchendaele on 2 December, 1917:

From his loving Mum and Dad, Sisters and Brothers, Bridge Street, Raunds."

On Sunday afternoon, **5 December**, Mr J P Archer gave an organ recital at the Parish Church. Mr Sidney Williamson, Diplomas, Royal College of Music, Leipzig, and inspector of music of Christchurch, New Zealand, sang solos and showed himself to be a real artiste.

The Church School managers met on Tuesday, **7 December**, when a letter of complaint was read from a town man alleging harsh treatment to his boy by Mrs W Spicer and asking for an interview with the managers. The man, Mrs Spicer and Miss Hull then met the managers, and after hearing the facts of the case, they decided that it was a "trivial complaint", that ought to have been settled by the man lodging his complaint direct to Miss Hull and Mrs Spicer. They felt that the accused had not unduly punished the boy, and exonerated her from all blame.

On Thursday evening, **9 December**, a whist drive and dance were held in the Church Institute, in aid of the Church School's football club. Mr H Martin was the MC for the whist drive; the winners being: Ladies, Miss E Chambers; Gentlemen, Mr S Wilmott. At the dance that followed, Mr C Cox (piano) supplied the music.

An accident occurred at Messrs Adams Bros factory on Saturday, **11 December**, when a youth named Cobley got his arm caught in the shafting, breaking it in several places. After examination he was taken to Northampton General Hospital.

On Monday evening, **13 December**, a lorry belonging to the Northampton Brewery Company, whilst going up Marshall's Road, backed into the side of the stables belonging to Mr Nunley, and also knocked down a lamp post. It appears that the engine was working, but owing to the slippery conditions of the road, the wheels would not revolve, and the lorry backed down the hill into the side of the stables. The driver of the lorry was injured about the head.

At the Urban Council meeting attention was called by Mr Batchelor to the prevalent unemployment, and he asked whether it would be wise to set up a committee to find ways and means to dispel the hardship. There were, he said, between 30 and 40 very bad cases in the town. He thought the best plan would be to appeal for these cases, and to set up a distress fund. He moved that a town meeting be called to form a distress committee, this was carried unanimously.

Mr T H Warth, with seconds in both the "Pen of two pigs over 300 lbs" and "Pen of two pigs under 300 lbs" classes, was the only Raunds success at the 22nd Thrapston Fat Stock Show on Tuesday, **14 December**. This was the first show for three years after the suspension imposed by the Board of Agriculture.

On Friday, **17 December**, a private limited liability company, under the name of Smith and Son (Raunds), was registered with a capital of £5,000 in £1 shares (£4,000 6% preferential) to take over the business of a builder and contractor carried on by G E Smith at Raunds. The subscribers (each with one ordinary share) were: G E Smith and Mrs E L Smith; G E Smith being the permanent governing director and chairman.

On Saturday, **18 December**, the flag sellers and other helpers, who had assisted Mrs A Camozzi during the past year, were entertained to a dance in the Central Hall of the Church School by Mr and Mrs Camozzi. Songs were rendered by Miss Wills (Cambridge), who also gave an exhibition of the toe dance. Supper was partaken of; Mr J Shelmerdine, JP, proposed thanks to the hostess and host; and Mr C and Mr R Cox supplied music for dancing, with Mr Herbert Betts as MC.

The annual musical service in aid of the Northampton General Hospital was held in the Wesleyan Church on Sunday, **19 December**. The chapel was full. The service was interspersed with vocal and instrumental music which included solos by Miss Letha Spicer and Mr O D Hall; a euphonium solo by Mr E Vickers; and an instrumental quartette by members of the Temperance Band.

At the annual meeting of the Rushden and District Working Men's Clubs' Fund for Blind and Crippled Children on Monday, **20 December**, the accounts showed receipts from Raunds of: Mr J Sale, donation, £4-5s-0d; Woodbine Club concert, £21-13s-3d; Corresponding Number competition, £6-13s-10d; Corresponding Number competition for boots, £3-14s-10d; Woodbine and Conservative Clubs' donations, £10s-6d each; Special Appeal (Factory collection), £22-19s-0d. Expenditure to Raunds included: Grants to blind persons, £8; surgical appliances and treatment of crippled children, £59-16s-8d.

And today, over at Deenethorpe, baby Lilian Margaret was born.

A well-attended town meeting was held at the Temperance Hall on Thursday evening, **23 December**, called to find some means of alleviating the distress caused in the town by the prevalence of unemployment. It was said that there were up to 50 men between the ages of 40 and 65, who had been out of work for over 12 months, and nearly 30 that had no means of income whatsoever. After considerable discussion, it was moved and carried that a distress committee be formed for Raunds. A resolution was also passed that the committee should apply to the Ministry of Health for a loan for road improvements, so as to employ some of those who were out of work.

On **Christmas Eve**, it was reported that a Raunds ex-soldier had been committed for trial at the Assizes, charged with feloniously marrying a Raunds woman in October 1918, while his first wife was still alive in Leeds!

Members of the Baptist Church for 40 years, Mr and Mrs R Eady celebrated their Golden Wedding on Monday, **27 December**. The couple were presented with a handsome bound volume of "Denham's Hymn" by the deacons of the Church.

On **New Year's Eve**, the Temperance Band held a dance in the Temperance Hall, Mr J Haynes acting as MC and the band supplying the music; whilst at the Church Schools, the Dancing Class held a dance, with Mr C Abbott as MC and Messrs C and R Cox providing the music.

The year closed with the announcement that during the month in Raunds, the temperature had fallen to one degree (F) below zero on the 13th, and then had risen to 60 degrees by Boxing Day, a temperature range of 61 degrees within a fortnight!

So "a land fit for heroes" had not quite proved to be the case for many of the old soldiers, and the coming year would see even more hardship for the traditional craftsmen of the town's principle industry.

11 – January to October 1921

The last casualty and wells are wrecked!

JANUARY – The annual tea and dance of the Young Men's Vicarage Class was held in the Church Schools on Monday, **3 January**. Around 150 sat down to tea; Messrs C and R Cox (piano) providing the music for the dance.

On Tuesday, **4 January**, a Raunds contractor was summoned to the Thrapston Petty Sessions for failing to relieve and maintain his daughter, a poor person who had been chargeable to the Thrapston Poor Law Guardians since 16 October 1920. After hearing conflicting evidence as to the defendant's means, the case was adjourned for two months to enable witnesses to attend to give evidence.

Friday, **7 January**, "Official Notice – 1921 Road Vehicles Registration and Licensing: To All Users of all Kinds of Mechanically-Propelled Vehicles; Within one month from 1 January 1921, every owner of a mechanically-propelled vehicle, other than a tramcar, used on public roads must register, or re-register, the vehicle with, and obtain an excise licence from, the County Council or County Borough Council within whose area the vehicle is ordinarily kept."

The Urban Council met on Monday, **10 January**, and the surveyor reported that the depth of water in the reservoir to be 4 feet 2 inches (4 feet last month), and 9 feet in the well (8 feet last month). He had submitted two schemes to the Waterworks Committee; one being a new well with a capacity of 10,000 gallons (cost £750). A letter was received from the Distress Committee urging the Council to apply for a loan for road improvements, however, Mr Camozzi queried where the other 70% of the cost of labour, and the whole cost of materials might come from as no grant could be obtained for such improvements.

On Tuesday afternoon, **18 January**, damage to the extent of £50 was done to the premises occupied by the Woodbine WMC, by the terrific gale that raged over the district. The roof of the newly erected building at the back of the club was lifted clean off and carried over a tree into the next field, while parts of the roof were found as far away as The Square. Fortunately there were no injuries.

A fine rendition of Handel's "Messiah" was given by the Wesleyan Choral Society (under the conductorship of Mr W W Hall) on Thursday, **20 January**, in the Wesleyan Church before a large and appreciative audience.

Mrs Turner, The Square, aged 88 years, died on Saturday, **22 January**, leaving 3 sons, 5 daughters, 43 grand children, and 28 great-grand children!

The main talking point at the Co-operative Society's half-yearly meeting on Tuesday, **25 January**, was the deficiency of over £800 on the farm account. It was said that the poor crop made the account bad; heated discussions then followed principally regarding the management of sheep and the new piggeries.

FEBRUARY – The magistrates at Thrapston on Tuesday, **1 February**, ordered a Raunds shoehand of Marshall's Road, to pay 2s-0d per week towards the maintenance of his two children instead of 1s-0d.

On Friday, **4 February**, it was reported that the Boot Operatives' Union were preparing the following set of modest demands to be presented to the employers: "A minimum wage of £5 per week for men over 21, and £3-10s-0d for women over 20, and a 5 day working week; boy labour to be restricted to 1 boy for every 5 men; and the employment of women with men in the clicking, press, lasting and finishing rooms to be declared 'undesirable', and that where it exists it should gradually cease and no fresh female labour be employed in such departments!"

"New Companies – Walter Lawrence Ltd (172853), Private company, Registered 28 January, Capital £10,000 in £1 shares; to carry on the business of boot and shoe manufacturers, hide and leather merchants etc; the directors are: W Lawrence (chairman), Raunds, boot manufacturer, H W Lawrence (managing director), Raunds, boot manufacturer; Registered office: High Street, Raunds."

Sunday afternoon, **6 February**, saw a large congregation representative of all the interests of the religious and social life of the town, assembled in the Primitive Methodist Church to witness the unveiling of a memorial tablet to the memory of **Wallace Payne (87)**, who made the supreme sacrifice two days before the signing of the Armistice. The tablet was inscribed:

"In loving memory of Wallace Payne, who fell asleep, 9 November, 1918, aged 33 years. He faithfully served the church as Sunday School Superintendent, President of the Christian Endeavor, and Society Steward; At Rest."

Miss Wootton, of Stanwick, beautifully rendered as a solo, "When I Survey the Wondrous Cross", and Mr J Harrison presided over the meeting.

On Friday, **11 February**, it was reported that the following had been sent to the Prime Minister, on behalf of the unemployed hand-sewn men of Raunds:

"The Premier, 10 Downing Street, London: For God's Sake find work for the hand-sewn Army boot makers of Raunds, who have mostly been unemployed for the past 2 years. During 1915 these men made 1,000 pairs of hand-sewn boots, and today not a man is employed. A number of those are ex-Servicemen, to whom work was promised on leaving the Army. Many of the older men have lost sons in the war, who were the mainstay of their homes. Your unemployment dole has now expired, if immediate action is not taken the wives and children of those men must starve. Nothing will relieve the situation but an issue of hand-sewn, signed: Councillor J Hodson, Councillor E Batchelor."

A fatal accident occurred near to Raunds on Friday morning, **18 February**, at about 11 o'clock, when Mr J Wm Rawlins, son of Mr Thos Rawlins, of Denford, was driving an engine attached to his father's threshing apparatus to Mr Farrington's Lodge. As he was leaning over the side of the engine it suddenly jerked and he was thrown out. The wheels of the heavy engine passed over him, and he was instantly killed. The coroner returned a verdict of "accidental death".

Today the town's boot manufacturers announced they were tendering for 90,000 pairs of Navy boots which would keep the factories busy for a month or two.

It was announced on Friday, **25 February**, that local telephone calls, which had previously been free of charge, would now be charged for 3 minute periods. This would mean that calls to Raunds from the Wellingborough exchange would be 3d and from Kettering 4½d.

A tablet was erected in the belfry of the Parish Church on Saturday, **26 February**, to commemorate the ringing of a peel of Double Norwich Court Bob Major, of 5,120 changes, in the space of 3 hours 25 months, on 6 November, 1920.

* *

MARCH – Two Raunds men appeared before the Sharnbrook Police Court on Friday, **4 March**, charged with having in their possession 8 rabbits and 13 purse nets when searched under the Poaching Regulation Act, by PC Robinson, at Dean on 11 February. Both men had given false names and addresses during the search but the constable had since identified them, although the identification of one was hampered by him being one of five brothers who all looked very much alike! Despite both defendants claiming that it was a case of misidentification, the Chairman said that as it was their word against that of the constable, he could only find them both guilty, and fined them £2 each.

Over the weekend of Saturday, **12** and Sunday, **13 March**, the War Memorials at Podington and Newton Bromswold were unveiled and dedicated.

Covington's War Memorial was unveiled on Easter Monday, **28 March**.

Tuesday, 29 March, John James Coles (40a), died.

The last of the town's war casualties to be named on the Town War Memorial, John James Coles was born in Ringstead in 1883, the eldest of the five children of William and Elizabeth Marie Coles. In 1903, after his father died, his widowed mother moved the family to Raunds and married John Parker, who already had four children. John first worked as a shoehand but then joined a company of travelling amusement caterers as a showman and was in this occupation when he enlisted in the Middlesex Regiment before transferring to the 1st Battalion, The Buffs (East Kent Regiment).

He was still with The Buffs when he received an honourable discharge in March 1919, but by now he was suffering the savage effects of the war as he had been admitted to the Upton Military Hospital, Northampton in January of the previous year, and it was here, 3 years 3 months and 23 days after admission, that he died, aged 38; the details on his death certificate suggesting that he was a victim of the extreme symptoms of what has popularly become known as "shellshock".

He was brought home to Raunds and buried in the Cemetery on 1 April, in an unmarked grave. His brothers, **Enos Owen Coles**, **Luther William Coles (41)**, and step-brother, **Ernest Parker (86)**, were also Great War victims, thus making his mother's composite family the hardest hit in Raunds, losing four out of six serving sons – a fifth son was also believed missing, but that is another story!

"Notice of Sales – Raunds, Monday, 4 April: 46 acres of Rich Upland and Meadow Grass Keeping to 1 December next; in 3 lots, full particulars by posters and in next week's newspapers; Sale at 5pm, Arthur G Brown & Sons."

* *

APRIL – On Friday afternoon, **1 April**, the Hargrave War Memorial Cross was unveiled and dedicated by the Rev C C Aldred, formerly vicar of Raunds. The ten names listed include Raunds-born **Arthur Abbott (8a)**.

Also today, all coal miners in the country began a strike against the Government's de-control of the industry; the National Union of Railwaymen also expressed their determination to support the miners. It would prove to be an action that would bite deep into the workings of the nation, and even Raunds would feel the full effects!

On a brighter note, the town's boot manufacturers today secured contracts for the supply of 80,000 pairs of box calf ankle boots for the Royal Marines.

"In Memoriam – In ever loving memory of our dear son, Pte **William Henry Groom (56)**, of the Northumberland Fusiliers, who was wounded and missing in France, 28 March, 1917.

From his sorrowing Father, Mother, Brother and Fiancée (Edith), 80c High Street, Raunds."

Friday, **8 April**, "In Memoriam – In loving memory of Pte **Ralph Pentelow (91)**, of the 12th Suffolk Regiment, who was killed in action in France on 9 April, 1918

From his sorrowing Wife and Children, 155 King Street, Kettering; and Mother, Father, Brothers, and Sisters, Raunds."

A party was held at Raunds this week on the occasion of the 80th birthday of Mr Enos Smith. Ten of his old friends attended, every one of them having attained octogenarian status, and who had, during that span of time, played an important part in the progress and development of the town viz: William Lawrence, 80; Christopher Coles, 80; George Pulpher, 82; Samuel Pettitt, 82; Frederick Pentelow, 81; Thomas Haynes, 81; Owen Knighton, 81, George Lee, 80; George Bass, 82, and John Horrell, 80, who, together with Mr Smith, totalled 889 years!

The Rothwell War Memorial was unveiled on Sunday, **10 April**, bearing the inscription "They were a wall unto us both day and night"; now where have we heard that before?

At the Thrapston Police Court on Tuesday, **12 April**, a Raunds omnibus conductor was summoned by his wife for a common assault on 3 April. It was said that the defendant had accused his wife of watching him so had hit her with his fist on the back of her head and had also bruised her left arm. She had previously applied for a separation order after he accused her of going with another man, but that was dropped and he returned home. After hearing the evidence, the magistrates had a talk with both parties, with a view to inducing them to sink their differences; the couple eventually agreed to "wipe the slate clean and make a fresh start".

Mr A Camozzi was elected chairman of the Urban Council for the new administrative year on Monday, **18 April**. A native of Wolverton, he moved to Raunds in 1888. The town also lost a well known public figure today, with the death of Mr E A Milligan, JP, of "The Crossways", aged 66.

There was success for Raunds at the 10th North Northants Musical Festival held in the Great Hall of Oundle School on Friday **22** and Saturday, **23 April**, when Miss Evelyn Bailey won the "Pianoforte Solo" class with her renditions of "a small prelude in C" by J S Bach and, "A Morning Canter" by C M Spurling.

On Friday, **29 April**, with the effects of the on-going miners strike already threatening to paralyse the country, it was reported that the Raunds Gas Works would have to close down next week if further supplies of coal were not forthcoming. Elsewhere in the town, if the expected 5 tons failed to appear soon there would be no coal available for household purposes except for 2 tons which had been reserved for distribution on receipt of doctor's certificates for the sick and aged. The bakers had enough in reserve to keep going for about three weeks, and the factories were burning anthracite, however, as they also relied on town gas for heating their machines, the factories would also have to close down soon.

"Raunds Urban District Council – Tenders are invited by 12 noon, Monday, 9 May, for the Hospital Building situated in Brooks Road, consisting of two rooms, 18 feet square, and one room, 12 feet square, together with a veranda of lavatories. The Building is one of corrugated iron, lined with match boarding, and in good condition. Tenders are also invited for two double-lined tents, one 22 feet by 14 feet, and one 18 feet by 9 feet; By order of the Council, W F Corby, Clerk."

* *

MAY – Friday, **6 May**, "In Memoriam – In loving memory of **John Brackley Higby (63)**, 7th Bedfords, who died of wounds in France, 15 March, 1917, aged 26 years; Also **Ralph Higby (64)**, 7th Bedfords, missing, 3 May, 1917, aged 19 years; From Mother, Father, Sisters, and Brothers, High Street, Raunds."

Raunds Town FC retained the Scott Gatty Cup on Saturday, **7 May**, defeating the Raunds Woodbine FC at Huntingdon by six goals to one, or as the local newspapers put it: "The town team defeated the popular brand of cigarettes' side!"

This weekend, the Stanwick War Memorial was unveiled.

Published on Friday, **13 May**, the medical officer's report for 1920 showed an estimated town population of 4,205; the number of births registered as 80 (41 male, 39 female), a ratio of 19 per 1,000 against the national ratio of 25.5 per 1,000; deaths registered 45 (half over 65, five under one year old); notified diseases: 1 of dysentery, 1 of diphtheria, 11 of tuberculosis, and 6 of pneumonia.

Local newspapers of Friday, **20 May**, recalled that 100 years ago this week (1821), Mr Benjamin Lever, of Raunds Lodge, had paid over to the Northampton General Infirmary, seventeen shillings, being a fine inflicted by a Justice of the Peace on two of his labourers for "the most culpable neglect in thrashing a quantity of wheat, a considerable part of which was thrown away in the straw!"

Raunds Town FC held its annual meeting in the Temperance Hall and the treasurer had to report a deficit of over £30 on the past season's proceedings, despite the club's success in retaining the Scott Gatty Cup. Undaunted, the committee decided that the first XI should still compete in the Northants League and that a second XI be formed to run in the Wellingborough and District League.

On Monday evening, **23 May**, the deeds of conveyance of the new Wesleyan Recreation Club grounds in Wellington Road were handed over by Mr W F Corby, CC, (the donor of the field) to Mr L G H Lee, secretary of the trustees. After reciprocal expressions of thanks, the tennis courts and bowling green were thrown open to the members, and soon games were being indulged in. The Temperance Band was also in attendance playing popular music.

Also this evening, the Woodbine FC held its annual meeting and unlike their Shopmate neighbours, heard that their season's exploits had actually produced a balance in hand of 2s-2½d! Its first season had been most successful, finishing 3rd in the Rushden and District League, winning the East Northants Medal Competition, and being runners up in the Scott Gatty Cup.

The Islip Recreation Ground was opened by Major Brassey on Empire Day, Tuesday, **24 May**, as a peace memorial to the Great War.

It was the Raunds Co-operative Society annual treat for member's children on Saturday, **27 May**. As usual, several hundred children paraded the town, and sang hymns at intervals. Tea was then taken in the National and Wesleyan Schools, followed by sports in the Co-operative Field in Thorpe Street.

The Co-operative Society boot factory in Ringstead was gutted by fire on Tuesday morning, **31 May**, and it was the sad tale of three separate fire brigades being unable to attend that almost certainly contributed to the total destruction of the building. The factory manager first called the Thrapston brigade, only to be told that there were no horses available for the engine; he then tried Raunds, but they had no fire engine; finally, Kettering was contacted, but again he was rebuffed, being informed that Ringstead was outside of their area of responsibility! Damage was estimated at £20,000, and 70 to 80 folk were thrown out of work.

JUNE – The Raunds Distress Fund Committee held a meeting in the Council Schools on Thursday evening, **2 June**, to revue the balance sheet and secretaries report. The receipts (by donations) amounted to £177-4s-10d and expenditure to £176-3s-0d (including vouchers issued for food, coal etc for £171-7s-0d), leaving a balance in hand of £1-1s-10d. The secretary then explained that owing to a lack of funds the committee had to close and wind up the fund, not because there was no distress, as at the present time there was more than when the fund was set up! The small balance had now been distributed to the neediest cases; and in all, over 50 severely distressed cases had received assistance.

Also this evening, an "Al Fresco" concert by the Wesleyan Church was held in the grounds of "Ashfields" as a special effort to realise the sum of £75 as their contribution to the Raunds Wesleyan Circuit Funds. The programme included items by the Choral Society, Misses M Sanders, L Spicer, and W Pentelow, and Messrs O D Hall, C Coles, and R Sanders.

The Raunds Cinema Company were summoned at Thrapston Police Court on Tuesday, **7 June**, for allowing the Palace Theatre to be used for the exhibition of pictures by means of a cinematograph without having in force a licence as required, between 29 September 1920 and 28 March 1921. The secretary of the company admitted the charges but claimed that this was due to an oversight that only came to light on the departure of the previous manager; and that as soon as the error was discovered a new licence was applied for. Sgt Osborn said that he was satisfied with the explanation as the place was now well run. A retrospective licence was approved but the Bench also imposed a fine of £30.

Two town men also appeared before the Bench today, each charged with riding a bicycle without lights on the Denford Road on 23 May. PC Parker gave evidence that one offender had ridden off when challenged and the other had given him a false name. The "false name" was fined 15s-0d, and the "rider off" 7s-6d, having successfully pleaded that he was unemployed with six children.

Wollaston's War Memorial Cross was unveiled on Saturday, **11 June**, by Viscount Althorp; and on Sunday, **19 June**, Desborough's War Memorial was dedicated, with touching eulogies by Lt-Col J Brown and the Bishop of Peterborough.

The town's annual parade and demonstration on behalf of Northampton Hospital took place on Saturday, **25 June**, and followed the usual lines of a parade and open-air meeting in the grounds of "The Hall". Mr W F Corby read out letters of apology from Lord Lilford (who sent a £10 cheque), Mr J Bruce (ten guineas), Mr A B Conyers (£5), and Mr A Sudborough (two guineas), after which the various guests gave their carefully chosen words.

Winners in the fancy dress competition were: "*Children's individual get-up*", Willie Stanley (Stephens' Ink); "*Children's group of five of less*", Bertie Hodson and Arthur Sykes (Indian Chiefs); "*Children's group over five*", Miss Sharp's Party (Flowers); "*Best individual get-up*", F Bugby (Tarzan of the Apes); "*Best artistic or historic group*", BWTA 'Y' Branch (Dominoes).

Winners in the sports events held in the Green House Field were: "*100 yards handicap, boys under 14*", E Maddison (Irthlingborough) and A Keach (Burton Latimer), dead heat; "*80 yards handicap, girls under 15*", Kathleen Saddington; "*100 yards handicap, open*", H Pleasance (Rushden); "*80 yards veterans' handicap*", C Sparkes, (Rushden); "*220 yards, open*", H Foreman (Rushden); "*Half-mile handicap*", T E Oates; "*Fire Brigade Competition*", Raunds 'B'.

After the sports many adjourned to the Hall grounds, where an al fresco concert was given by artistes from Northampton. In the sports field the Temperance Silver Prize Band played for dancing.

At the close of the afternoon, the principle speaker, the Rt Hon C A McCurdy, KC MP, received in one of the rooms of "The Hall", a deputation from the town's Army hand-sewn operatives relative to their lack of employment. He agreed that he would investigate whether any assistance could be obtained from the Navy, Army or Air Force when they come to review their future boot requirements.

On Sunday, **26 June**, Denford's War Memorial was unveiled by Sir Ryland Adkins.

* *

JULY – Friday, **1 July**, "In Memoriam – In fond and loving memory of our dear wife and mother, Elsie Kathleen Lucas (née Sanders), who passed away at Raunds on 15 June, 1919:

'Sadly Missed'

Inserted by her loving husband, Ernest Lucas (late A I F) and little daughter Ina; Derby, Tasmania, Australia."

Under the auspices of the Raunds local Labour Party, a fete was held at "Northdale", kindly lent by the committee of the Raunds Distributive Co-operative Society, on Saturday, **2 July**. Amongst the attractions was a cricket match between "Ladies" and "Gentlemen", the men winning by 11 runs; there were also cake and doll guessing competitions, football kicks, quoits and darts. The public tea was held at four o'clock followed by a public meeting at 6 o'clock.

The children of the Parish Church enjoyed their annual treat on Saturday, **9 July**, favoured by fine weather. About 250 children paraded the town and were entertained to tea. Many sports etc were held in the Vicarage grounds, the attractions and side-shows being most popular. The highlight of the sports was the marathon race of about 3 miles, for which eight runners turned out; the winner was Dennis Bettles. The bowling competition was won by Mr G Kirk, and after the sports the Temperance Band played for dancing on the lawn.

Woodford's War Memorial was unveiled and dedicated on Feast Sunday, **10 July**.

At the council meeting of Monday, **11 July**, the "nuisance" caused by the condition of the culvert arch near Messrs Own Smith's factory was discussed; the coal stocks of the town's bakers were becoming critical and the members endorsed the Surveyor's decision to order a truck load at £5 per ton; the state of the town's water supply was also giving concern, and with no immediate prospect of rain, it was decided to approach the owner of "Page Well" with a view to reopening it for the public; the question of unsanitary houses, and the need to proceed with the building of 40 houses without further delay, were also discussed.

Mr W F Corby represented Raunds at the Northants County Council quarterly meeting on Thursday, **14 July**, and complained that the 5 or 6 acres of land purchased by the County Council in the town some months ago was now growing nothing but weeds and was an absolute disgrace. The area was a nuisance to the allotments and school gardens nearby. It was explained that the land would soon be cleared thoroughly and cropped, although it had been purchased for a recreation ground in connection with the proposed secondary school.

The extreme shortage of water in the town came to a dramatic climax on Friday evening, **15 July**, when between 80 and 100 townspeople made three raids on pumping equipment in fields at the bottom of Meadow Lane, the property of an absent landowner believed to be a wealthy manufacturer and financier living at Bailrigg, Lancaster. The residents believed that water had regularly been pumped from the wells on the site to water the farmer's fields and for his stock, drawing away supplies of the precious liquid from the council's nearby pumping station as a consequence. After luring the local constabulary away from the area with hoax telephone calls, the raiders dismantled the equipment and threw it down the wells, and also destroyed a hut used for storage, then disappeared into the fields in all directions before the bailiff and constables arrived. ***(Plate 21)***

This evening, the proceeds of the "motors" at the Feast were generously given by Mr Thurston to the town's Hospital Week Committee for Northampton Hospital. The net result was 12s-9d.

At an auction sale held at the "Robin Hood Inn" on Thursday, **21 July**, ten £10 shares in the Raunds Gas Light and Coke Co fetched £12-10s-0d each, Mr Owen Young being the purchaser.

There was a good attendance at the Co-operative Society's half-yearly meeting in the Temperance Hall on Monday evening, **25 July**. The balance sheet showed sales for the half-year to have been £1,402 in excess of the previous year, and it was decided by the committee that the available surplus of £1,186 should be paid as a dividend of 11d in the £ to all members.

Friday, **29 July**, "In Memoriam – In loving memory of Pte **Cyril J Clarke (38)**, who died of wounds in France, 3 August, 1917.

From his loving Mother, Father, Sisters, and Brothers, 13 High Street, Raunds."

*

AUGUST – At the Boot Operatives' Union local branch meeting on Monday evening, **8 August**, another protest was made against the employment of married women in boot factories whilst single girls were out of work. And continuing the (un)employment strain, over the border at Cardington, it was claimed that the Government's ban on building airships had resulted in over 2,000 people being thrown out of work, with more jobs at risk in the near future.

However, the future of the industry would not be helped by the loss of the R38, which crashed into the River Humber later this month, killing 44 of the 49 crew.

Friday, **12 August**, "In Memoriam – In loving memory of Ptes **P Watson (119)** and **S Brayfield (27)** of Raunds, lost on board the 'Royal Edward', which was torpedoed in the Aegean Sea, 13 August, 1915; C.W.W."

"Auction Sales – Brook Street, Raunds; Valuable Copyhold Shops and Dwelling Houses to be sold by auction by John S Mason, on Monday, 29 August, at the "Globe Inn", at 6pm; Auctioneer's Offices: 30 High Street, Rushden."

Just four months after the remarkable gathering to celebrate his 80th birthday, the death occurred on Tuesday, **16 August**, of Mr Enos Smith, JP, of Thorpe Street. He had seemed in his usual health but while on a visit to his sister, Mrs George Lee, had complained of feeling tired and on sitting down, immediately expired.

"Little White Ribboners" belonging to the Raunds branch of the British Women's Temperance Association held their birthday party in the Temperance Hall on Wednesday, **17 August**. Owing to the rain the picnic had to be postponed. After two short addresses, the roll was called and each child received a small present.

On Friday, **19 August**, the end of the drought was gratefully reported. In the six months between February and July 1921, only 3.69 inches had fallen compared the average of 11.3 inches; but now the rain was falling again!

"In Memoriam – In memory of Privates **S Brayfield (27)** and **P Watson (119)**, RAMC(T), of Raunds, drowned by the sinking of the transport 'Royal Edward', torpedoed 13 August, 1915 – H.H."

On Sunday afternoon, **21 August**, the members of the Raunds Fire Brigade were entertained at "Stanwick House" by Captain and Mrs F Adams and a most enjoyable time was spent. A whist drive was held and games were indulged in, including bowls and cricket. Afterwards a capital spread was provided, ably presided over by Mrs Adams, assisted by Miss Johnson.

The results of the 1921 Census were announced on Friday, **26 August**, and for Raunds showed an official total population of 3762, 1875 male and 1887 female; this compared to 3873 in 1911 (1976 male and 1897 female).

* *

SEPTEMBER – Friday, **2 September**, "In Memoriam – In loving memory of Pte **Evelyn Wood (135)**, 12th East Surrey Regiment, killed in action in France, 3 September, 1918.

From his loving Wife and Children, Thrapston."

On Friday, **9 September**, it was recalled how, this week in 1896, a poll of the town of Raunds – in which over half of the ratepayers took the trouble to vote, expressed approval of steps being taken to form an Urban Council.

The Higham Ferrers War Memorial, including the name of Raunds' **George Henry Hall MSM (59)**, was unveiled by Lord Downe on Sunday, **11 September**; also today, the War Memorials at Sharnbrook and Souldrop were dedicated.

On Wednesday, **14 September**, Raunds Town Football Club resigned from the Northants League citing an inability to raise a team up to the League's standard. Their resignation was accepted, however, the League's secretary stated his regret as the Shopmates were the oldest club in the league having first joined in 1896/7.

The Raunds Manor Boot Company, boot manufacturers, had gone into voluntary liquidation on 31 August, and at a meeting of the creditors at Wellingborough on Tuesday, **20 September**, a deficiency of £2,476 was shown, in addition to £931 to the shareholders. The liquidator stated that the reason the company had failed was due to bad trading, and no attempt to keep accounts.

Several of the town's football clubs were in trouble at the Rushden League meeting of Friday, **23 September**. St Peter's were forced to resign from the league and were also fined 2s-6d for fielding an ineligible player who had already appeared for the Woodbine; The Woodbine were deducted two points for fielding an ineligible player who had already appeared for the Coffee Tavern; and of the two players in question, both Raunds men, one was suspended for 14 days, and the other severely reprimanded.

The Rushden War Memorial was unveiled on Sunday, **25 September**.

At the Thrapston Police Court on Tuesday, **27 September**, seven young men from Raunds were summoned for playing pitch and toss in a public place in the town on 11 September. All the defendants pleaded guilty. PC Newberry said he saw the men playing on the public footpath leading from Thorpe Street to Chelveston, and several people had to walk through them while the accused used obscene language. As this was their first offence, each was fined 10s-0d.

"For Sale – Bees, Surplus Stock; A few very strong stocks of Italian Hybrids on 8, 10 and 12 frames, full of brood and feed; 1921 queens; guaranteed healthy; inspection invited; 25 years experience; Price on application to J H Willmott, 'Apiaries', Stanwick."

* *

OCTOBER – The Little Irchester War Memorial was unveiled and dedicated on Sunday, **2 October**.

On Monday, **3 October**, Mr G Pulpher, the veteran organist of the Raunds Baptist Chapel, celebrated his 83rd birthday, and a tea in honour of the event was given by his daughter, Mrs W H Lovell, of Stanwick. There was a large attendance of relatives and friends, including Mr Pulpher's sister, 89 year old Mrs H Hall.

Mrs Lovell presented to the trustees a large framed portrait of her father, to be hung in the schoolroom; the portrait was inscribed: "George Pulpher, 45 years organist, Baptist Chapel; October 1921". On behalf of the church, the deacons presented Mr Pulpher with a large beautifully framed hymn book, together with a tune book. In the 45 years he had never once been late at his post, and had only been absent through illness three times.

* *

* *

SUNDAY, 9 OCTOBER, THE DEDICATION OF THE RAUNDS WAR MEMORIAL

On Sunday afternoon Raunds, which already possessed a fine mural memorial in its ancient Parish Church, dedicated its town War Memorial, erected on The Square. ***(Plate 22)***

The representative committee for carrying through the scheme consisted of twelve members of the Urban Council, twelve representatives of ex-servicemen, and twelve representatives of the general public, with Mr A Hazeldine (who was chairman of the Urban Council at the time the movement was started) as chairman; Mr H W Lawrence treasurer, and Mr W F Corby, CC, and Mr V H Sykes as the very efficient hon secretaries. The total estimated cost was about £600, which was raised by public subscription.

With a population of just under four thousand, Raunds during the war laboured at high pressure in turning out boots for HM Forces and for our Allies; it sent a high percentage of its men to serve, and of these no fewer than one hundred and six made the supreme sacrifice.

The memorial was unveiled by the Rev C C Aldred, MA, Rector of Abington, who was vicar of Raunds during the major period of the war; and the address was given by Sir W Ryland Adkins, KC MP.

The memorial, erected upon a very suitable site in The Square, takes the form of a Gothic clustered column of delicate proportions, enriched with the ball-flower ornament, rising from a sub-base in the form of a Greek cross upon a very substantial base with steps, and is surmounted by a small square tabernacle with carved panels. The total height is about twenty-two feet. The steps are of Derbyshire stone, the column and base are of Weldon stone with bronze tablets – one on each side – bearing the names of the fallen.

The dedicatory inscription is upon a stone tablet in the front panel of the main base. It is cut into stone, and is as follows:

"Raunds to its Honoured Dead:"
"1914-1919"
"They were a wall unto us both by day and by night."

The whole of the work was skilfully and sympathetically executed by Mr W Partrick, of Raunds, under the supervision of the architect, Lieut-Col John Brown, A.R.I.B.A., of Northampton, whose beautiful design met with general appreciation. The bronze tablets were the work of Messrs Pullen and Co, of Northampton; the names are inscribed in raised lettering on the two bronze tablets (53 on each).

The service on The Square was fixed to commence at 2.45pm, and half-an-hour earlier a procession was formed several hundred yards away, on the main thoroughfare near "The Hall". This comprised the K.R.R. Cadets (Raunds St Mary's Company), with band; The Raunds Temperance Prize Band; the Parish Church surpliced choir, with cross-bearer; the Reverends C Curtis MA, (Vicar of Raunds), C C Aldred, and J Wells (Superintendent Wesleyan Minister, Raunds); the Wesleyan Choral Society (over a hundred); Comrades of the Fallen (ex-servicemen, over a hundred strong); the Memorial Committee; and others. Mr A Camozzi, JP, chairman of the urban council, was in front of the cadets; and Mr John Hodson, an ex-serviceman and former member of the Temperance Band, walked at the head of the band, carrying a wreath from the bandsmen.

All being in readiness, the procession slowly proceeded up the street – accompanied on either side by other sympathisers – singing the stirring hymn "For all the Saints who from their labours rest," to the Temperance Band accompaniment.

Meanwhile on The Square the members of the Fire Brigade and a number of Special Constables attended to the prescribed seating and space arrangements, everything being carried out smoothly and reverently. Relatives of the departed friends (a great many carrying wreaths) were shown to seats in a large semi-circle in front of, and some little distance from, the memorial. The Sunday School children of the various religious bodies, totalling several hundreds, occupied a space with their teachers on rising ground above the memorial (to the left of those facing the front of the memorial); while the general public assembled in large numbers.

On arrival of the long procession the ex-servicemen lined up three or four deep at the back of the relatives, forming as it were a guard of honour; the Church Choir, the Choral Society, the Temperance Band, and the Company of Cadets took up positions to the right of these facing the memorial; the members of the Memorial Committee, Sir Ryland Adkins, and the others had seats to the left (below the school children), and immediately in front of them were the clergy. The general public stretched all round The Square and into adjoining properties, and it was estimated that the gathering numbered at least four thousand.

"O God, our Help in ages past," to the Temperance Band accompaniment, was sung with much fervour; after which the vicar said the first three sublime sentences of the Church Burial Service, followed by the lesson – those very appropriate first nine verses of the third chapter of the Book of Wisdom, "But the souls of the righteous are in the hand of God," etc.

The unveiling of the memorial was performed by the Rev C C Aldred, who (after the Union Jacks around the base had been removed) used the following terms of dedication, "To the glory of God, and in proud and thankful remembrance of the men of this parish who fell in the Great War, I unveil this memorial in the name of the Father, and of the Son, and of the Holy Ghost, Amen."

A number of prayers and responses were led by the Church choir, with Mr J P Archer at the piano. The names were distinctly and reverently read out in nine sections, with the response after each, "We praise thee, O God." During an interval for this purpose, the Temperance Band playing fitting music, a very large number of beautiful floral tributes were lovingly placed on the memorial and a temporary wreath platform by relatives and friends, this portion of the proceedings being very effective.

Sir Ryland D Adkins, KC MP, having advanced to the wreath platform, gave an address, speaking with force and eloquence. Having alluded to the beautiful monument and the stately ceremony, he remarked that that day they thought with gratitude of those who had given their lives; they reflected with pride that Raunds had done its duty and been worthy of its character. They also thought with tenderness and sympathy of those whose loss was nearest and greatest, and to whom it would be a privilege as well as a duty to show all kindness possible as long as they lived. And should they not keep in mind two or three things which the war was teaching? It taught them as never before the duty which could not be escaped, that of national defence. Secondly, they had to realise as fully as possible the horrors of war; war was the most horrible, most un-Christlike, most devilish thing which human beings could take part in; and was only justifiable when necessary to defend our rights and libeties. The third lesson he ventured to recall to their minds was the lesson of unity, loyalty to the religious or political or economic society to which they belonged could be blended with a sense of brotherhood and a sense of unity.

Mr A Hazeldine, chairman of the Memorial Committee, then handed "this beautiful memorial" to the Raunds Urban District Council, and asked them to take care of it and to preserve it for evermore. Mr A Camozzi, JP, chairman of the Urban Council, accepted the memorial on behalf of the council. No one, he remarked, could listen without emotion to the long list of names of those who had given their lives, and whom had been so familiar to them, and who a few years ago were their fellow citizens.

The Rev C Curtis having pronounced the Blessing, the "Last Post" and "Reveille" were sounded by Buglers Albert Ward, Fred Richardson, Kenneth Hodson, and Jack Hodson, of the Cadets; after which the National Anthem by the Temperance Band brought a very appropriate, impressive, and reverent service to a close.

Muffled peals were rung on the church bells both before and after the service.

* *

And so we end the journey with our forebears through the tumultuous Great War years and into the brave new world that followed.

**Angels or devils, rebels or rogues, they were all Rance folk,
And we bless them all!**

DEMOBILISATION AT THE END OF THE GREAT WAR

Shortly after the start of the war, a call went out for volunteers and men came forward in their thousands, far exceeding the numbers expected. The system had to adapt in order to turn these men into soldiers at a vastly higher rate than ever before.

By the end of the war Britain had around 3,750,000 men under arms, a number of whom had served for a considerable period of time. This was far higher than after any previous conflict and presented the country with many problems. With the Armistice of 11 November 1918 there came an end to the fighting, but the peace had yet to be formalised. So a great number of men would still be needed, but that said, a far greater number now needed to be returned to civilian life to begin rebuilding Britain's economy.

The Government did not want a mass of men leaving the army and facing unemployment, so the Demobilisation sub-committee was set up under the auspices of the Ministry of Reconstruction. To that end a steady release was organised, whereby men left in groups. The first being civil servants who would monitor the whole process. Next were the "pivotal men"; those who it was believed would be able to work to create more jobs for others. The next group were the so called "slip men", those who had been promised employment at home on their return. They had to produce an employment form or slip, filled out by their future employer. They were released in stages according to the importance of their skills in rebuilding post war Britain. A number of Raunds men were released under this category, as the shoe factories had large orders to fulfil. The last two groups were the men whom it was felt would be able to find work in civilian life, followed by those whom it was believed would possibly be unemployed.

The system was not without its problems; men who had served for a long period of the war would be held back and sent out to the Rhine Army and also to Russia, whilst men with a shorter service and more recent contact with their former employers were able to be demobilised earlier. This system was also very slow and complicated, resulting in a number of demonstrations by dissatisfied troops, some of whom had refused to board troop ships to return to France at the end of their leave and others demonstrating in Brighton and Whitehall. At the instigation of Winston Churchill the system was changed and those that had served the longest were the first to go. Within a few weeks 56 per cent of the Officers and 78 percent of the men that were eligible had been released. At the peak of the process as many as 14,000 men were being released daily and after a year the strength of the army was down to 380,000.

All soldiers were released with a 28 day furlough and would then be formerly discharged at the end of it. Prior to their leave they would report to one of the 26 dispersal centres in the UK where each soldier would receive pay to cover his leave, a ration book and either a clothing allowance or a Government "demob suit"; they could also keep their uniform and greatcoat. The state would also pay unemployment insurance for up to twenty weeks.

As the Peace Treaty had not yet been signed, most men were transferred to the reserves, the Raunds men that we have been able to trace mostly went to the Class "Z". This Class was established by Army Order on the 3 December 1918, to guard against the possibility of any emergency re-mobilisation that may have been required in the event of Germany refusing to accept the terms of a peace treaty. The Class Z Reserve was abolished as a result of AO (Army Order) 98 on the 29 March 1920, which said that "All soldiers in Class Z of the Army Reserve will be deemed to have been discharged as from the 31 March 1920."

This was the time of "A land fit for heroes", but the fact was that as well as paying a high price with the lives of her sons, Britain had also paid financially. By the end of the war Britain had a debt of some £9,300,000,000 and needed to get back on its feet. Only just over 200,000 of the planned 800,000 new homes to replace unsafe slum housing were built, the cost proving too high, when weighed against the need to make goods for export.

The women that had gone into jobs in order to release men for the army were just as quickly sent home to allow those men to have their jobs back. It was a short taste of emancipation, but was a catalyst for women's rights movements in the forthcoming years. The women of Raunds suffered in this way as the shoe factories took back those men whom they had sent away.

But despite all the problems, the state of the country and the lack of decent housing, we are sure that many a demobilised Raunds man stepped onto the platform at Raunds Station with a sense of relief in his heart for having survived the "War to end all Wars". But sadly that would not be the case for less than 20 years later their sons would be stepping off the same platform bound for another world war, against the same enemy!

* *

Sources: the Great War Forum, Yahoo, Wikipedia

INDEX

RANCE LIFE

RANCE FOLK